Politics, Religion and Literature in the Seventeenth Century

Edited, with an introduction and notes, by
William Lamont,
Reader in History, University of Sussex
and
Sybil Oldfield,
Lecturer in English, University of Sussex

Dent, London
Rowman and Littlefield, Totowa, N.J.

820.4

Made in Great Britain
at the
Aldine Press · Letchworth · Herts
for
J. M. DENT AND SONS LTD
Aldine House · Albemarle Street · London
First published 1975

Dent edition
Hardback ISBN: 0 460 10632 5
Paperback ISBN: 0 460 11632 0

200286654

Rowman and Littlefield edition
Library of Congress Cataloging in Publication Data
Lamont, William M   comp.
Politics, religion, and literature in the seventeenth century

Bibliography: p.
1. Great Britain—History—Stuarts, 1603–1714—Sources.
2. English literature—Early modern, 1500–1700.
I. Oldfield, Sybil, joint comp. II. Title.
DA370.L35 1975   914.2'03'608   74-12113
ISBN 0-87471-575-X
ISBN 0-87471-576-8 (pbk.)

Contents

Preface

For a number of years Sybil Oldfield and I have taught a course at the University of Sussex on 'English Literature and the Civil War'. She is an English specialist and I am an historian; our students were drawn from a number of different disciplines. The idea of this book grew out of that experience. We both felt that we had gained something from looking at literary and historical problems together. Collections of source materials on the seventeenth century, however, tended to keep the literature and the history apart. We hope that this volume will be helpful to other students and teachers who want to bring the two together.

The seventeenth century offers an embarrassing richness of choice. We have organized our material around eight themes. They seem to us to offer a useful perspective for the study of politics, religion and literature in the seventeenth century, but not the only perspective. Other editors might have chosen other themes—and supporting texts—and their choice would have been equally valid. It seemed to us therefore to be a good idea to come clean with our own prejudices: in the literary and historical introductions that follow this preface, Sybil Oldfield and I explain what guided our choice of material for this volume. In all cases the extracts have been taken from the original editions, unless otherwise indicated.

We would never have embarked on this joint enterprise if, in addition to our general interest in inter-disciplinary work, we had not believed that there is a special sense in which history and literature complement each other when we try to understand the English Revolution of the seventeenth century. I know no better exposition of the 'two truths' about the English Revolution than in Professor Laurence

Stone's recent monograph, *The Causes of the English Revolution*. His words are worth quoting at length:

> What was important about the English Revolution was not its success in permanently changing the face of England—for this was slight—but the intellectual content of the various opposition programmes and achievements after 1640. For the first time in history an anointed King was brought to trial for breach of faith with his subjects, his head was publicly cut off, and his office was declared abolished. An established church was abolished, its property was seized, and fairly wide religious toleration for all forms of Protestantism was proclaimed and even enforced. For a short time, and perhaps for the first time, there came on to the stage of history a group of men proclaiming ideas of liberty not liberties, equality not privilege, fraternity not deference. These were ideas that were to live on, and to revive again in other societies in other ages. In 1647 the Puritan John Davenport forecast correctly that 'the light which is now discovered in England . . . will never be wholly put out, though I suspect that contrary opinions will prevail for a time'.

We need to have both truths about the English Revolution. From the literary evidence alone, we have marvellous access to one truth: we can understand Davenport's light; we can see how, as early as the 1630s, armed camps were forming (the theme of Sybil Oldfield's second section); we can see how, as the actual Civil War developed, each side stereotyped—and misunderstood—the other (the theme of her third and fourth sections); we can see how the experience of war affected a generation whose lack of moral fibre was put down by Bishop Wren in the 1630s to an over-long exposure to peace (the theme of her final, seventh, section). But contrary truths need to be asserted, for which the literary evidence is less impressive. There is the truth that Puritans were as devoted to monarchy as their Anglican opponents were, although Milton for propaganda purposes joined his Anglican opponents in the pursuit of the contrary fiction. The theme of my first section is, therefore, King-worship. There is the truth that regicide was an attack upon the man rather than the office: the theme of my fifth section on the execution of Charles I. There is the truth that Cromwell—for and against—invoked a response that was more ambivalent than party propaganda, on either side, would lead us to expect (my sixth section). There is the truth that the English Revolution of the mid-seventeenth century did less to change the permanent face of English political life than did the 1688 Glorious Revolution. Laurence Stone hints at this in the passage quoted above: it is an argument developed at greater length, and with great conviction, in Professor J. R. Jones's recent study, *The Revolution of 1688 in England*. But that Revolution itself was the product of Protestant *consensus*: it was a Whig *and* Tory Settlement. That consensus might be explained away as a negative reflex—anti-Popery, and nothing much else. I argue the opposite, in my eighth and final section of the book, and through the argument of Thomas Barlow trace a continuity back to the first section of the book. But even if this continuity did not exist, and the consensus were only a negative one, my point would stand unaffected: that Sybil Oldfield's literature of conflict in the early sections of the volume prepared us for the penultimate Protestant conflict of the Civil War, and not for the ultimate consensus of the Revolutionary Settlement. But to rest on that consensus, and to deny Davenport's light, would be to revive Whiggery with a vengeance. We need both truths. Historical pyrrhonism reached the point, in the early nineteenth century, when a popular pamphlet could be written, *Some Historic Doubts Concerning the Existence of Napoleon*. But Napoleon did exist; the English Civil War did happen. And the literature of the time gives a unique insight into the fears and aspirations of the men that fought that war. We need to turn to the historical context to set these fears and aspirations in perspective. And then to go back to the literature again to honour John Davenport's insight.

1975   W. M. LAMONT

Literary Introduction

This anthology of selections from seventeenth-century controversy assaults the reader's inner ear with a multitude of differing voices—some uplifted in hope for mankind, some bitterly disillusioned, some mocking, some indignant, some querulous, some ferocious, some resigned. 'The subjective, not the objective, alone is true,'[1] maintained Kierkegaard, and Blake insisted that 'everything possible to be believed is a portion of truth.'[2] What we are concerned with here are the multitudinous subjective truths in the phenomenology of men and women in seventeenth-century England. Each extract, therefore, necessarily presents a different perspective, and if at first we are bewildered, perhaps it is a healthy bewilderment, for we may then in fact be closely approximating to the state of mind of a mid seventeenth-century Englishman. Implied in this approach is a scepticism regarding the possibility of ever attaining to any absolute objective insight into the truth about the past. Did Charles I sneer at his accusers or did he gaze imperturbably on them? Was Cromwell a hypocrite or not? Which was the dragon and which the dragon-slayer in this whole central conflict of the 1640s? In other words was the Civil War a case of 'Damnè'd Treason' or was it 'The Good Old Cause'? The answers in every case are inseparable from the people who try to answer—both then and ever since.

Poets do not usually feature very largely in collections of historical documents, but because this book is concerned not only with what *did* happen, but with what people felt about what they thought was happening, poets with their exceptional skill at rendering the truth of their own feelings have contributed very largely to the volume—not least because they felt impelled during this period to write about

xiii

the great public events, not just about their mistress's eyebrow.

Having admitted that this book contains a welter of conflicting testimony, is it possible to make any generalizations at all about the reactions of these individuals to their time?

What first emerged in preparing this book was the sheer obsessiveness of the recurrent subject of religion and the forms of worship. Coarse ballads, innumerable mock-litanies, even the chapbooks of jokes of the period, all focus on religion.

Secondly, it emerged that many of the witnesses here assembled did not hold a simplistic, black and white view either of the issues or of the men engaged on either side. The Nonconformist leader Richard Baxter, for example, loved the poetry of the Anglican George Herbert and was deeply suspicious of Cromwell; Sir Edmund Verney, the King's own standard-bearer, believed his master to be in the wrong in his championing of episcopacy; Marvell's ambivalent attitude to the issues is still the subject of critical argument and uncertainty, whilst it is to the Puritan Lucy Hutchinson that we owe a devastating portrait of two bogus Puritans:

> Sir John Gell . . . had . . . so highly misdemeaned himself that he looked for punishment from the parliament; to prevent it, he very early put himself into their service . . . no man knows for what reason he chose that side; for he had not understanding enough to judge the equity of the cause, nor piety or holiness; being a foul adulterer all the time he served the parliament, and so unjust, that without any remorse, he suffered his men indifferently to plunder both honest men and cavaliers. . . .[3]

Another regrettable ally was the 'libidinous goat' Chadwick, who pretended to sanctity,

> cutting his hair, and taking up a form of godliness, the better to deceive. . . . Never was a truer Judas, since Iscariot's time, than he, for he would kiss the man he had in his heart to kill . . .[4]

Thirdly, one is struck time and again by the extraordinary *contemporary* relevance of very many of the arguments, temperamental divisions and issues of the mid seventeenth century. Speaking of the Thirty Years War, 1618–1648, Professor Golo Mann has written recently: 'All periods resemble one another, but this one resembles our own more than others.'[5] For instance, the perception that 'extremes meet', familiar to us from the many analogies drawn between Communist and Fascist authoritarian intolerance, was already intuited in seventeenth-century comparisons between Puritans and Papists. Both allegedly shared an equal indifference as to the ethics of the means necessary to attaining their fanatical ends:

> From Papists on one hand, and Phanatick
> o'th other,
> From Presbyter Jack, the Popes younger
> brother, . . .
> Libera nos.[6]

and Cowley's *The Puritan and The Papist* begins:

> So two rude *waves*, by stormes together throwne
> Roare at each other, fight, and then grow *one*.
> Religion is a *Circle*; men contend,
> And runne the round in dispute without end.
> Now in a *Circle* who goe contrary,
> Must at the last meet of necessity.
> The Roman to advance the *Catholicke* cause
> Allowes *a Lie*, and calls it *Pia Fraus*.
> The Puritan approves and does the same,
> Dislikes nought in it but the *Latin name*.[7]

Then again the insurmountable gulf in taste between the ascetic George Fox and the Shadwell who wrote, 'The Delights of the Bottle are turned out of doors/By Factious Fanatical sons of dammn'd whores',[8] is familiar in our own time when what is 'art' or a 'freely exploratory life-style' to some is seen as 'sickening indecency' by others. More important, many of the issues raised during the Civil War period are still as pressing and as unsolved now as they were then. We may no longer care about the power wielded by Anglican bishops (and Anglican bishops may themselves now be advocates of revolution), but we still ask ourselves: what is a Just Society? How is it to be realized? Can mutually exclusive ideologies possibly be tolerated within one society?

Instances of hatred, of unprincipled 'Trimming', of triumphing over the defeated—whether a Laud or a Hugh Peters—of steadfastness under oppression and genuine self-devotion to an altruistic cause are all to be found in the following pages. Examples of quite unforgettable personal statements—

nakedly emotional, subjective and unashamed—also abound
in the period before 1660:

> 'And for this I will spend and be spent, and be puld in ten
> thousand pieces; before I will in the least deny my God.'
>> (Lilburne, *Come out of her my People*.)

> 'To say, Sir that there hath not been a strife in me, were to
> make me less man than, God knoweth, my infirmities make me.'
>> (Strafford's last letter to Charles I.)

> 'I have no quarrell to any man, either for unbeleefe or mis-
> beleefe, because I judgeth no man beleeveth any thing, but
> what he cannot choose but beleeve.'
>> (William Walwyn, *A Still and Soft Voice*, 1647.)

> 'I beseech you, in the bowels of Christ, think it possible you
> may be mistaken. . . . There may be a *Covenant* made with
> Death and Hell.'
>> (Cromwell, letter no. 136 to the General
>> Assembly of the Kirk of Scotland.)

> 'What I have spoken, is the language of that which is not
> called amiss "The good old Cause:" . . . Thus much I should
> perhaps have said, though I was sure I should have spoken
> only to trees and stones; to tell the very soil itself, what her
> perverse inhabitants are deaf to. Nay, though what I have
> spoke should happen . . . to be the last words of our expiring
> liberty.'
>> (Milton, *A Ready and Easy Way to Establish a*
>> *Free Commonwealth*, 1660.)

But 'Human-kind cannot bear very much reality',[9] and
this also goes for the reality of naked emotion. After 1660 it is
a truism of English literary history that satire, already of
course an important part of the literature of the 1640s and
1650s, became the *dominant* literary mode—satire dressed in
its god-like robes of wrathful or mocking judgment. Satire is
denunciatory and therefore implies a maximum of moral
distance between the writer and his subject; its emotional
range is deep but narrow, encompassing only different shades
of anger or contempt. For it to carry conviction at all as
possessing general relevance it must assume a *mask* of
generalized objectivity, to quash accusations of merely personal
spite. With the exception of an aberrant 'mad tinker' like
Bunyan, English literature had to make do without the

writer's most intimate, unmasked 'I' until the poetry of William Cowper a hundred years later. This flight from subjectivism is often ascribed to the dual influences of the new scientific rationalism and of French neo-classicist aesthetics, but the traumatic phenomenon of the recent Civil War would seem a much more adequate reason for such a profound literary reaction. Would not the individualism of personal faith and opinion now be deeply suspect for its association with sectarian 'anarchy', and the passions themselves be feared as all too easily moved to brutal violence? The fabric of society had been, it was felt, temporarily rent; a civilized state of society had to be reordered, and to this end the range of permissible emotions, opinions and their expression, all had to be restricted. There was, of course, no issuing of a Court edict or a Party directive—the memory of past 'excesses' would be enough to ensure a dominant attitude that 'People don't do such things!' any more.

Historical Introduction

Towards the end of this volume will be found excerpts from a remarkable pamphlet by an Anglican bishop (**8.5**). Thomas Barlow wrote *Popery* in 1679. He offered his readers a potted history of English religion and politics in the seventeenth century. Where others had found discord, he found harmony. What united English Protestants, argued Barlow, was their imperial faith. England was an Empire, governed by one Supreme Head: this is what the preamble to the Act in Restraint of Appeals had asserted; it was for this belief that the martyrs, in John Foxe's great work, had given up their lives. The Gunpowder Plot, Archbishop Laud, the Civil War, the Protectorate, the Clarendon Code and now the Popish Plot (Barlow was writing in defence of Titus Oates) were all ruthlessly fitted into Barlow's pattern of history. In different ways they represented the continuation of that sixteenth-century struggle between the Christian Emperor and the Papal Antichrist chronicled first by Foxe and Jewel. This struggle was seen in apocalytic terms. Much was obscure in the Book of Revelation—had the millennium already happened, or was it to take place in the future? Was the Pope *the* Antichrist or merely *an* Antichrist? But one thing at least was clear: England, the Elect Nation, was locked in a momentous struggle with Roman Catholicism. And in that struggle the Royal Supremacy was the Catholic target, the Protestant shield.

There is a lot to be said against the Barlow view of seventeenth-century history. The man himself was a shameless turncoat. The work was a crude piece of propaganda: Barlow wanted to show Protestants why they should believe Titus Oates's preposterous stories of a Popish Plot. Most damaging of all, his thesis ran counter to common sense. The one safe generalization that can be made about English Protestantism

in the seventeenth century is that it was hopelessly divided.
The English Civil War was a *Protestant* Civil War. Recent
research has destroyed the myth that English Catholics were,
in the main, enthusiastic Royalists.[1] They chose neutralism;
when they did depart from this position, it was mainly a defensive response to attacks *on them* initiated by the Roundhead
Army. Nor was this Protestant division an aberration of the
1640s. It had been a long time coming. Sybil Oldfield rightly
calls her second chapter, dealing with the 1620s and 1630s,
'the coming storm': and her next two chapters show how
Civil War strengthened, for each side, the dehumanized image
of the other, the flattering image of self. The execution of the
King in 1649 is the logical end to this story of conflict.

But 1649 is not the end of the seventeenth century. Nor have
we made it the end of our volume. Had we done so we would
have saddled ourselves with at least three unacceptable propositions. One would be that what happened after 1649 is of
little intrinsic value. It has taken two good recent studies of
the Rump Parliament and the Protectorate, for instance, to
rescue those institutions from the shadow cast by the regicide
and for their true contribution to be recognized.[2] Another
falsity would be to accept the events of 1649 at the cosmic
valuation given them by the authors of *Eikon Basilike* and
Eikonoklastes. And a third would be to see English Puritanism
in the early part of the seventeenth century as a closed spiritual
brotherhood, preparing itself for the Revolution and the regicide. All these propositions will be challenged in the following
sections, but the last is the most plausible, and is worth refut-
ing immediately.

A number of separate myths are bound up with the myth
that English Protestantism was a gymnasium for revolution
in the early seventeenth century. *The first myth is that Calvinism is a creed for rebels*. This rests on a simplistic view of
Calvin's political philosophy, and upon the way it evolved in
different communities at different times. For instance, in
France under Coligny Huguenotism was a patriotic, centraliz-
ing force (as opposed to the pro-Spanish tendencies of the
Guise family). After 1572, and the massacre of St Bartholomew's Day, we see the development of Huguenot tyrannicide
theories: but only a decade or so later it is Huguenots who
are proclaiming the Divine Right of Kings against the Catholic
League.[3] In Holland Calvinists supported the Royal House of
Orange and Arminians were the revolutionaries: a point made

against the Arminians by the Presbyterian writer, Thomas Edwards, in 1646.[4] That Arminianism need be no barrier to revolutionary zeal is suggested by the careers of George Fox and his Quakers, John Goodwin and John Milton. Indeed in the eighteenth century Edward Thompson has shown how Calvinist dogma limited the revolutionary potential of Particular Baptism, and the importance of Wesley's Arminian theology to his evangelical success is only beginning to be properly understood.[5]

The second myth is that the English Puritan movement was in its most aggressive phase in the early seventeenth century. Historians would now see the high point of Puritan ideological commitment as being the 1570s and 1580s. The death of Field, and the collapse of the classical movement in the 1580s, marked a change in the character of English Puritanism. It took an inward turn; its great names were now Sibbes and Bolton, Preston and Gouge; its characteristics were a devotion to casuistry, the moral life and individual spiritual experience. It has even been suggested that, in this period of development, the popular mission of the Catholic clergy was more effectively to English Protestants than to English Catholics.[6] Thus the great English Puritan, Richard Baxter, could proclaim his profound debt to 'an old torn book . . . lent my father which was called *Bunny's Resolution* (being written by Parsons the Jesuit and corrected by Edward Bunny)'.[7]

The third myth is that James I alienated the affections of his English Protestant subjects by his absolutist claims for monarchy. This myth rests on two other myths: that James I's views on Kingship were offensive to the majority of his subjects; that he wrecked unity at the Hampton Court Conference. Both of these assumptions are discussed in the first section in this volume.

The fourth myth is that 'Court' and 'Country' were polarized in the 1620s and 1630s. Now it is true that there was nothing like this polarity in the Elizabethan period: even when Field's Presbyterians were developing an abrasive ideology, the Court was dominated by Puritan 'fellow travellers' like Walsingham, Cecil and Leicester. A far cry from Henrietta Maria's 'Popish' Court. Even so, we can underrate the fluidity of 'Court' and 'Country' concepts even in the later period. The struggle for office produced a competitiveness that undercut simple divisions along such lines. The Duke of Buckingham's flirtation with John Preston and his Puritan colleagues did not last long, but it opened up interesting possibilities of a Puritan 'Court' versus an Anglican 'Country'. It is to this period that we owe some of the most outspoken criticisms of the Royal Supremacy from Anglican sources (see John Cosin's embarrassments: (1.7)). The most recent student of Strafford's correspondence sensibly points out that the woolly rhetoric of the day made changes in political allegiance natural and legitimate. Thus Strafford in opposition may tiresomely play at the role of country bump-kin (1.8), but the real break in his career is not 1628, when he becomes Lord President, but 1630 when he begins the friend-ship with Archbishop Laud that takes him away from the middle ground of politics.[8]

The fifth myth is that the ideological innovators were, not the Laudians, but their Puritan critics. Only now, in the work of scholars like Dr Tyacke and Professor Bangs, are we beginning to appreciate the importance of Laud's break with his predeces-sors in an ideological commitment to Arminianism.[9] This claim was linked by Laud and his colleagues, to the parallel claim that bishops existed by divine right, not by virtue of the Royal Supremacy. The two claims are strictly not parallel. High Church Calvinists flourished in the reign of James I: men like Carleton and Downame. They were not extinct in Laud's time —witness Joseph Hall—but they were becoming rarer. The panic felt by English Protestants came from their perception of a twin menace; an assault on their Calvinist faith and on the Royal Supremacy from the same source: Arminian bishops. The Puritan pamphleteer Prynne wrote in 1637 a tract entitled *A Breviate of the Prelates Intollerable Usurpations Upon The Royall Prerogative.* This captures well the worried tone of Pro-testants at this time: men who saw the settled truths—the Calvinist doctrine of the Predestination of the Elect and the imperial case for the Royal Supremacy that Barlow was to expound in 1679—subverted by the Arminian clergy. Indeed, in an unfortunate but revealing analogy, Prynne compared Laud to Copernicus as the wrecker of established certitudes.

With these myths out of the way, we are in a better position to do justice to the King-worship of our first section, and to see that its appeal was much broader than is commonly supposed. But to argue that King-worship, on the imperial lines laid down by Barlow, was sincere and traditional is not the same thing as saying that it was unconditional. A pamphleteer in 1689 justified the deposition of James II because he had 'changed the form of Government, and Constitution from an English

Monarchy, and Independent; from an Imperial Crown, to a subjection to the Pope, and See of Rome'.[10] This was the other side of imperialism: Coke's assertion that the Kingdom of England should have no foreign power over it. The *suspicion* that Charles I—through the influence of Laud or of his wife— was a Papist and the *certain knowledge* that James II was one: they made possible, respectively, the regicide and the Glorious Revolution. They don't prove that Barlow was wrong in claiming that most English Protestants were sincerely devoted to their King; only that loyalty had its limits and that the Christian Emperor, who broke the rules of the imperial game, could expect no mercy from his subjects.

Select Bibliography

There are full references in the footnotes to the most helpful monographs on specific themes. But the following short list may be helpful to readers who are looking for general background works.

HISTORY

Christopher Hill	*The Century of Revolution* (1961).
William Lamont	*Godly Rule* (1969).
Christopher Hill	*Puritanism and Revolution* (1964).
Conrad Russell	*The Crisis of Parliaments* (Oxford, 1971).
Brian Manning (ed.)	*Politics, Religion and the English Civil War* (1973).
L. V. Bredvold	*The Intellectual Milieu of John Dryden* (Ann Arbor, 1956).
C. Webster (ed.)	*The Intellectual Revolution of the Seventeenth Century* (1974).
M. Walzer	*The Revolution of the Saints* (1966).
A. G. R. Smith (ed.)	*The Reign of James VI and I* (1973).
C. Russell (ed.)	*The Origins of the English Civil War* (1973).
G. Aylmer (ed.)	*The Interregnum* (1972).
A. S. P. Woodhouse	*Puritanism and Liberty* (1950).

LITERATURE

C. V. Wedgwood	*Poetry and Politics under the Stuarts* (Ann Arbor, 1960).
Frank Jessup	*Background to the English Civil War* (Oxford, 1966).

E. Dowden   *Puritan and Anglican* (1900).

H. Grierson   *Cross-currents in the Literature of the
                     Seventeenth Century* (1958).

E. Saillens   *John Milton, man, poet, polemist*
                     (Oxford, 1964).

D. Wolfe   *Milton in the Puritan Revolution* (1963)
                     and *Milton and his England* (Princeton,
                     1971).

W. Haller   *Rise of Puritanism* (New York, 1957).

Boris Ford (ed.)   *From Donne to Marvell*, Pelican Guide
                     to English Literature (1970).

Douglas Bush   *English Literature in the Earlier
                     Seventeenth Century 1600–1660* (1962).
                     Oxford History of English Literature.

Henry Kamen   *The Rise of Toleration* (1967).

Acknowledgments

The editors wish to extend their thanks to the following publishers:
Oxford University Press for permission to use material from
A. S. Knowland's *Six Caroline Plays*, 1962; the Royal Historical
Society for permission to use material from the *Wentworth Papers,
1597–1628*, ed. by J. P. Cooper, 1973; George Bell & Sons Ltd and
The Regents of the University of California for permission to
use material from their editions of *Pepys Diary*, ed. by Robert
Latham and William Mathews; the Clarendon Press for permission
to use material from *The Jacobean and Caroline Stage* by G. E.
Bentley, 1968, and from Samuel Butler's *Hudibras Parts I and II
and Selected Other Writings*, ed. by J. Wilders and H. de Quehen,
1973; New York University Press for permission to use material
from *Cavalier and Puritan: Ballads and Broadsides Illustrating the
Period of the Great Rebellion 1640–1660*, ed. by Hyder Rollins,
copyright 1923 by New York University.

I

KING-WORSHIP

James I has been given short shrift by schoolmasters. Successive generations of schoolchildren have learned to despise a pedantic boor, who wrecked the delicate Elizabethan balance by his attachment to alien ideologies of royal absolutism. This antipathy seems hard to explain. Did they find it harder to forgive James's pursuit of learning or of attractive young boys? But their profession is one not usually characterized by an excessive devotion to either ignorance or heterosexuality. And why, when they reach for the most damaging epithet to describe James I, do they come up with the term 'schoolmasterly'?

It is time to rescue James I from their self-flagellations. The researches of Professor Neale into the latter years of Elizabeth I's reign have shown us how tatty was much of the legacy that James I inherited. Interesting research recently has been done on James I's achievements in Scotland before he came to the English throne.[1] The effect of such studies is to enhance James's stature. He faced problems similar to those encountered by Elizabeth—Bothwell was James's Essex—and handled them with skill. The lordships of erection were—contrary to myth—not part of a conscious 'party-building' strategy, but his success was founded on co-operation with the magnates. His Scottish experience had not unfitted James for England, although it is possible to argue that later his English experience would weaken his grip on Scotland.

And what of his English experience? Did the sure touch he displayed in Scotland desert him in England? There is little ground for such a supposition. James was no more involved in a doctrinaire challenge to common law procedure than Coke was in a similar challenge to prerogative. If James had permanently antagonized his English Puritan subjects at the Hampton Court Conference, this would have been at variance

with the finesse that he showed in handling Scottish ecclesiastical matters, as is revealed in Professor Donaldson's researches.
There is no reason to posit such a decline. The version that
has come down to us of the Hampton Court Conference owes
much to the propagandist skill of William Barlow, Bishop of
Lincoln, who drew up the official record of the Conference. The
Conference had worked out better for Reynolds and his
Puritan colleagues than they had dared to hope: Barlow's
technique, in the extract that follows (1.6), is to put in their
mouths absurdly inflated claims for success. In this way he
hoped to mask the real success which they had won and to
conceal the bishops' own defeat.[2] The worst that can be said
against James I is that he did go into decline, in matters of
Church and State, in the latter years of his reign: whether this
can be put down to political theory or porphyria is open to
question.

James's political theory should anyway be put in perspective. What was shocking about a belief in the Divine Right
of Kings to Englishmen brought up in the imperial tradition
(discussed in the historical introduction earlier)? The answer
is: very little. Just how little can be measured by the response
of Richard Baxter. James had first produced his classic statement of Divine Right, *The Trew Law of Free Monarchies*,
anonymously in 1598 five years before the officially accredited
publication.[3] It was this anonymous tract that Baxter read in
his prison cell in 1686, and to which he responded angrily (1.2).
But his anger was not directed at the inflated claims for monarchy in the work, but at the 'nameless Scot's' dangerous
reliance on conquest as a basis for Kingship (1.1). This was to
put too *low* a valuation on monarchy: Baxter, in another passage at this same time, shows the importance to an English
Protestant of the imperial tradition (1.3). And for Baxter the
justification of King-worship was in Scripture, not in the
sword: above all, 'in the Apocalypse and former prophecies'.
What is striking about both these Baxter passages is that they
are from unpublished manuscripts and composed in prison.
They were not intended for public scrutiny, and there is no
sense in which they can be put down to Court flattery.

There is, of course, plenty of literary evidence of Court
flattery (1.10) and from Milton and other Puritans it produced
an angry response. But 'Court' and 'Country' polarities can
be exaggerated: in the passage from Strafford that follows
(1.8), for instance, the claims to a 'Country' purity are already

a form of self-parody. And a Laudian cleric like John Cosin could burn his fingers rather badly in 1628 with sneers at the Royal Supremacy at a time when Puritanism seemed the religion of 'Court' rather than 'Country' (**1.7**).

This in itself is a useful reminder to us that King-worship was a Protestant characteristic, and not an exclusively Anglican one. Its roots lay, as Baxter had indicated, in prophecy—and in magic.[4] As late as 23 June 1660 Pepys would note the poor people standing all morning in the rain to be touched 'for the King's evil' by Charles II. Thus a belief in the power of Kings to deal with the scrofulous survived the death of the father and the life of the son. Intellectuals had different reasons for valuing the Royal Supremacy. One would not have found John Selden waiting in the rain for the Royal Touch: his defence of Kingship is altogether more homely and domestic (**1.5**). The expressions of King-worship that follow vary very much in tone, but a common theme can be discerned.

That theme is the imperial one outlined by Baxter: Protestants serve the Christian Emperor against the Popish Antichrist. Baxter was wrong to think that this theme was absent from James I's claims for monarchy. Even Hobbes—*par excellence* the cynical apologist for conquest as the basis of Kingship—is now seen to have been touched by these apocalyptic intimations (**1.4**).[5]

It is no paradox then to insist that the Civil War was begun by King-worshippers. Apart from Henry Marten, it is hard to think of a first-class politician who was a Republican. The Civil War was fought between two sorts of King-worshipper: one rescuing the King from power-hungry opposition politicians, the other from sycophantic privy councillors. Hence the extreme slowness of theory to catch up with practice. Resistance theories develop very late in the English Civil War (contrasted with the French Wars of Religion) and when they do, tend to be imported from Scotland. But was there not always in Calvinist political theory that fatal loop-hole, which sanctioned resistance to the ungodly ruler? There was, but its reception in England was a cool one (*pace* Milton). If there is a case for linking Puritanism with rebellion, it is an oblique and long-term one, and only in those terms can it be justified. Hunton's *Treatise of Monarchy* is significant in this context (**1.9**). His devotion to monarchy is sincere; he has no time for resistance theories; he does not believe in the sovereignty of Parliament. But Hunton is not a neutral. He will fight for Parliament, not because it has an authoritative case—hence the dismay he caused in Roundhead colleagues—but because his *conscience* tells him to do so. It was not in full-blown resistance theories imported from Geneva, France or Scotland, but in an unstrident emphasis on conscience, that the true limits of Kingworship were set for English Protestants of the seventeenth century.

1.1 James I, from *The Trew Law of Free Monarchies*
(London, 1598)

In this extract from his pamphlet, *The Trew Law of Free Monarchies*, written before he came to the throne of England, James I (1566–1625) puts forward the case for the English monarchy derived from conquest. Historians have disagreed about the extent to which Royalists as a whole relied upon the Norman Conquest to buttress their cause. At one time it was thought that James I was unusual in making such a claim,[6] but this view was open to one serious objection, for if the 'balanced polity' was the ideal common to Royalists *and* Parliamentarians in the period before the Civil War why did the Parliamentarians spend so much energy on attacking a view that nobody held?[7] In fact it has been shown that neither Hobbes nor James I were as eccentric in stating this view as the frequent outraged response to their views in pamphlets would suggest.[8]

And according to the fundamental Lawes already alledged we daily see that in the Parliament (which is nothing else but the head Court of the King and his vassals) the lawes are but craved by his subjects, and only made by him at their rogation, and with their advice. For albeit the king make daily statutes and ordinances, enjoying such paines thereto as hee thinkes meet, without any advice of Parliament or estates; yet it lies in the power of no Parliament, to make any kinde of Law or Statute, without his Scepter be to it, for giving it the force of a Law. And although divers changes have been in other countries of the blood Royall and kingly house, the kingdom being rest by conquest from one to another, as in our neighbour country in England (which was never in ours) yet the same ground of the king's right over all the land, and subjects thereof remaineth alike in all other free Monarchies, as well as in this: for when the Bastard of Normandie came into England, and made himself king, was it not by force, and with a mighty army? Where he gave the Law, and tooke none, changed the Lawes, invested the order of government, set down the strangers his followers in many of the old possessours roomes, as at this day well appeareth a great part of the Gentlemen in England, beeing come of the Norman blood, and their old Lawes, which to this day they are ruled by, are written in his language and not in theirs: And yet his successours have with great happinesse enjoyed the Crowne to this day; whereof the like was also done by all them that conquested them before.

1.2 and 3 Doctor Williams's Library from *Baxter Treatises*

The two extracts that follow are interesting for the light which they throw upon the depth of the attachment to monarchy shown by the Puritan, Richard Baxter (1615–1691). Baxter reacts with horror to a crude 'conquest' theory of Kingship. The identity of the 'namelesse Scot' was not known to him; thus he attacked James I for pitching his claims for monarchy too low. The other extract shows why Baxter pitched his claims so high: he saw, as John Foxe (1516–1587) the great martyrologist had done, that the millennium had begun with Constantine, the Christian Emperor. It is a useful summary of Erastian millenarianism: a combination that seems odd to us, but natural to seventeenth-century Protestants. From this position (which, incidentally, despite this particular passage, James I shared with Baxter and many Protestants) Baxter rejected clericalist claims (Laudian, Presbyterian or Papist) to superiority over the King on the soul/body analogy as 'the sense of the Revelation perverted'. He also similarly rejected arguments for a future millennium from friends like Thomas Beverley on the grounds: 'Would we not have Christian Kings? Was not Constantines Reign a grand blessing to the Church?'. The extracts are the more interesting because they are part of his private manuscript collection, not intended for publication. One minister owned up in 1647 to the need to utter 'soft and silken phrases' publicly for the magistrate's benefit.[9] The argument in this section is that there was a *King-worship* among Puritans as well as this judicious sycophancy: it is easier to separate the one from the other in private correspondence than in public statement.

There is a little booke written by a namelesse Scot, 1603 called the Law of free Monarchies agt all Rebellion which concontaineth much of what I have said. But when he foundeth the originall right of Monarchy uppon strugle and Conquest by which only Kings are made Kings, and then they only make all Laws and are prime proprietors of the land, I shall say, 1) that I dare not think Hobs and Spinoza in the right that thought Right was nothing but strugle to get and keep possession 2) nor dare I so farre encourage Rebels, nor did I ever believe that Cromwell's (enforced) conquest gave any usurper Right 3) Nor while France is stronger than England, Holland or other Kings, I dare not say that if that Kingdom conquer them he is their rightfull monarch, lest such doctrine entice him to attempt it. (i., f. 172 v.)

It is a great cause of all our Church confusions, that the usurpation of the Romane Clergy hath by appropriating to themselves the title of the CHURCH and the Ministers or Vicars of Christ, obscured the true dignity of Christian Princes and Magistrates, and blinded the world (and too many Rulers) into a false and base conceit, that Princes are but for the Body, and Priests only for the Soule, and so that the office of every sorry priest is as much above the Kings as the soule is above the body: And as the Soule must rule the Body, so must the Pope, prelates and priests rule Kings and Magistrates: And hereby the Glory of Christs Kingdome as set up in Power, by Christian Emperours and Kings is clouded, and the sense of the Revelation perverted by Papists and too many protestants; who call for the exercise of Christs Kingly office by a vile mistake as if it were only in the hands of pope, prelates, presbyters or popular congregations: And God hath given the world too few good Princes, because we do not sufficiently value and pray for such. Whereas a due consideration of scripture would tell us, that Christian Princes are as Sacred persons as priests, and are bound as much to understand the Law of God, and are the Rulers of priests by the sword, tho' priests may Guide them by the word as their physicians when they choose may direct them

for their health: And as Moses was above Aaron . . . so is the
King above the Archbishop and the rest: And that Christs
Kingdome was but in its Infancy till he visibly ruled by the
sword, by Christian Princes. And as God did in the time of the
Judges rule by Prophets and Imperial Deliverers, till Kings
were settled, and then let Government run in the naturall
course, so did he by propheticall Apostles and Inspired teachers
Keep up his Church, till he had ripened it for a Christian
Empire, and then let it run in the natural channel. . . . This is
the forme of Government that Christ expressly offered the
Jews and owned and claimed in the world: As he is King of
Kings and Lord of Lords; and commissioned him Apostles to
Disciple Nations; and would have naturally gathered the Jewes
as their King, and as he here gathereth his Christians: which
no part of Scripture more fully sheweth than the Apocalypse,
and former prophecies. (vii, f. 330 v.)

1.4 Thomas Hobbes, from *Leviathan*

(London 1651) (Everyman's Library Edition)

The exact date of publication of *Leviathan* by Thomas Hobbes
(1588–1679) is not known, but it was within the first half of 1651.
It has been argued that in publishing it at that time, one of
Hobbes's main aims was to contribute to the debate about the
rights of *de facto* powers which had been precipitated by the
Rump Parliament's requirement in January 1650 that the entire
adult male population swear an oath of 'engagement' to its
authority.[10] Clarendon's dismissal, therefore, of the work as a
'sly address to Oliver' is unjust as a description of its *conception*—
the theme was implicit in Hobbes's earlier work, *De Cive*, which
had appeared abroad as early as 1642—but not of its *effect*, when
it appeared at the time that it did. Against the Royalist and
Laudian insistence that Cromwell was a usurper who could not
be obeyed, Hobbes enormously strengthened the hands of the
political theorists who insisted on Cromwell's *de facto* entitlement
to obedience: Ascham, Warren, Needham and the anti-Laudian
Anglican, Sanderson. Even the rejection of religious independence
in this passage is ambivalent: it is not seen here simply as a re-

lapse to the state of nature, but acknowledged as 'perhaps the best' form of government if contention could be avoided.

. . . Now seeing it is manifest, that the Civill Power, and the Power of the Common-wealth is the same thing; and that Supremacy, and the Power of making Canons, and granting Faculties implyeth a Common-wealth; it followeth, that where one is Soveraign, another Supreme; where one can make Lawes, and another make Canons; there must needs be two Common-wealths, of one & the same Subjects; which is a Kingdome divided in it selfe, and cannot stand. For notwithstanding the insignificant distinction of *Temporall*, and *Ghostly*, they are still two Kingdomes, and every Subject is subject to two Masters. For seeing the *Ghostly* Power challengeth the Right to declare what is Sinne it challengeth by consequence to declare what is Law, (Sinne being nothing but the transgression of the Law;) and again, the Civill Power challenging to declare what is Law, every Subject must obey two Masters, who both will have their Commands be observed as Law; which is impossible. Or, if it be but one Kingdome, either the *Civill*, which is the Power of the Common-wealth, must be subordinate to the *Ghostly*, and then there is no Soveraignty but the *Ghostly*; or the *Ghostly* must be subordinate to the *Temporall*, and then there is no *Supremacy* but the *Temporall*. When therefore these two Powers oppose one another, the Common-wealth cannot but be in great danger of Civill warre, and Dissolution. For the *Civill* Authority being more visible, and standing in the cleerer light of naturall reason, cannot choose but draw to it in all times a very considerable part of the people: And the *Spirituall*, though it stand in the darknesse of Schoole distinctions, and hard words; yet because the fear of Darknesse, and Ghosts, is greater than other fears, cannot want a party sufficient to Trouble, and sometimes to Destroy a Common-wealth, And this is a Disease which not unfitly may be compared to the Epilepsie, or Falling-sicknesse (which the Jewes took to be one kind of possession by Spirits) in the Body Naturall. For as in this Disease, there is an unnaturall spirit, or wind in the head that obstructeth the roots of the Nerves, and moving them violently, taketh away the motion which naturally they should have from the power of the Soule in the Brain, and thereby causeth violent, and irregular motions (which men call Convulsions) in the parts; insomuch as he that is seized there-with, falleth down sometimes into the water, and sometimes into the fire, as a man deprived of his senses; so also in the Body Politique, when the spirituall power, moveth the Members of a Common-wealth, by the terrour of punishments, and hope of rewards (which are the Nerves of it,) otherwise than by the Civill Power (which is the Soule of the Common-wealth) they ought to be moved; and by strange, and hard words suffocates their understanding, it must needs thereby Distract the people, and either Overwhelm the Common-wealth with Oppression, or cast it into the Fire of a Civill warre. . . .

. . . But as the Inventions of men are woven, so also are they ravelled out; the way is the same, but the order is inverted: The web begins at the first Elements of Power, which are Wisdom, Humility, Sincerity, and other vertues of the Apostles, whom the people converted, obeyed, out of Reverence, not by Obligation: Their Consciences were free, and their Words and Actions subject to none but the Civill Power. Afterwards the Presbyters (as the Flocks of Christ encreased) assembling to consider what they should teach, and thereby obliging themselves to teach nothing against the Decrees of their Assemblies, made it to be thought the people were thereby obliged to follow their Doctrine, and when they refused, refused to keep them company, (that was then called Excommunication,) not as being Infidels, but as being disobedient: And this was the first knot upon their Liberty. And the number of Presbyters encreasing, the Presbyters of the chief City or Province, got themselves an authority over the Parochiall Presbyters, and appropriated to themselves the names of Bishops: And this was a second knot on Christian Liberty. Lastly, the Bishop of Rome, in regard of the Imperiall City, took upon him an Authority (partly by the wills of the Emperours themselves, and by the title of *Pontifex Maximus*, and at last when the Emperours were grown weak, by the priviledges of St Peter) over all other Bishops of the Empire: Which was the third and last knot, and the whole *Synthesis* and *Construction* of the Pontificiall Power.

And therefore the *Analysis*, or *Resolution* is by the same way; but beginneth with the knot that was last tyed; as wee may see in the dissolution of the præter-politicall Church Government in England. First, the Power of the Popes was dissolved totally by Queen Elizabeth; and the Bishops, who before exercised their Functions in Right of the Pope, did afterwards exercise the same in Right of the Queen and her Successours; though by retaining the phrase of *Jure Divino*, they were thought to demand it by immediate Right from God: And so was untyed the first knot. After this, the Presbyterians lately in England obtained the putting down of Episcopacy: And so was the second knot dissolved: And almost at the same time, the Power was taken also from the Presbyterians: And so we are reduced to the Independency of the Primitive Christians to follow Paul, or Cephas, or Apollos, every man as he liketh best: Which, if it be without contention, and without measuring the Doctrine of Christ, by our affection to the Person of his Minister, (the fault which the Apostle reprehended in the Corinthians,) is perhaps the best: First, because there ought to be no Power over the Consciences of men, but of the Word it selfe, working Faith in every one, not alwayes according to the purpose of them that Plant and Water, but of God himself, that giveth the Increase: and secondly, because it is unreasonable in them, who teach there is such danger in every little Errour, to require of a man endued with reason of his own, to follow the Reason of any other man, or of the most voices of many other men; Which is little better, then to venture his Salvation at crosse and pile. Nor ought those Teachers to be displeased with this losse of their antient Authority: For there is none should know better then they, that power is preserved by the same Vertues by which it is acquired; that is to say, by Wisdome, Humility, Clearnesse of Doctrine, and sincerity of Conversation; and not by suppression of the Naturall Sciences, and of the Morality of Naturall Reason; nor by obscure Language; nor by Arrogating to themselves more Knowledge than they make appear; nor by Pious Frauds; nor by such other faults, as in the Pastors of Gods Church are not only Faults, but also scandalls, apt to make men stumble one time or other upon the suppression of their Authority.

But after this Doctrine, *that the Church now Militant is the Kingdome of God spoken of in the Old and New Testament*, was received in the World; the ambition, and canvasing for the Offices that belong thereunto, and especially for that great Office of being | Christs Lieutenant, and the Pompe of them that obtained therein the principall Publique Charges, became by degrees so evident, that they lost the inward Reverence due to the Pastorall Function: in so much as the Wisest men, of them that had any power in the Civill State, needed nothing but the authority of their Princes, to deny them any further Obedience. For, from the time that the Bishop of Rome had gotten to be acknowledged for Bishop Universall by pretence of Succession to St Peter, their whole Hierarchy, or Kingdome of Darknesse, may be compared not unfitly to the *Kingdome of Fairies*; that is, to the old wives *Fables* in England, concerning *Ghosts* and *Spirits*, and the feats they play in the night. And if a man consider the originall of this great Ecclesiasticall Dominion, he will easily perceive, that the *Papacy*, is no other, than the *Ghost* of the deceased *Romane Empire*, sitting crowned upon the grave thereof: For so did the Papacy start up on a Sudden out of the Ruines of that Heathen Power.

The *Language* also, which they use, both in the Churches, and in their Publique Acts, being *Latine*, which is not commonly used by any Nation now in the world, what is it but the *Ghost* of the Old *Romane Language*?

The *Fairies* in what Nation soever they converse, have but one Universall King, which some Poets of ours call King *Oberon*; but the Scripture calls *Beelzebub*, Prince of *Dæmons*. The *Ecclesiastiques* likewise, in whose Dominions soever they be found, acknowledge but one Universall King, the *Pope*.

The *Ecclesiastiques* are *Spirituall* men, and *Ghostly* Fathers. The Fairies are *Spirits*, and *Ghosts*. *Fairies* and *Ghosts* inhabite Darknesse, Solitudes, and Graves. The *Ecclesiastiques* walke in Obscurity of Doctrine, in Monasteries, Churches, and Church-yards.

The *Ecclesiastiques* have their Cathedral Churches; which, in what Towne soever they be erected, by vertue of Holy Water, and certain Charmes called Exorcismes, have the power to make those Townes, Cities, that is to say, Seats of Empire. The *Fairies* also have their enchanted Castles, and certain Gigantique Ghosts, that domineer over the Regions round about them.

The *Fairies* are not to be seized on; and brought to answer for the hurt they do. So also the *Ecclesiastiques* vanish away from the Tribunals of Civill Justice.

The *Ecclesiastiques* take from young men, the use of Reason, by certain Charms compounded of Metaphysiques, and Miracles, and Traditions, and Abused Scripture, whereby they are good for nothing else, but to execute what they command them. The *Fairies* likewise are said to take young Children out of their Cradles, and to change them into Naturall Fools, which Common people do therefore call *Elves*, and are apt to mischief.

In what Shop, or Operatory the Fairies make their Enchantment, the old Wives have not determined. But the Operatories of the *Clergy*, are well enough known to be the

Universities, that received their Discipline from Authority Pontificiall.

When the *Fairies* are displeased with any body, they are said to send their Elves, to pinch them. The *Ecclesiastiques*, when they are displeased with any Civill State, make also their Elves, that is, Superstitious, Enchanted Subjects, to pinch their Princes, by preaching Sedition; or one Prince enchanted with promises, to pinch another.

The *Fairies* marry not; but there be amongst them *Incubi*, that have copulation with flesh and bloud. The *Priests* also marry not.

The *Ecclesiastiques* take the Cream of the Land, by Donations of ignorant men, that stand in aw of them, and by Tythes: So also it is in the Fable of *Fairies*, that they enter into the Dairies, and Feast upon the Cream, which they skim from the Milk.

What kind of Money is currant in the Kingdome of *Fairies*, is not recorded in the Story. But the *Ecclesiastiques* in their Receipts accept of the same Money that we doe; though when they are to make any Payment, it is in Canonizations, Indulgences, and Masses.

To this, and such like resemblances between the *Papacy*, and the Kingdome of *Fairies*, may be added this, that as the *Fairies* have no existence, but in the Fancies of ignorant people, rising from the Traditions of old Wives, or old Poets: so the Spirituall Power of the *Pope* (without the bounds of his own Civill Dominion) consisteth onely in the Fear that Seduced people stand in, of their Excommunications; upon hearing of false Miracles, false Traditions, and false Interpretations of the Scripture.

It was not therefore a very difficult matter, for Henry 8. by his Exorcisme; nor Qu. Elizabeth by hers, to cast them out. But who knows that this Spirit of Rome, now gone out, and walking by Missions through the dry places of China, Japan, and the Indies, that yeeld him little fruit, may not return, or rather an Assembly of Spirits worse than he, enter, and inhabite this clean swept house, and make the End thereof worse than the Beginning? For it is not the Romane Clergy onely, that pretends the Kingdome of God to be of this World, and thereby to have a Power therein, distinct from that of the Civill State. And this is all I had a designe to say, concerning the Doctrine of the POLITIQUES. Which when I have reviewed, I shall willingly expose it to the censure of my Countrey.

1.5 John Selden, from *Table Talk*

(ed. F. Pollock, London, 1927)

John Selden (1584–1654), the great Erastian jurist, was opposed to divine right claims from clergymen, whether they were Laudian or Presbyterian. His view that 'a King is a thing men have made for their owne sakes for quietness sake' has obvious links with the position of his friend Hobbes, although his cynicism was more far-reaching: it extended even to those apocalyptic and prophetic insights which underlay Hobbes's support for the civil magistrate.

The puritans who will alow noe free will, but God do's all, yet will allow the subject his liberty to doe or not doe notwithstanding the King, the God upon earth. The Arminians who hold we have free will; yet say when wee come to the King there must be all obedience, and noe liberty must be stood for. . . . A King is a thing men have made for their owne sakes for quietness sake. Just as in a family one man is appointed to buy the Meate, if every man should buy, or if there were many buyers they would never agree, one would buy what the other liked not, or what the other had bought before, so there would bee a confusion, but that charge being committed to one, hee according to his discretion pleases all, if they have not what they would have one day, they shall have it the next, or something as good.

1.6 William Barlow, from *The Summe and Substance of the Conference,*

(London, 1638)

William Barlow (d. 1613), Bishop of Lincoln, took part in the Hampton Court Conference between James I, the Bishops and Puritan dissenters in 1604. He was also entrusted with the official report of the proceedings and this has come down, in diluted form in history textbooks, as the classic confrontation between James I and his Puritan opponents. Modern research has established, however, that Barlow's account was distorting.

Some of the speeches that are bruted upon M. Doctor Reynolds returne to Oxon concerning the late conference before his Majesty.

1. That the Kings Majesty did gratifie Master Doctor Reynolds in every thing which he proposed: or that Doctor Reynolds obtained, and prevailed in every thing he did desire.
2. That if any man report the contrary, he doth lye, or that they should give him the lye, from M. Doctor Reynolds.
3. That these things now obtained by the reformers, were but the beginning of reformation: the greater matters are yet to come.
4. That my Lord of Winton stood mute, and said little or nothing.
5. That my Lord of London called Doctor Reynolds Schismaticke indeed (he thankes him for it) but otherwise said little to purpose.
6. That the Kings Majesty used the Bishops with very hard words, but imbraced Master Doctor Reynolds, and used most kind speeches to him.
7. That my Lord of Canterbury, or my Lord of London, falling on his knees, besought his Majesty to take their cause into his owne hands, and to make some good end of if, such as might stand with their credit.

1.7 From John Cosin
Correspondence
(ed. G. Ornsby, Surtees Society, 52, 1869, pp. 147–152)

John Cosin (1594–1672), later to become Bishop of Durham at the Restoration, was a close friend of Archbishop Laud and Richard Montague. That in November 1628 he was also engaged in the task of clearing himself of the suspicion that he was out to destroy the Royal Supremacy through his *iure divino* claims for bishops is very revealing. This is the necessary background against which to understand the mentality of Puritans like

Prynne in the 1630s, who wrote pamphlets with titles like *A Breviate of the Prelates Intollerable Usurpations Upon the Royall Prerogative*. And this is why (although the charge was subsequently dropped in 1643) Archbishop Laud was accused, in the fifth Article in the original list of charges that Pym drew up in 1640, of seeking to undermine the Royal Supremacy through the Canons issued in that year. Laud saw the reason for the change of mind in October 1643, when the ten Additional Articles against him were sent up from the Commons to the Lords. This charge was hardly compatible with the general one, that he had sought to enlarge the royal prerogative: 'To advance it, and yet made contrary Canons against it, which is the way to destroy it? What pretty nonsense is this?'[11] Because the charge against the Archbishop of destroying the Royal Supremacy was then quietly dropped for tactical reasons, we are slow to give enough credit to the genuineness of such fears earlier among King-worshipping Puritans: what seemed paranoid in 1643 bore a different complexion in 1640, let alone in 1628.

Relation by John Cosin, Prebendary of Durham, of the particulars of a conversation as to the Royal Supremacy.
This was the summe of those speeches which passed from me in our casuall discourse at Tyler's house in Durham, April 28. . . .

1. The first question being put (upon occasion of some discourse between Mr Robson and me about the Canon law) from whom the power of excommunication proceeded, I answered 'that we had our power of excommunication from Christ': and Mr Pleasance interposing that we had it from the King, and that he might excommunicate as well as wee, this I said:—

'That no man ever said or held it before him, that our Church disclaym'd it, that it was a slander laid upon us by the Papists; that the exercise of it indeed was under the King, but the power of it only from Christ, and by virtue of Holy Orders. And, lastly, that our Kings had never taken any such power upon them.'

2. The second question (upon occasion of the former) being presently made by Mr Pleasance, 'How the King then cold be said to be Head of the Church?' I demanded of him, 'Who said it now? for the lawes said it not, the Canons said it not, our best writers said it not, specially in his sense, Queen Elizabeth refused it, our Kings since liked it not, that the oath of Supremacie itself expressed it not, that in my

judgment [*In margine:* Here was I questioned, why I used not the title of Head of the Church in my prayer before my sermons.] it was unsafe for us private men to set forth any other title of the King than what himself or his state had ordeyned, that the stile was the more misliked (howsoever in a generall sense it might be well enough interpreted) because the Pope's flatterers had given it to him, and because it doth most properly belong unto Christ, who was the only Head of his Church, precisely taken, which is but one bodie it self, and therefore not capable of many heads. And lastly, that they did but cause themselves to be pittyed or condemned; whosoever did affirme that we gave power of administering the sacraments, or of excommunication unto Princes themselves, whom, nevertheless, we acknowledged (and I would be as redy to maintain and set forth as any man) to be Supreme Govenor both of Church and State, and that by their power of supreme dominion they might command churchmen at any time to doe their office, or punish them for the neglect of it.' I added further, to Mr Robson's sayings, 'That externall coaction, indeed, whereby men were forced to obey the jurisdiction of the Church, was only from the King, but the *power* of spirituall jurisdiction it self was from Christ, who had given it unto his Apostles, and they to their successors in ordination.'

This was the utmost of that I said: and being urged as I was in a companie of schollers and other understanding men, I think I should have betrayed the truth if I had said lesse. The whole companie, or the best of them, often interposed and assented to what I spake; unless it were Mr Pleasance and G. Walton. But as for any irreverent words of his Majestie, my most gracious Lord and Sovereign, they yet did never, and never shall they come either in my mouth or into my hart.

                                                    JOHN COSIN

The Testimony of Sir William Belayse and others as to Mr Cosin's expression of opinion with regard to the Royal Supremacy.
Whereas in a casuall conference which passed between Mr John Cosin and others, at a Court dinner kept by the Dean and Prebendaries of Durham, in Widdow Tyler's house there, upon the 28th day of April last past, some persons seeking to wound the honest name and reputation of the said Mr Cosin have lately given out that he should speak certain disloyall

words, tending to the denyall of the King's supremacie, and namely that he shold say, the King had no more power to officiate in the Church or to excommunicate then his man, as some, or then his horse-keeper, as others more odiously have bruited it.

These are to testifie unto all men to whom these presents may be addressed, that wee, who were then present and weere auditors of all speeches then passing from Mr Cosin, heard no such words by him uttered, nor any other words tending to disloyaltie, or irreverence of his sacred Majestie, his person or his power, but further that we apprehended nothing by him then discoursed or spoken, but what we approved, and might well have spoken ourselves in the like case, he there professing openly and freely, 'That according to his bounden dutie, he was as ready to defend and set forth the King's supremacie and power of Ecclesisticall dominion (though no man attributed unto him the power of excommunication or other priestly functions) as any man shold be to oppose the same.'

In witness whereof we have hereunto subscribed our names, as giving testimonie to the truth, if at any time the said Mr Cosin shall have cause for the cleering of himselfe to make use hereof. Dated the 6th day of November 1628

WILL BELAYS   WILL. JAMES
MARM. BLAKISTON   JO. BROWNE

This is a true copie of the original testimonie.

FRA. BURGOINE
WILL. JAMES

1.8 From *Wentworth Papers 1597–1628*
(ed. J. P. Cooper, Camden Fourth Series, Volume 12, London, 1973)

Thomas Wentworth (1593–1641), first Earl of Strafford, wrote this letter to Christopher Wandesford in 1624 when he was outside the Court influence, and his letter makes great play with that fact.

Yow charge mee that I writt of stagges and foxes from Rufford
where yow say I might have sunge of secretaries displaced,
messages dissavowed. But, by yow leave, that was not so
sutable to my low condicion, nay if you had bene so well
read in my domesticke Ovid as yow might, had yow but
grace, yow might have found a quaint art in that forbearance
*Triste petis munus, quis enim sue proelia victus commemorare
velit?* God helpe yow man there is as well Cuntry as Court
crafte; But that yow may know wee live not here altogether in
a palpable, in an Egiptian darknes, bee yow advertized that,
the French Ambassador came back to Darby with a fresh
alarume that all should goe on with all perseuarance, only that
the hands were to be changed thorowe which it is to passe and
so the match presently to be concluded. What your more
refined witts will make of this, as workinge upon your proper
subject the affaires of Princes and Potentates, I know not,
but wee plaine Swaines after our ordinary manner resort to an
old adage and cry out that there is art in daubinge. . . .

1.9 Philip Hunton, from
A Treatise of Monarchy
(London, 1643)

Philip Hunton (1604–1682), later to become provost of Cromwell's
University of Durham, 1657–1660, here gives in 1643 the classic
exposition of the problems of continuing to believe in a 'balanced
polity' while fighting a Civil War to claim the balance for one
side. This was the humbug of Ferne on the Royalist side but
also of Herle on the Parliamentary side. Both claimed to be
fighting for *King and Parliament*; both claimed to *believe* in mixed
government. But Hunton's logic is remorseless: in a mixed
government there can be no 'legal constituted judge'. Make
King or Commons the umpire, and you make that body sovereign
and then farewell 'balance'. Belatedly Henry Parker (for Parliament) and Digges (for the King) were saying the same thing as
they moved from arguments of 'balance' to claims to sovereignty
for their respective sides. Hunton's *analysis* may resemble theirs,
but his *prescription* is radically different. He still believes in
'balance', and cannot accept that royal absolutism or Parlia-

mentary sovereignty is the way of the English constitution.
What then? If balance *has* demonstrably broken down, are we
not then left with anarchy? Or neutrality? Hunton says: neither.
The individual conscience must be the arbiter. In Hunton's own
case the choice is clear: he will opt for Parliament against the
destructive acts of the King's agents, without fooling himself that
Parliament *has* the authoritative power to judge such acts as
destructive.

If it be demanded then, 'How this cause can be decided? and
which way must the people turn in such a contention?' I
answer; if the non-decision be tolerable, it must remain un-
decided, whilst the principle of legal decision is thus divided,
and by that division each suspends the other's power. If it
be such as is destructive, and necessitates a determination,
this must be evident, and then every person must aid that
part, which, in his best reason and judgment, stands for
publick good against the destructive. And the laws and
government which he stands for, and is sworn to, justify and
hear him out in it; yea, bind him to it. If any wonder I should
justify a power in the two houses, to resist and command
aid against any agents of destructive commands of the king,
and yet not allow them power of judging when those agents
or commands are destructive? I answer, I do not simply deny
them a power of judging and declaring this; but I deny them
to be a legal court ordained to judge of this case authoritatively, so as to bind all people to receive and rest in their
judgment for convenience of its authority, and because they
have voted it. It is the evidence, not the power of their votes,
must bind our reason and practice in this case. We ought to
conceive their votes the discoveries made by the best eyes of
the kingdom, and which in likelihood, should see most: but,
when they vote a thing against the proceedings of the third
and supreme estate, our consciences must have evidence of
truth to guide them, and not the sole authority of votes; and
that for the reason so often alleged.

1.10 Literary Evidence

Although most convinced 'Puritans' of the 1630s felt a deep
allegiance to the King, the adulatory terms in which the Court

poets addressed Charles and Henrietta must have smacked of 'Pagan Idolatry' in a God-fearing ear:

> Jove rivalls your great vertues, Royall Sir,
> And Juno, Madam, your attractive graces.
>> (Carew, from *Coelum Britannicum* (1633).)

and

> Such huge extremes inhabit thy great mind,
> Godlike, unmoved, and yet, like woman, kind!
> Which of the ancient poets had not brought
> Our Charles's pedigree from Heaven, and taught
> How some bright dame, compress'd by mighty Jove,
> Produced this mix'd Divinity and Love?
>> (Waller, from *Of His Majesty's receiving the
>> news of the Duke of Buckingham's Death* (1628).)

(a) SIR WILLIAM DAVENANT, *To the King on New-Year's Day* (1630).

This ode by the Poet-Laureat would also have struck some worrying notes. Not only would the unabashed worldliness of the references to Wine and Wealth, or the near-blasphemous juxtaposition of the joys of love-making and of spiritual sanctity in the first stanza have seemed offensive, but also the inadequate militancy in the poet's view of Charles as Protestant ally of Gustavus Adolphus the Swedish king. Admittedly, Davenant hopes that Parliament will vote money to Charles, 'To make the Northerne Victors Fame/No more our envy, nor our shame', but he also hopes that the victory (over Catholic Spain and Austria) will be obtained by Fame or pray'r—not by actual fighting.

> The joyes of eager Youth, of Wine, and Wealth,
> Of Faith untroubled, and unphysick'd Health;
>> Of Lovers, when their Nuptials nie,
>> Of Saints forgiven when they die;
>>> Let this yeare bring
>>> To *Charles* our King:
> To Charles: who is the 'xample and the Law,
> By whom the good are taught, not kept in awe.

Long proffer'd Peace, and that not compass'd by
Expensive Treaties but a Victorie;
  A Victory by Fame obtain'd
  Or pray'r, and not by slaughter gain'd;
     Let this yeare bring
     To Charles our King:
To Charles: who is the 'xample and the Law,
By whom the good are taught, not kept in awe.

A Session too, of such who can obey,
As they were gather'd to consult, not sway:
  Who not rebell, in hope to git
  Some office to reclaime their wit;
     Let this yeare bring
     To *Charles* our King:
To *Charles;* who is the 'xample and the Law,
By whom the good are taught, not kept in awe.

Praetors, who will the publique cause defend,
With timely gifts, not Speeches finely pend;
  To make the Northerne Victors Fame
  No more our envy, nor our shame;
     Let this yeare bring
     To *Charles* our King:
To *Charles;* who is th'xample and the Law
By whom the good are taught, not kept in awe.

(b) CAREW, from *In Answer of an Elegiacal letter upon the Death of the King of Sweden from Aurelian Townsend, inviting me to write on that subject* (late 1632).

After Gustavus Adolphus' death, Carew went even further in escapist quietism—very unpopular among his more committed Protestant compatriots—as he here affirmed Charles I's non-involvement in the ferocious religious struggle on the Continent.

But let us that in myrtle bowers sit
Under secure shades, use the benefit
Of peace and plenty, which the blessed hand
Of our good King gives this obdurate Land,
Let us of Revels sing, and let thy breath
(Which filled Fames trumpet with *Gustavus* death,
Blowing his name to heaven) gently inspire
Thy past'rall pipe . . .

But these are subjects proper to our clime
Tourneyes, Masques, Theaters, better become
Our Halcyon dayes: what though the German Drum
Bellow for freedome and revenge, the noyse
Concernes not us, nor should divert our joyes:
Nor ought the thunder of their Carabins
Drowne the sweet Ayres of our tun'd Violins;
Beleeve me friend, if their prevailing powers
Gaine them a calme securitie like ours,
They'le hang their Armes up on the Olive bough,
And dance, and revell then, as we doe now.

(c) CAREW, from _Coelum Britannicum, A Masque performed at Whitehall in 1633_.

This masque exemplifies the adulation of the King at its most exquisitely absurd, but the very baselessness of the flattery lends it in retrospect a pathetic irony. For within less than ten years this same Monarch had to fight for his crown and later his life—so little Concord was there in fact among his subjects concerning his possession of True Religion, or Wisdom, or a Reputation for Good Government. Far from Time standing still at the sight of Charles' perfections, it drove him inexorably to a public scaffold.

The revels being past, and the King's Majesty seated under the State by the Queen, for conclusion to this masque there appears coming forth from one of the sides, as moving by a gentle wind, a great cloud, which, arriving at the middle of the heaven, stayeth; this was of several colours, and so great, that it covered the whole scene. Out of the further part of the heaven, begins to break forth two other clouds, differing in colour and shape; and being fully discovered, there appeared sitting in one of them _Religion, Truth_, and _Wisdom_. Religion was apparelled in white, and part of her face was covered with a light veil, in one hand a book, and in the other a flame of fire: Truth in a watchet robe, a sun upon her fore-head, and bearing in her hand a palm: Wisdom in a mantle wrought with eyes and hands, golden rays about her head, and Apollo's cithara in her hand. In the other cloud sat _Concord, Government_, and _Reputation_. The habit of _Concord_ was carnation, bearing in her hand a little faggot of sticks bound together, and on the top of it a heart, and a garland of corn on her head. _Government_ was figured in a coat of armour, bearing a shield, and on it a Medusa's head; upon her head a plumed helm, and in her right hand a lance. Reputation, a young man in purple robe wrought with gold, and wearing a laurel wreath on his head. These being come down in an equal distance to the middle part of the air, the great cloud began to break open, out of which struck beams of light; in the midst, suspended in the air, sat *Eternity* on a globe; his garment was long, of a light blue, wrought all over with stars of gold, and bearing in his hand a serpent bent into a circle, with his tail in his mouth. In the firmament about him was a troop of fifteen stars, expressing the stellifying of our British heroes; but one more great and eminent than the rest, which was over his head, figured his Majesty. And in the lower part was seen, afar off, the prospect of Windsor Castle, the famous seat of the most honourable Order of the Garter.

THE FOURTH SONG

Eternity, Religion, Truth, Wisdom, Concord,
Government, Reputation

ETERNITY

Be fixed, you rapid orbs, that bear
The changing seasons of the year
On your swift wings, and see the old
Decrepit sphere grown dark and cold;
Nor did Jove quench her fires: these bright
Flames have eclipsed her sullen light,
   This Royal Pair, for whom Fate will
   Make motion cease, and time stand still:
Since good is here so perfect, as no worth
Is left for after-ages to bring forth.

RELIGION

Mortality cannot with more
Religious zeal the Gods adore.

TRUTH

My truths, from human eyes conceal'd
Are naked to their sight reveal'd.

WISDOM

Nor do their actions from the guide
Of my exactest precepts slide.

CONCORD

And as their own pure souls entwined,
So are their subjects' hearts combined.

GOVERNMENT

So just, so gentle is their sway,
As it seems empire to obey.

REPUTATION

And their fair fame, like incense hurl'd
On altars, hath perfumed the world.

ETERNITY

Brave spirits, whose advent'rous feet
    Have to the mountain's top aspired,
Where fair desert and honour meet,
    Here form the toiling press retired,
Secure from all disturbing evil,
For ever in my temple revel.

With wreaths of stars circled about,
    Gild all the spacious firmament,
And, smiling on the panting routs
    That labour in the steep ascent,
With your resistless influence guide
Of human change th'incertain tide.

RELIGION, TRUTH, WISDOM

But oh, you Royal Turtles, shed,
    When you from earth remove,
On the ripe fruit of your chaste bed
Those sacred seeds of love.

CHORUS

Which no power can but yours dispense,
Since you the pattern bear from thence.

CONCORD, GOVERNMENT, REPUTATION

Then from your fruitful race shall flow
    Endless Succession:
Sceptres shall bud, and laurels blow
    'Bout their immortal throne.

CHORUS

Propitious stars shall crown each birth
Whilst you rule them, and they the earth.

The song ended, the two clouds, with the persons sitting on them, ascend; the great cloud closeth again, and so passeth away overthwart the scene, leaving behind it nothing but a serene sky. After which, the masquers dance their last dance, and the curtain was let fall.

(d) DAVENANT, *To the Queen, entertained at night by the Countess of Anglesey.*

The poems to the Queen were often written in the Courtly Love tradition, adoring from afar, which in itself was more attuned to the Catholic veneration of Mary and of the Female Saints than to a strenuous Protestant suspicion of all human idols and all sexual vanities:

Fair as unshaded light, or as the day
In its first birth, when all the year was May;
Sweet as the altar's smoke, or as the new
Unfolded bud, swelled by the early dew;
Smooth as the face of waters first appeared,
Ere tides began to strive or winds were heard;
Kind as the willing saints, and calmer far
Than in their sleeps forgiven hermits are:
You, that are more than our discreeter fear
Dares praise with such dull art, what make you here?
Here, where the summer is so little seen
That leaves (her cheapest wealth) scarce reach at green;
You come, as if the silver planet were
Misled a while from her much injured sphere,
And to ease the travails of her beams to-night,
In this small lanthorne would contract her light.

(e) WALLER, from *Of the Queen.*

In this poem, the Court with Henrietta as Sun-Queen is fancied to be Heaven on Earth. We note the tactlessness of the name Gloriana, first used by Edmund Spenser for the English Protestant Queen Elizabeth, now being applied to the French Catholic Henrietta Maria. Waller next plays with the conventions of hopeless 'Courtly Love'; the Queen of course is a forbidden subject for amorous worship, but the poet indulges in vain surmise. His flattery escalates ever more wildly until at last the Queen is likened to immortal Pagan goddesses, and little Prince Charles is assured of becoming another heroic Aeneas, simply because he was born of her:

> The lark, that shuns on lofty boughs to build
> Her Humble nest, lies silent in the field;
> But if (the promise of a cloudless day)
> Aurora smiling bids her rise and play,
> Then straight she shows 'twas not for want of voice,
> Or power to climb, she made so low a choice;
> Singing she mounts; her airy wings are stretch'd
> T'ward heaven, as if from heaven her note she fetch'd.
> So we, retiring from the busy throng,
> Use to restrain the ambition of our song;
> But since the light which now informs our age
> Breaks from the Court, indulgent to her rage,
> Thither my Muse, like bold Prometheus, flies,
> To light her torch at Gloriana's eyes . . .
> She saves the lover as we gangrenes stay,
> By cutting hope, like a lopp'd limb, away;
> This makes her bleeding patients to accuse
> High Heaven, and these expostulations use:
> 'Could Nature then no private woman grace,
> Whom we might dare to love, with such a face,
> Such a complexion, and so radiant eyes,
> Such lovely motion, and such sharp replies?
> Beyond our reach, and yet within our sight,
> What envious power has placed this glorious light?' . . .
> A brave romance who would exactly frame,
> First brings his knight from some immortal dame,
> And then a weapon, and a flaming shield,
> Bright as his mother's eyes, he makes him wield.
> None might the mother of Achilles be,
> But the fair pearl and glory of the sea;
> The man to whom great Maro gives such fame,
> From the high bed of heavenly Venus came;
> And our next Charles, whom all the stars design
> Like wonders to accomplish, springs from thine.

(f) WALLER, from *Puerperium* (1640).

Edmund Waller's last poem to Henrietta Maria was written on the birth of the Queen's fourth son. Although he is forced to admit that rage and tumult are abroad in England, he still persists in gallantly reassuring his royal patroness with

soothing words about England's happiness, glory and peace,
all secured through her fertility:

> Fair Venus! in thy soft arms
> The God of Rage confine;
> For thy whispers are the charms
> Which only can divert his fierce design.
>
> What though he frown, and to tumult do incline?
> Thou the flame
> Kindled in his breast canst tame,
> With that snow which unmelted lies on thine.
>
> Great goddess! give this thy sacred island rest;
> Make heaven smile,
> That no storm disturb us while
> Thy chief care, our halcyon, builds her nest.
>
> Great Gloriana! fair Gloriana!
> Bright as high heaven is, and fertile as earth,
> Whose beauty relieves us,
> Whose royal bed gives us
> Both glory and peace,
> Our present joy, and all our hopes' increase.

(g) MILTON, *The Readie and Easy Way to Establish a Free
Commonwealth* (1660).

The outstanding *attack* on King-worship in this period in
England was that delivered by Milton, denouncing his
countrymen for their sentimental remorse after the King's
execution. He called them 'an image-doting rabble, a credulous and hapless herd begotten to servility, . . . and enchanted
with tyranny' (conclusion to *Eikonoklastes*). In response to
the Court poets' exploitation of classical mythology to flatter
their monarch, the more Hebraic Milton acidly reminded his
readers that:

> God in much displeasure gave a king to the Israelites, and
> imputed it a sin in them that they sought one. How unmanly
> must it needs be, to count such a one the breath of our nostrils,
> to hang all our felicity on him, all our safety, our well-being,
> for which if we be aught else but sluggards or babies, we need
> depend on none but God and our own counsels, our own
> active virtue and industry! . . . Is it such an unspeakable joy
> to serve, such felicity to wear a yoke? to clink our shackles,

locked on by pretended law of subjection, more intolerable
and hopeless to be ever shaken off, than those which are
knocked on by illegal injury and violence?

Milton loathed every facet of Court-culture, as the final
extract in this section shows:

> ... a king must be adored like a demigod, with a dissolute
> and haughty court about him, of vast expense and luxury,
> masks and revels to the debauching of our prime gentry, both
> male and female: not in their pastimes only, but in earnest, by
> the loose-employments of court-service ... to the multiplying
> of a servile crew, bred up then to the hope not of public, but of
> court-offices, to be stewards, chamberlains, ushers, grooms
> even of the close-stool. We may well remember this not long
> since at home.

2

THE DIVIDE OF THE 1630s: THE COMING STORM

Although only a few men in the 1630s were intransigently committed either to the authority of King and Bishops or to a more radical Reformation and Parliamentary liberty, yet, with the wisdom of hindsight, we know that it was these non-compromisers who came so to dominate and polarize the situation that the country was ultimately divided into two armed camps. Therefore, this section focuses on the under-lying conflicts in taste, in values, and in ideology for which we already have documentary evidence in the 1630s, although it should never be forgotten that at this stage most people were far from committing themselves either to one 'side' or another. Indeed the 'sides' themselves were still just in the process of definition. Thus Milton's sense of poetry as being 'sensuous and passionate' was far from inimical to that of the Courtly School of Ben Jonson and a conscious corrective to the too-common Puritan suspicion of beauty and of art. The Anglican poet and parson, George Herbert, on the other hand, was vividly aware of the need for a radical purification and spiritual renewal of the slothful and corrupt English clergy— as indeed was Laud himself; and Clarendon, later to see himself as a devoted servant of the King and his cause, was, during the 1630s, very critical of Royal policy, and even associated himself at first with the assertion of Parliamentary rights.

The two lyrics which follow, though probably written in the 1620s, serve as prologue and may stand as an evocative sum-mary of some of the conflicting values of the period. *Farewell, Rewards and Fairies* (attributed to Richard Corbet) clearly mourns the passing of Catholic old England, which is here associated with folk-festivity, the holy days kept as holidays and the unworried proximity of Mother Church and peasant paganism:

A PROPER NEW BALLAD, ENTITLED THE FAIRIES'
FAREWELL OR GOD-A-MERCY WILL; TO BE SUNG OR
WHISTLED TO THE TUNE OF THE MEADOW BROW BY
THE LEARNED; BY THE UNLEARNED, TO THE TUNE
OF FORTUNE

Farewell, rewards and fairies,
  Good housewives now may say,
For now foul sluts in dairies
  Do fare as well as they;
And, though they sweep their hearths no less
  Than maids were wont to do,
Yet who of late for cleanliness
  Finds sixpence in her shoes?

Lament, lament old abbeys,
  The fairies lost command,
They did but change priests' babies,
  But some have changed your land;
And all your children stol'n from thence
  Are now grown puritanes
Who live as changelings ever since
  For love of your demaines.

At morning and at evening both,
  You merry were and glad;
So little care of sleep and sloth
  These pretty ladies had;
When Tom came home from labour,
  Or Ciss to milking rose,
Then merrily went their tabor,
  And nimbly went their toes.

Witness those rings and roundelays
  Of theirs which yet remain,
Were footed in Queen Mary's days
  On many a grassy plain.
But since of late Elizabeth
  And later James came in,
They never danced on any heath
  As when the time had been.

By which we note the fairies
  Were of the old profession,

> Their songs were *Ave Maries*,
>   Their dances were procession;
> But now, alas, they all are dead
>   Or gone beyond the seas,
> Or further from religion fled,
>   Or else they take their ease.
>
> A tell-tale in their company
>   They never could endure,
> And whoso kept not secretly
>   Their mirth, was punished sure.
> It was a just and Christian deed
>   To pinch such black and blue;
> Oh, how the commonwealth doth need
>   Such justices as you! [1]

But in *The Bounty of Our Age* (which is attributed to Henry Farley) the poet is dismayed that the people are still un-regenerate, too brutalized in their pleasures to centre their lives on God:

> To see a strange outlandish fowl,
> A quaint baboon, an ape, an owl,
> A dancing bear, a giant's bone,
> A foolish engine move alone,
> A morris dance, a puppet-play,
> Mad Tom to sing a roundelay,
> A woman dancing on a rope,
> Bull-baiting also at the *Hope*,
> A rhymer's jests, a juggler's cheats,
> A tumbler showibg cunning feats,
> Or players acting on the stage,—
> There goes the bounty of our age:
> But unto any pious motion
> There's little coin and less devotion. [2]

Both these poets feel that the other 'side' has already won, and the issues have been defined as 'Joylessness' versus 'Godlessness'.

2.1 Reactions to Drama and Art in the 1630s

(a) The theatre was in the front line of all attacks by militant Protestants on the present state of the country.

The premier theatre in England at this time was Black-friars. Run by the company of the King's Men, it was patronized by a coterie of gentry, aristocrats and even Royalty. The *district* of Blackfriars, however, was strongly Puritan.[3] This led to many civic petitions for the theatre to be closed, as well as to protests against particular offensive productions. In November 1629, for example, a visiting company presented a French farce in which French *actresses*

> ... did attempt, thereby giving just offence to all vertuous and well-disposed persons in this town, to act a certain lascivious and unchaste comedye, in the French tong at the Black-fryers. Glad I am to saye they were hissed, hooted, and pippin-pelted from the stage, so as I do not thinke they will soone be ready to trie the same againe.[4]

In November 1632,

> The Players of the Blackfryers were on Thursday called before the High Commission at Lambeth, and were bound over to answere such articles as should be objected against them. And it is said to be for uttring some prophane speeches in abuse of Scripture and wholly thinges, which they found penned, for them to act and playe, in Ben Jonsons newe comedy called the *Magnetique lady*.[5]

In October 1633, the Master of the Revels, Sir Henry Herbert, who was responsible for stage censorship to the Star Chamber, suppressed a performance of Fletcher's *The Tamer Tam'd, or Woman's Prize* (1605) 'upon complaints of foule and offensive matters conteyned therein'.[6] Sir Henry then 'purgd' the actors' text of 'oaths, prophaness, and ribaldrye' and made the following policy statement:

> All ould plays ought to bee brought to the Master of the Revels, and have his allowance to them for which he should have his fee, since they may be full of offensive things against church and state; ye rather that in former time the poetts tooke greater liberty than is allowed them by mee.

Just what was so offensive in the dialogue or situations of plays produced for a 1630s audience in the centre of Puritan London? Sex and violence were fused with their customary success in John Ford's tragedy of incest *'Tis Pity She's a Whore* (1634). And the comedies of the period were almost equally outrageous to a Puritan view. A few short extracts from two comedies follow.

Aretina, the heroine of Shirley's *Lady of Pleasure* (1635), is the original of all the maddeningly languid, frivolous-minded Restoration ladies of fashion, living for extravagant fripperies and risky sexual adventures behind her husband's back. A lady's morning work she sums up as:

> . . . we rise, make fine,
> Sit for our picture, and 'tis time to dine.
> *Littleworth:* Praying's forgot.
> *Alexander* (a wit and Aretina's beau): Tis out of fashion.
>
> (Exeunt)

Aretina's own fashionable procuress, *Madame Decoy*, later assures her:

> I have done offices, and not a few
> Of the nobility but have done feats
> Within my house, which is convenient
> For situation, and artful chambers,
> And pretty pictures to provoke the fancy.

The Captain, the randy hero of *The Parson's Wedding* (1642) by Killigrew, a Court Wit, has for friends three dashing young bloods called Jolly, Wild and Careless, who are held up for admiration as they bait the tradespeople whose bills they refuse to pay, and mock their religion as 'Brownists', only fit to be jeered at and kicked down the stairs. The Captain, whose idea of a capital joke it is to force a Parson to marry a whore and sleep with a trull in full view of the gallants on stage and in the audience, himself descants on the pleasure of being left alone all night to cook 'a bird of paradise':

> *Wild:*   A bird of paradise? What's that?
> *Captain:* A girl of fifteen, smooth as satin, white as her Sunday
>   apron, plump, and of the first down. I'll take her
>   with her guts in her belly and warm her with a
>   country dance or two, then pluck her and lay her dry
>   betwixt a couple of sheets; then pour her into so much

oil of wit as will make her turn to a man, and stick
into her heart three corns of whole love, to make her
taste of what she is doing; then, have strewed a man
all over her, shut the door and leave us—we'll work
ourselves into such a sauce as you can never surfeit
on, . . .⁷

PRYNNE'S FULMINATIONS AGAINST STAGE-PLAYS (FROM HISTRIOMASTIX, 1633)

[It is against this background of risqué plots and dialogue that the
notorious attack on the theatre by William Prynne in 1633 should
be read. The following is only a short sample of his diatribe.]

For having from my first arrivall here in London, heard and
seene in foure severall Playes (to which the pressing im-
portunity of some ill acquaintance drew me whiles I was yet
a novice) such wickedness, such lewdness as then made my
persistent heart to loath, my conscience to abhore all stage-
plays ever since . . . had not then my HISTRIOMASTIX
overgrowne its just intended pigimies statute, it had never
been able to foyle these many Giantlike Enemies. ('Ben
Johnson, Shackspeers and others': marginal note) . . . the
universall overspreading still-increasing evills . . . Dancing,
Musicke, Apparell, Effeminacy, Lascivious Songs, Laughter,
Adultery, obscene Pictures, Bonefires, New-years gifts, Grand
Christmasses, Health-drinking, long haire, Lords-dayes Dic-
ing . . . most of all our English Churches at first devoted unto
Masse, and Popish Idolatrie, are now designed to Gods publike
worship; whence the Brownists stile them, Idole Synagogues,
Bauls Temples, abominable sties, and would have them rased
to the ground, for which we all condeme them: yet it cannot
be held in case of Stage-Playes . . . sophisticall . . . to
argue . . . they may be regulated, and reduced to good and
lawfull uses; therefore they are lawfull unto Christians now;
I take it for my own part; that Christians should rather
argue thus: They are duceable to good, and Lawfull ends,
but they are not yet reduced: their abuses may be reformed,
but as yet they are not corrected; therefore we must take
them as we finde them, as we finde them now, unpurged,
uncorrected; and so we must needs avoyde them, yea

condemne them . . . as a reverend worthy of our Church observes . . . there is nothing more dangerous in a State than for the Stage and Poet to describe sinne, which by the Bishops and Pastours of the Church is gravely and severely to be reproved; because it causeth Magistrates, Ministers and Statesmen to lose their reputation, and sinne to be lesse feared . . . causing them to seeme that in outward appearances which they are not in truth; therefore it must needs bee odious to the God of truth . . . (on the sin of 'contributing to Players Boxes':) The maine end why God bestowes abundance of earthly riches upon some man, more than others, being only this; that there super-abundant plenty might supply the wants of others . . . Magistrates must take care that no filthinesse or obscenity be shewed neither in Shewes, nor Pictures. . . . Thus Aristotle, whose words I would our Magistrates, our Priests would consider . . . (on the Emperor Constantine:) that very first and most famous Christian Romane Emperour, (whose name we English men have speciall cause to honour, he being borne, bred and first crowned King and Emperour here in England . . .) that he wholy withdrew himselfe from the Secular Stage-playes of the Gentiles . . . (Bale, Chaucer and Skelton excepted:) penned only to be read, not acted; their subjects being al serious, sacred, divine, not scurrilous Wanton or prophan, as al modern Plays poems are . . .

2.2 Cavalier Lyrics of the 1630s— 'Wine, Women and Song'

(a) WILLIAM CARTWRIGHT, 'Drinking Song' from *The Royal Slave*, 1636.

Although Charles I's own personal life bore no resemblance to that later enjoyed by his son, his more sensual courtiers were already clearly anticipating the pleasures of the Restoration. The delights of the bottle had not yet been 'turned out of doors by Factious Fanatical sons of damn'd whores' (Shadwell) as is shown by the countless Drinking Songs of the period, of which this is a typical example. The writer of these

happily Pagan stanzas was not only a favourite of Charles I,
but also in Holy Orders as an Anglican Divine:

> Now, now the sun is fled
> Down into Tethys' bed,
> Ceasing his solemn course awhile. What then?
> 'Tis not to sleep, but be
> Merry all night, as we:
> Gods can be mad sometimes as well as men.
> *Then laugh we, and quaff we, until our rich noses*
> *Grow red and contest with our chaplets of roses.*
>
> Thus then we chase the night
> With these true floods of light,
> This Lesbian wine, which with its sparkling streams,
> Darting diviner graces,
> Casts glories round our faces,
> And dulls the tapers with majestic beams.
> *Then laugh we, and quaff we, until our rich noses*
> *Grow red and contest with our chaplets of roses.*

(b) SIR JOHN SUCKLING, *To a Lady That Forbad To Love
Before Company.*

Another favourite at the Court was Sir John Suckling, according to Aubrey 'the greatest gallant of his time, and the
greatest gamester'. His love songs are frankly sensual and
equally emotionally uncommitted:

> What! no more favours? Not a ribbon more,
> Not fan nor muff to hold as heretofore?
> Must all the little blisses then be left,
> And what was once love's gift, become our theft?
> Teach our souls parley at our eyes, not glance,
> Not touch the hand, not by soft wringing there
> Whisper a love that only yes can hear?
> Not free a sigh, a sign that's there for you?
> Dear, must I love you, and not love you too?
> Be wise, nice, fair; for sooner shall they trace
> The feather'd choristers from place to place,
> By prints they make in th' air, and sooner say
> By what right line the last star made his way,

That fled from heaven to earth, than guess to know
How our loves first did spring, or how they grow.
Love is all spirit: fairies sooner may
Be taken tardy, when they night-tricks play,
Than we, we are too dull and lumpish rather,
Would they could find us both in bed together!

2.3 Comments on the State of the Anglican Church

(a) GEORGE HERBERT

Herbert's own short, exemplary time as an Anglican pastor of the parish of Bemerton was his way of actively contributing to 'a cure for the wickedness and growing Atheism of our age'.

... above all, I will be sure to live well, because the vertuous life of a Clergyman, is the most powerful eloquence to perswade all that see it, to reverence and love, and at least, to desire to live like him. And this I will do, because I know we live in an age that hath more need of good examples than precepts ...

In another of his *Salisbury* walks, he met with a Neighbour Minister, and after some friendly Discourse betwixt them, and some Condolement for the decay of Piety, and too general Contempt of the Clergy, Mr *Herbert* took occasion to say,

One Cure for these Distempers would be for the Clergy themselves to keep the Ember-weeks strictly, and beg of their Parishioners to joyn with them in Fasting and Prayers for a more Religious Clergy.

And another Cure would be, for themselves to restore the great and neglected duty of Catechising, on which the salvation of so many of the poor and ignorant Laypeople does depend; but principally, that the Clergy themselves would be sure to live unblameably; and that the dignifi'd Clergy especially, which preach Temperance, would avoid Surfeiting, and take all occasions to express a visible humility and charity in their lives; ...

And, my dear Brother, till this be done by us, and done in earnest, let no man expect a reformation of the manners of the

Laity: for 'tis not learning, but this, this only, that must do it; and till then, the fault must lye at our doors.[8]

From THE CHURCH-PORCH

[16]

O England! full of sinne, but most of sloth;
Spit out this flegme, and fill thy brest with glorie:
Thy Gentrie bleats, as if thy native cloth
Transfus'd a sheepishness into thy storie:
   Not that they all are so; but that the most
   Are gone to grasse, and in the pasture lost.

From THE CHURCH MILITANT

... Religion stands on tip-toe in our land
Readie to passe to the *American* strand [9]
When heights of malice, and prodigious lusts,
Impudent sinning, witchcrafts, and distrusts
(The marks of future bane) shall fill our cup
Unto the brimme, and make our measure up;
When *Sein* shall swallow *Tiber*, and the *Thames*
By letting in them both pollutes her streams:
When *Italie* of us shall have her will,
And all her calender of sinnes fulfill;
Whereby one may foretell, what sinnes next yeare
Shall both in *France* and *England* domineer:
Then shall Religion to *America* flee:
They have their times of Gospel, ev'n as we,
My God, thou dost prepare for them a way
By carrying first their gold from them away:
For gold and grace did never yet agree:
Religion alwaies sides with povertie. ...

But none of the current abuses in the Anglican Church could destroy Herbert's fundamental allegiance to its fabric, its ritual or the language of its Common Prayer:

THE BRITISH CHURCH

I joy, deare Mother, when I view
Thy perfect lineaments and hue
        Both sweet and bright.

> Beautie in thee takes up her place,
> And dates her letters from thy face,
>> When she doth write.

> A fine aspect in fit array.
> Neither too mean, nor yet too gay.
>> Shows who is best.
> Outlandish looks may not compare:
> For all they either painted are,
>> Or else undrest.

(b) JOHN MILTON

For Milton, however, who felt himself to have been 'church-outed by the prelates',[10] the whole body of the Anglican clergy consisted of

> Anow of such as for their bellies sake,
> Creep and intrude, and climb into the fold?
> Of other care they little reck'ning make,
> Then how to scramble at the shearers feast,
> And shove away the worthy bidden guest.
> Blind mouthes! that scarce themselves know hold to hold
> A Sheep-hook, or have learn'd ought els the least
> That to the faithfull Herdmans art belongs!
> What recks it them? What need they? They are sped;
> And when they list, their lean and flashy songs
> Grate on their scrannel Pipes of wretched straw,
> The hungry Sheep look up, and are not fed,
> But swoln with wind, and the rank mist they draw,
> Rot inwardly, and foul contagion spread:
> Besides what the grim Woolf with privy paw
> Daily devours apace, and nothing sed,
> But that two-handed engine at the door,
> Stands ready to smite once, and smite no more.

Milton's prose pamphlets, *The Reason of Church Government Urged against Prelaty* (from which the next extract is taken) and *Of Reformation in England* (1641), are even more intemperate on the spiritual unfitness and gross fleshly appetites of the Anglican clergy, and above all of the prelacy:

yea, they and their seminaries shame not to profess, to petition, and never leave pealing our ears, that unless we fat them like boars, and cram them as they list with wealth, with deaneries and pluralities, with baronies and stately preferments, all learning and religion will go underfoot. Which is such a shameless, such a bestial plea, and of that odious impudence in churchmen, who should be to us a pattern of temperance and frugal mediocrity, who should teach us to contemn this world and the gaudy things thereof, according to the promise which they themselves require from us in baptism, that should the scripture stand by and be mute, there is not that sect of philosophers among the heathen so dissolute, no not Epicurus, nor Aristippus with all his Cyrenaic rout, but would shut his school-doors against such greasy sophisters; not any college of mountebanks, but would think scorn to discover in themselves with such a brazen forehead the outrageous desire of filthy lucre. Which the prelates make so little conscience of, that they are ready to fight, and if it lay in their power, to massacre all good Christians under the names of horrible schismatics, for only finding fault with their temporal dignities, their unconscionable wealth and revenues, their cruel authority over their brethren, that labour in the word, while they snore in their luxurious excess: openly proclaiming themselves now in the sight of all men, to be those which for a while they sought to cover under sheep's clothing, ravenous and savage wolves, threatening inroads and bloody incursions upon the flock of Christ, which they took upon them to feed, but now claim to devour as their prey. More like that huge dragon of Egypt, breathing out waste and desolation to the land, unless he were daily fattened with virgin's blood.

In his *Of Reformation in England* Milton accuses the Anglican Establishment of coming between the people and their God:

the table of communion, now become a table of separation, stands like an exalted platform upon the brow of the quire, fortified with bulwark and barricado, to keep off the profane touch of the laics, whilst the obscene and surfeited priest scruples not to paw and mammoc the sacramental bread, as familiarly as his tavern biscuit. And thus the people, vilified and rejected by them, give over the earnest study of virtue and godliness, as a thing of greater purity than they need, and the search of divine knowledge as a mystery too high for their capacities, and only for churchmen to meddle with; which is what the prelates desire, that when they have brought us back to popish blindness, we might commit to their dispose the whole managing of our salvation; for they think it was never fair world with them since that time. But he that will mould a modern bishop into a primitive, must yield him to be elected by the popular voice, undiocesed, unrevenued, unlorded, and leave him nothing but brotherly equality, matchless temperance, frequent fasting, incessant prayer and preaching, continual watchings and labours in his ministry; which what a rich booty it would be, what a plump endowment to the many-benefice-gaping-mouth of a prelate, what a relish it would give to his canary-sucking and swan-eating palate, let old bishop Mountain judge for me.

Milton ends with a revolutionary demand for the abolition of the entire temporal and spiritual power of the Bishops who

beseech us that we would think them fit to be our justices of peace, our lords, our highest officers of state, though they come furnished with no more experience than they learnt between the cook and the manciple, or more profoundly at the college audit, or the regent house, or to come to their deepest insight, at their patron's table; they would request us to endure still the rustling of their silken cassocks, and that we would burst our midriffs, rather than laugh to see them under sail in all their lawn and sarcenet, their shrouds and tackle, with a geometrical rhomboides upon their heads: they would bear us in hand that we must of duty still appear before them once a year in Jerusalem, like good circumcised males and females, to be taxed by the poll, to be sconced our head-money, our twopences, in their chandlerly shopbook of Easter. They pray us that it would please us to let them still hale us, and worry us with their bandogs and pursuivants; and that it would please the parliament that they may yet have the whipping, fleecing, and flaying of us in their diabolical courts, to tear the flesh from our bones, and into our wide wounds instead of balm, to pour in the oil of tartar, vitriol, and mercury: surely, a right reasonable, innocent, and soft-hearted petition. O the relenting bowels of the fathers! Can this be granted them, unless God have smitten us with frenzy from above, and with a dazzling giddiness at noonday? Should not those men rather be heard that come to plead against their own preferments, their worldly advantages, their own abundance; for honour and obedience to God's word, the conversion of souls, the Christian peace of the land, and union of the reformed catholic church, the unappropriating and un-monopolizing the rewards of learning and industry, from the greasy clutch of ignorance and high feeding? We have tried already, and miserably felt what ambition, worldly glory, and immoderate wealth, can do; what the boisterous and contradictional hand of a temporal, earthly, and corporeal spirituality can avail to the edifying of Christ's holy church; were it such a desperate hazard to put to the venture the universal votes of Christ's congregation, and fellowly and friendly yoke of a teaching and laborious ministry, the pastorlike and apostolic imitation of meek and unlordly discipline, the gentle and benevolent mediocrity of church-maintenance, without the ignoble hucksterage of piddling tithes? Were it such an incurable mischief to make a little trial, what all this would do to the flourishing and growing up of Christ's mystical body? as rather to use every poor shift, and if that serve not, to threaten uproar and combustion, and shake the brand of civil discord?

O, sir, I do now feel myself inwrapped on the sudden into those mazes and labyrinths of dreadful and hideous thoughts, that which way to get aut, or which way to end, I know not, unless I turn mine eyes, and with your help lift up my hands to that eternal and propitious throne, where nothing is readier than grace and refuge to the distresses of mortal suppliants: and it were a shame to leave these serious thoughts less piously than the heathen were wont to conclude their graver discourses.

Thou, therefore, that sittest in light and glory unapproachable, parent of angels and men! next, thee I implore, omnipotent King, Redeemer of that lost remnant whose nature thou didst assume, ineffable and everlasting Love! and thou, the third subsistence of divine infinitude, illumining Spirit, the joy and solace of created things! one Tripersonal godhead! look upon this thy poor and almost spent and expiring church, leave her not thus a prey to these importunate wolves, that wait and think long till they devour thy tender flock; these wild boars that have broke into thy vineyard, and left the print of their polluting hoofs on the souls of thy servants. O let them not bring about their damned designs, that stand now at the entrance of the bottomless pit, expecting the watchword to open and let out those dreadful locusts and scorpions, to reinvolve us in that pitchy cloud of infernal darkness, where we shall never more see the sun of thy truth again, never hope for the cheerful dawn, never more hear the bird of morning sing.

(c) FRANCIS QUARLES, 'On Those that Deserve it' from *Divine Fancies* (1632).

Quarles believed that the Church should be served for Christ's sake despite the vanities and worldliness of its Bishops. Like Herbert he hoped that the Church could be gradually purified from within:

O When our Clergie, at the dreadful Day,
Shall make their Audit; when the judge shall say,
Give your accompts: What, have my Lambs been fed?
Say, do they all stand sound? Is there none dead
By your defaults? Come Shephards bring them forth
That I may crowne your labours in their worth.
O what an answer will be given by some!
We have been silenc'd: Canons struck us dumb;
The Great ones would not let us feed thy flock,
Unless we play'd the fools, and wore a Frock:
We were forbid unless we'd yeeld to signe
And cross their browes, they say, a mark of thine.
To say the truth, great Judge, they were not fed;
Lord, here they be; but Lord, they be all dead.
Ah cruel Shephards! Could your conscience serve
Not to be fooles, and yet to let them sterve?
What if your Fiery spirits had been bound
To Antick Habits; or your heads been crown'd
With *Peacock* Plumes; had ye been forc'd to feed
Your Saviour's dear-bought Flock in a fools weed;
He that was scorn'd, revil'd, endur'd the Curse
Of a base death, in your behalfs; nay worse,
Swallow'd the cup of wrath charg'd up to th' brim;
Durst ye not stoop to play the fooles for him?

(d) JOHN LILBURNE, from *Come Out of Her, My People* (1639).

Moving though Quarles's plea was, the far more popular view, in London at least, was that of John Lilburne. To him the Bishops were actually the Devil incarnate, and to hear them would be to sin against the Holy Ghost. Writing from prison, where he had been committed after a public whipping for smuggling into England anti-episcopal tracts from the Netherlands, Lilburne declared:

... for my owne part, if I should never heare a Sermon while I live, yet I should never dare to heare one from any man, good or bad, that is made a Minister by the Prelates, or any of their Creatures, or by vertue of any of their muddy Antichristian Lawes, neither dare I have any spirituall communion with them, so long as they stand in their calling, in regard I am perswaded that he that heareth them sinneth, . . . and by undenyable consequence I will prove it, that whosoever heares them so long as they Officiat by vertue of their calling and power which they have received from the Bishops to preach, doth heare the Devill; . . .

Now Jesus Christ saith to his Disciples, he that heares you, heareth me, and he that heareth me heareth him that sent me.

So on the contrary, he that heares the Ministers, heares the Prelates that made and sent them; And he that heares the Prelates, heares the Pope, that authorised and gave them their authority; And he that heares the Pope, heares the Devill, that gave him his power; . . .

And for this I will spend and be spent, and be puld in ten thousand pieces: before I will in the least deny my God, and his naked truth, . . . And further knowe that all my kindred according to the flesh, had deserted and forsaken me, in my present condition. But if all my friends (yea and Christian Brethren also) in the world, should be offended with me, for sticking close to my good cause, . . . yea though I starve and rott in Prison, . . . yet the Lord will stand by mee, support and uphold me, . . .

2.4 Archbishop Laud

(a) ARCHBISHOP WILLIAM LAUD (1573–1645) (see Introduction, p. xxii) was naturally the focal point of militant antiepiscopal feeling in the 1630s. As we see below he was in the habit of recording his dreams as one element in his anxious soul-searching.[11] Prynne produced an edited version of Laud's journal at his trial, but his hopes that erotic dreams about the Duke of Buckingham would make good political capital were disappointed. Puritan colleagues, like Henry Robinson, reacted sympathetically to Laud's confessional approach. Prynne's attack was entitled *Rome's Masterpeece*, but the Leveller William Walwyn called it 'the Archbishop's Master-peece'.

(i) In my sleep it seemed to me that the Duke of Buckingham got into my bed, where he showed me much love (*ubi multo erga me amore se gessit*), and it seemed to me that many people entered the bedroom and saw this. (3 July 1625: in Latin)

(ii) I dreamt that I was reconciled to the Church of Rome. This troubled me much; and I wondered exceedingly, how it should happen. Nor was I aggrieved with myself only by reason of the errors of that Church, but also on account of the scandal, which from that my fall would be cast upon many eminent and learned men in the Church of England. Going with this resolution, a certain priest met me, and would have stopped me. But moved with indignation, I went on my way. And while I wearied myself with these troublesome thoughts, I awoke. Herein I felt such strong impressions, that I could scarce believe it to be a dream. (1 March 1627)

(b) *Archbishop Laud's Apologia:* delivered in Star Chamber, 14 June 1637, at the condemnation of Bastwick, Burton and Prynne.

Laud's address condemning the Puritans Bastwick, Burton and Prynne in Star Chamber, in 1637, to have their ears cut off (**2.5**) adopts a curiously defensive tone. His argument is that his *iure divino* claim for episcopacy (as opposed to the humbler *iure humano* defence of his Tudor predecessors) does not threaten the Royal Supremacy. His opponents had argued that it did. Nine years earlier, Laud's crony, John Cosin (see above, **1.7**), had landed himself in serious trouble with such a claim (or alleged claim).

... 'Tis unworthy in itself, and preposterous in demeanour, for a man to be ashamed for doing good because other men glory in speaking ill. And I can say it clearly and truly, as in the presence of God, I have done nothing as a prelate, to the uttermost of what I am conscious, but with a single heart, and with a sincere intention for the good government and honour of the Church, and the maintenance of the orthodox truth and religion of Christ, professed, established and maintained in this Church of England.

For my care of this Church, the reducing of it into order, the upholding of the external worship of God in it, and the settling of it to the rules of its first reformation, are the causes (and the sole causes, whatever are pretended) of all this malicious storm, which hath lowered so black upon me and some of my brethren. And in the meantime, they, which are the only or the chief innovators of the Christian world having nothing to say, accuse us of innovation; they themselves and their complices in the meantime being the greatest innovators that the Christian world hath almost ever known. I deny not but others have spread more dangerous errors in the Church of Christ; but no men, in any age of it, have been more guilty of innovation than they, while (they) themselves cry out against it. *Quis tulerit Gracchos?*

And I said well, *Quis tulerit Gracchos?* For 'tis most apparent to any man that will not wink, that the intention of these men and their abettors was and is to raise a sedition, being as great incendiaries in the State (where they get power) as they have ever been in the Church. . . .

Our main crime is (would they all speak out, as some of them do) that we are bishops; were we not so, some of us might be as passable as other men. And a great trouble 'tis to them that we maintain that our calling of bishops is *jure divino*, by divine right: of this I have said enough, and in this place, in Leighton's case, nor will I repeat (it). Only this I will say, and abide by it, that the calling of bishops is *jure divino*, by divine right, though not all adjuncts to their calling. And this I say in as direct opposition to the *Church of Rome*, as to the Puritan humour. And I say further, that from the Apostles' times, in all ages, in all places, the Church of Christ was governed by bishops, and lay elders never heard of till Calvin's newfangled device at Geneva.

Now this is made by those men as if it were *contra regem*, against the King, in right or in power. But that's a mere ignorant shift, for our being bishops *jure divino*, by divine right, takes nothing from the King's right or power over us. For though our office be from God and Christ immediately, yet we may not exercise that power, either of order or jurisdiction, but as God hath appointed us, that is, not in his Majesty's or any Christian king's kingdoms, but by and under the power of the King given us so to do. And were this a good argument against us, as bishops, it must needs be good against priests and ministers too, for themselves grant that their calling is *jure divino*, by divine right; and yet I hope they will not say that to be priests and ministers is against the King, or any his royal prerogatives.

Next, suppose our calling as bishops could not be made good *jure divino,* by divine right, yet *jure ecclesiastico,* by ecclesiastical right, it cannot be denied. And here in England the bishops are confirmed, both in their power and means, by Act of Parliament. So that here we stand in as good case as the present laws of the realm can make us. And so we must stand till the laws shall be repealed by the same power that made them.

. . . No man can libel against our calling (as these men do), be it in pulpit, print or otherwise, but he libels against the King and the State, by whose laws we are established. Therefore all these libels, so far forth as they are against our calling, are against the King and the Law, and can have no other purpose than to stir up sedition among the people. . . .

2.5 Wallington, from Historical Notices

Nehemiah Wallington (1598–1658) gives here a good contemporary description of the outrage on the Puritan pamphleteers, Prynne, Burton and Bastwick. Wallington was a rather timid Puritan. He himself had a minor skirmish with the authorities for possessing one of the three pamphleteers' works. His journal records his anguish of mind, although he faced nothing comparable to their ordeal. What steeled him was the knowledge of their ordeal: 'It made me rejoice that I was partakers of Saints Sufferings, it made me to pray more often and more fervently': a useful illustration of the symbolic value of the confrontation.

The Execution of the Lords' Censure in Star Chamber upon DR BASTWICK, MR PRYNNE, and MR BURTON *in the Palace Yard at Westminster.*

The 30th day of June last, 1637, at the spectation whereof the number of people was so great (the place being very large) that it caused admiration in all that beheld them, who came with tender affections to behold those three renowned soldiers and servants of Jesus Christ, who came with most undaunted and magnanimous courage thereunto, having their way strawed with sweet herbs from the house out of which they came, to the Pillory, with all the honour that could be done unto them.

Dr Bastwick and Mr Burton first meeting, they did close one in the other's arms three times, with as much expressions of love as might be, rejoicing that they met at such a place, upon such an occasion, and that God had so highly honoured them, as to call them forth to suffer for His glorious truth. Then immediately after came Mr Prynne, the Doctor and he saluting each other, as Mr Burton and he did before. The Doctor then went up first on the scaffold, and his wife, immediately following, came up to him, and, like a loving spouse, saluted each ear with a kiss, and then his mouth; whose tender love, boldness, and cheerfulness so wrought upon the people's affections that they gave a marvellous great shout with joy to behold it. Her husband desired her not to be in the least manner dismayed at his sufferings, and so for a while they parted, she using these words, 'Farewell, my dearest, be of good comfort, I am nothing dismayed', and then the Doctor began to speak these words:—

'There are many that are this day spectators of our standing here as delinquents; though not delinquents, we bless God for it. I am not conscious to myself wherein I have committed the least trespass (to take this outward shame) either against my God or my King. And I do the rather speak it, that you that are now beholders, may take notice how far innocency will preserve you in such a day as this is, for we come here in the strength of our God, Who hath mightily supported us, and filled our hearts with greater joy and comfort than our shame or contempt can be. The first occasion of my trouble was by the Prelates, for writing a book against the Pope; and the Pope of Canterbury said I wrote against him, and therefore questioned me. But if the presses were as open to us as they formerly have been, we would shatter his kingdom about his ears. But be ye not deterred by their power, neither be affrighted at our sufferings. Let none determine to turn from the ways of the Lord, but go on; fight courageously against Gog and Magog. I know there are many here who have set many days apart for our behalf (let the Prelates take notice of it) and they have sent up strong prayers to heaven for us. We feel the strength and benefit of your prayers all along this cause. In a word, so free I am from base fear, or caring for anything they can do, or cast upon me, that, had I as much blood as would swell the Thames, I would shed it every drop in this cause. Therefore be not any of you discouraged, be not daunted at their power; ever labouring to preserve innocency, and keep peace within, go on in the strength of your God, and He will never fail you in such a day as this. As I said before, so I say again, had I as many lives as I have hairs on my head, or drops of blood in my veins, I would give them up all for this cause. This plot of sending us to those remote places was first consulted and agitated by the Jesuits, as I can make it plainly appear. Oh see what times we are fallen into, that the Lords must sit to act the Jesuits' plots! For our own parts we owe no malice to the persons of any of the prelates, but would lay our necks under their feet to do them good, as they are men; but against the usurpation of their power, as they are bishops, we do profess ourselves enemies till Doomsday.'

Mr Prynne, shaking the Doctor by the hand, desired him that he might speak a word or two.

'With all my heart,' said the Doctor.

'The cause' (said Mr Prynne) 'of my standing here is for not bringing in my Answer, for which my cause is taken *pro confesso* against me. What endeavours I used for the bringing in thereof, that God, and my own conscience, and my Counsel knows, whose cowardice stands upon record to all ages; for, rather than I will have my cause a leading cause to deprive the subjects of that liberty which I seek to maintain, I expose my person to a leading example to bear this punishment. And I beseech you all to take notice of their proceedings in this cause. When I was served with a sub-pœna into this Court, I was shut up close prisoner, that I could have no access to Counsel, nor admitted pen, ink, or paper to draw up my Answer by my instructions, for which I feed them twice, though to no purpose; yet when all was done, my Answer would not be accepted into the Court, though I tendered it upon my oath. I appeal to all the world if this be a legal or just proceeding. Our accusation is in point of libel (but supposedly) against the prelates. To clear this now I will give you a little light what the law is in point of libel (of which profession I have some times been, and still profess myself to have some knowledge in). You shall find in the case of libel two statutes, the one in the second of Queen Mary the one in the seventh of Queen Elizabeth. That in the second of Queen Mary the extremity and height of it runs thus: That if a libeller doth go so far and so high as to libel against King or

Queen by denomination, the height and extremity of the law is, that they lay no greater fine on him than a hundred pounds, with a month's imprisonment and no corporal punishment, except he do refuse to pay his fine, and then to inflict some punishment in lieu of that fine at the month's end. Neither was this censure to be passed on him except it were fully proved by two witnesses, who were to produce a certificate of their good demeanour for the credit of their report, or else confessed by the libeller. You shall find in that statute 7 Elizabeth some further addition to the former of 2 Mary, and that only in point of fine and punishment, and it must still reach as high as the person of the King and Queen. Here this statute doth set a fine of two hundred pounds, the other, but one, so that therein only they differ. But in this they both agree, namely, at the end of his imprisonment to pay his fine, and so to go free without any further questioning; but if he refuse to pay his fine, then the Court is to inflict some punishment on him, correspondent to his fine. Now see the disparity between those times of theirs and ours; a libeller in Queen Mary's days was fined but an hundred pounds, in Queen Elizabeth's time, two hundred. In Queen Mary's days but a month's imprisonment, in Queen Elizabeth's, three months, and so great a fine, if they libelled against King or Queen. Formerly the greatest fine was but two hundred pounds, though against King or Queen. Now, five thousand pounds, but against the prelates, and that but supposedly, which cannot be proved. Formerly, but three months' imprisonment now, perpetual imprisonment. Then, upon paying the fine, no corporal punishment was to be inflicted; but now, infamous punishment with the loss of blood, and all other circumstances that may aggravate it. See now what times we are fallen into, when that libelling (if it were so) against prelates only shall fall higher than if it touched kings or princes.

'That which I have to speak of next, is this. The prelates find themselves exceedingly aggrieved and vexed against what we have written concerning the usurpation of their calling, where indeed we declare their calling not to be *Jure Divino*. I make no doubt but there are some intelligencers or abettors within the hearing, whom I would have well to know and take notice of what I now say. I here in this place make this offer to them, That if I may be admitted a fair dispute, on fair terms, for my cause that I will maintain, and do here make the challenge against all the Prelates in the King's dominions, and against all the Prelates in Christendom (let them take in the Pope, and all to help them) that their calling is not *Jure Divino*. I will speak it again, I make the challenge against all the Prelates in the King's dominions and all Christendom, to maintain that their calling is not *Jure Divino*. If I make it not good, let me be hanged up at the Hall Gate;' whereupon the people gave a great shout. 'The next thing I have to speak of is this: the Prelates find themselves exceedingly aggrieved and vexed against what I have written in point of law concerning their writs and process. That the sending forth of writs and process in their own name is against all law and justice, and doth entrench on his Majesty's prerogative Royal, and the subject's liberties. And here now I make a second challenge against all the lawyers in the Kingdom in the way of fair dispute. That I will maintain the prelates sending forth of writs and process in their own names, to be against all law and justice, and entrencheth on his Majesty's prerogative Royal and the subject's liberty. Lest it should be forgotten, I speak it again, I here challenge all the whole society of the law upon a fair dispute to maintain, That the sending forth of writs and process in the prelates' own names to be against law and justice, and entrencheth on the King's prerogative Royal, and the subject's liberty. If I be not able to make it good, let me be put to the tormentingest death they can devise.

'We praise the Lord, we fear none but God and the King; had we respected our liberties, we had not stood here at this time; it was for the general good and liberties of you all that we have now thus far engaged our own liberties in this cause; for did you know how deeply they have entrenched on your liberties in point of popery, if you knew but into what times you were cast, it would make you look about you. And if you did but see what changes and revolutions of persons, causes, and actions have been made by one man, you would more narrowly look into your privileges, and see how far your liberty did lawfully extend, and so maintain it.

'This is the second time that I have been brought to this place; who hath been the author of it, I think you all well know. For the first time, if I could have had leave given me, I could easily have cleared myself of that which was then laid to my charge as also I could have done now if I might have been permitted to speak. That book, for which I suffered formerly, especially for some particular words therein written, which I quoted out of God's Word, and ancient Fathers, for which, notwithstanding, they passed censure on me, that same book was twice licensed by public authority, and the same words I then suffered for, they are again made use of and applied in the same sense by Heytin in his book, lately printed, and dedicated to the King, and no exception taken against them, but are very well taken.'

'Aye,' said Dr Bastwick, 'and there is another book of his licensed, wherein he rails against us there at his pleasure, and against all the martyrs that suffered in Queen Mary's days, calling them schismatic heretics; and there is another book of Pocklington's licensed, they be as full of lies as dogs be full of fleas. But were the presses as open to us, as they are to them, we would pay them and their great Master that upholds them, and charge them with notorious blasphemy.'

Said Master Prynne, 'You all at this present see there be no degrees of men exempted: Here is a Reverend Divine for the soul, a physician for the body, and a lawyer for the Estate. I had thought they would have let alone their own Society, and not have meddled with any of them. And the next (for ought I know) may be a Bishop; you see they spare none, of what Society or calling soever; none are exempted who cross their own ends. Gentlemen, look to yourselves; if all the Martyrs that suffered in Queen Mary's days are accounted and called Schismatical Heretics and Factious Fellows, who shall we look for? Yet so they are called in a book lately called forth under authority; and such Factious Fellows are we, for discovering a plot of popery. Alas! poor England, what will become of thee if thou look not the sooner into thine own privileges, and maintainest not thine own lawful liberty? Christian people, I beseech you all, stand firm, and be zealous for the cause of God and His true Religion, to the shedding of your dearest blood, otherwise you will bring yourselves and all your posterities into perpetual bondage and slavery.'

Now, the Executioner being come to sear him and cut off his ears, Mr Prynne spake these words to him, 'Come, friend, come, burn me, cut me, I fear it not; I have learned to fear the fire of Hell, and not what man can do unto me; come, sear me, sear me. I shall bear in my body the marks of the Lord Jesus,' which the bloody executioner performed with extraordinary cruelty, heating his iron vice to burn one cheek, and cut off one of his ears so close that he cut off a piece of his cheek. At which exquisite torture he never moved with his body, or so much as changed his countenance, even to the astonishment of all the beholders, and uttering (as soon as the executioner had done) this heavenly sentence, 'The more I am beaten down, the more I am lift up.' And, returning from the execution in a boat, made, as I hear, these two verses by the way on the two characters branded on his cheeks:

'S. L. LAUD'S SCARS

Triumphant I return, my face descries

Laud's searching Scars, God's grateful sacrifice.'

2.6 The Anti-Laudian Reaction in the early 1640s, as mirrored in ballads

The popular clamour for Laud's death was not pretty. Not only is it clear that the London populace was quite mistakenly convinced that Laud was a secret Papist, but it is also plain that the crowd greatly enjoyed the prospect of his suffering. That he was never forgiven for his ordering the mutilation of Prynne, Bastwick and Burton is shown by the last ballads, the ominous 'Keep Thy Head On Thy Shoulders', and the more jolly 'Thanks to the Parliament'. They show how all the issues at stake, cultural, economic, religious and political, had by 1641–2 grown into *one* great movement of those backing Parliament against the King.

From *A Prognostication on Will Laud, Late Archbishop of Canterbury*.

My little lord, methinks 'tis strange,
    That you should suffer such a change,
    In such a little space.
You, that so proudly t'other day,
    Did rule the king, and country sway,
    Must budge to 'nother place.

Remember now from whence you came,
And that your grandsires of your name,

Were dressers of old cloth
Go, bid the dead men bring their shears,
And dress your coat to save your ears,
　　Or pawn your head for both . . .

The king by heark'ning to your charms,
Hugg'd our destruction in his arms,
　　And gates to foes did ope;
Your staff would strike his sceptre down,
Your mitre would o'ertop the crown,
　　If you should be a Pope.

But you that did so firmly stand.
To bring in Popery in this land,
　　Have missed your hellish aim;
Your saints fall down, your angels fly,
Your crosses on yourself do lie,
　　Your craft will be your shame . . .

Within this six years six ears have
Been cropt off worthy men and grave,
　　For speaking what was true;
But if your subtle head and ears
Can satisfy those six of theirs,
　　Expect but what's your due, . . .

Your white lawn sleeves that were the wings,
Whereon you soared to lofty things,
　　Must be your fins to swim;
Th' Archbishop's see by Thames must go,
With him unto the Tower below,
　　There to be rack'd like him.

Your oath cuts deep, your lies hurt sore,
Your canons made Scot's cannons roar,
　　But now I hope you'll find,
That there are cannons in the Tower,
Will quickly batter down your power,
　　And sink your haughty mind.

The Commonalty have made a vow,
No oath, no canons to allow,
　　No Bishop's Common Prayer;
No lazy prelates that shall spend
Such great revenues to no end,
　　But virtue to impair.

Dumb dogs that wallow in such store,
That would suffice above a score,
   Pastors of upright will;
Now they'll make all the bishops teach,
And you must in the pulpit preach,
   That stands on Tower Hill.[12]

From *Keep Thy Head On Thy Shoulders* (1641).

Though Wentworths beheaded,
Should any Repyne,
Thers others may come
To the Blocke besides he:
Keepe thy head on thy Shoulders
I will keepe mine;
For what is all this to thee or to mee?
Then merrily and cherrily
Lets drink off our Beere,
Let who as will run for it
   Wee will stay heere.

What meanes our brave gallants
So fast for to flye:
Because they are afraid
That some danger might be,
They car'd not for seeing
The Deputy dye,
But what is all this to thee or to me:
Then merrily and cherrily
Lets drink off our Beere,
Let who as will run for it,
   We will stay heere . . .

A man to doe evill
And have too much Grace,
Me thinkes its a wonder
Most strange for to see,
So little in person,
Yet great by his place:
But what is all this to thee or to me,
Then merrily and cherrily
Lets drinke off our wine
Keepe thy head on thy shoulders,
   I will keepe mine.

Since no Canterbury,
Nor old womans tale
Or dissimulation
Will credited be,
The Popish Supporters
Begin for to faile,
But what is all this to thee or to me?
Then merrily and cherrily
Lets drinke off our wine,
Keepe thy head on thy shoulders,
    I will keepe mine.

Though some with much patience
Hath suffered long:
Who after much tryall
(Are la)tely set free:
And others be punish'd
Which did them such wrong,
But what is all this to thee or to me?
Then merrily and cherrily &c. . .

If that all false Traytors,
Were banisht our Land,
And that from all Popery
It once might be free,
Then England and Scotland
Might joyne hand in hand
Then times will prove better to thee & to me.
So merrily and cherrily
Weel drinke wine and Beere,
Let who as will run for it,
    We will stay heere.[13]

From *Thanks to the Parliament* (1642).

Come let us cheere our hearts with lusty wine,
Though *Papists* at the Parliament repine;
And Rattle-Heads so busily combine
That thou canst call thy Wife and Children thine,
    Thanke the great Counsell of the King,
    And the Kings great Counsells.

Like silly Sheepe they did us daily sheare,
Like Asses strong our backes were made to beare,

Intollerable burdens, yeare by yeare,
No hope, no helpe, no comfort did appeare,
   But from the great Counsell of the King,
   And the Kings great Counsell.

With taxes and Monopolies opprest,
Ship-mony, Souldiers, Knighthood, and the rest,
The Coate and Conduct-mony was no jest,
Then think good neighbour how much we are blest
   In the great Counsell of the King,
   And the Kings great Counsell.

Were not these plagues worse then a sweeping rot,
O how unkindly did they use the Scot;
But those bould blades did prove so fiery hot
This swinging Bowle to them this other Pot
   To the great Counsell of the King,
   And the Kings great Counsell.

Who did regard our povertie, our teares,
Our wants, our miseries, our many feares,
Whipt, stript, and fairely banisht as appeares;
You that are masters, now of your owne eares
Blesse the great Counsell of the King
   And the Kings great Counsell.

Great paine to till the land ere it be sowne,
And yet the bread we eate was not our owne,
So greedy were those Catterpillers growne
But now the nest of filthy Birds are flowne
   From the great Counsell of the King,
   And the Kings great Counsell . . .

Had not these theeves an Ore in every Boate,
And still their wicked mallice is afloate,
Would they not now perswad's to cut our throate,
By printed Proclamations against the Vote,
   Of the great Counsell of the King,
   And the Kings great Counsell . . .

Now tell me Tom, shall we thus cheated be,
By Papists, Atheists, and the Hirarchie
To fall from those who faine would set us free,
And undergoe such care for thee and me,
   That great Counsell of the King,
   And the Kings great Counsell . . .

Where's our defence if we cut off our hand,
Shall we to fire our houses light a brand,
And joyne with those who would destroy the Land,
For my part I resolve to fall or stand,
With the great Counsell of the King,
    And the Kings great Counsell . . .[14]

3
THE DEHUMANIZED IMAGE OF 'THE ENEMY'

Wars have been and still are being fought in our own century to wipe out 'Capitalist Hyenas', 'Imperialist Dogs', 'Fascist Pigs', 'Jewish Vermin', 'Vietcong Gooks' and Chinese 'Blue Ants'—amongst others[1]—but the seventeenth century was already quite familiar with the idea of righteous armed conflict between Man and Beast.

The Puritans, of course, had Scriptural authority for this interpretation of their struggle in the terrible words contained in the Book of Revelation about The Beast, or Anti-Christ, who must be defeated by God's Angels in this world before Christ can come again:

> And I stood upon the sand of the sea, and saw a beast rise up out of the sea, having seven heads and ten horns, and upon his horns ten crowns, and upon his heads, the name of blasphemy. And the beast which I saw was like unto a leopard, and his feet were as the feet of a bear, and his mouth as the mouth of a lion: and the dragon gave him his power, and his seat, and great authority . . .
> and all the world wondered after the beast.
> And they worshipped the dragon which gave power unto the beast: and they worshipped the beast, saying 'Who is like unto the beast? who is able to make war with him?' . . .
> And it was given unto him to make war with the saints, and to overcome them: and power was given him over all kindreds, and tongues, and nations.
> And all that dwell upon the earth shall worship him whose names are not written in the book of life of the Lamb slain from the foundation of the world.
> If any man have an ear, let him hear . . .
> And I beheld another beast coming up out of

the earth; and he had two horns like a
lamb, and he spoke as a dragon. . . .
And he causeth all, both small and great
rich and poor, free and bond, to receive
a mark in their right hand, or in their
foreheads: And that no man might buy
or sell, save he that had the mark, or
the name of the beast, or the number of
his name. Here is wisdom. Let him that
hath understanding count the number of the
beast: for it is the number of a man: and
his number is Six hundred threescore and
six.[2]

These nightmarish, enigmatic words were scanned over
and over during this period, the most common definition of
the Beast being Papal Rome; but the Beast extended his
incarnation into all the servants of Rome, from Anglican
Bishops to the barbarous Irish. Not just the above passage,
but the whole Book of Revelation was the ultimate source of
all the apocalyptic rhetoric of Milton, Lilburne, Prynne and
the most riveting Puritan Preachers of the 1630s and 1640s.
Lilburne's very title, *Come Out of Her My People* (see above
(2.3), was a well-known quotation from Revelation, chapter 18.
Lilburne identified himself with the voice from heaven crying
to the righteous to forsake the wicked city of Babylon (i.e.
London) at its moment of Judgement:

Come out of her, my people, that ye be not
partakers of her sins and that ye receive not
of her plagues.
For her sins have reached unto heaven, and God
hath remembered her iniquities.

Similarly, Milton's invective against the prelates—'there
may be a sanctified bitterness against the enemies of truth'[3]—
constantly likened them, in the language of Revelation, to
'wild boars', 'ravening wolves', 'dreadful locusts and scorpions', or the huge, virgin-fattened 'dragon of Egypt' (pp. 40
and 42 above). In one passage of tremendous vituperative
indictment against the 'Babylonish merchant of souls' (i.e.
Bishops), Milton is so beside himself that he mixes his animal
imagery, again all familiar from the Book of Revelation:

> Believe it, sir, right truly it may be said,
> that Anti-christ is Mammon's son. The sour
> leaven of human traditions, mixed in one
> putrefied mass with the poisonous dregs of
> hypocrisy in the hearts of prelates, that
> lie basking in the sunny warmth of wealth
> and promotion, is the serpent's egg that
> will hatch an Antichrist wheresoever, and
> engender the same monster as big, or little,
> as the lump is which breeds him. If the
> splendour of gold and silver begin to lord
> it once again in the church of England, we
> shall see Antichrist shortly wallow here,
> though his chief kennel be at Rome.
>
> (From *Of Reformation in England*.)

Milton also used animal imagery in direct counter-attacks on other opponents in controversy—his Presbyterian detractors on the Divorce question he refers to as 'Owles and Cuckoes, Asses, Apes and Dogs'[4] and the hapless critic of the English regicides, Salmasius, is called:

> 'You slug', 'You ass', 'you brute beast . . .
> for you deserve not the name of a man . . .'
> 'you apostate and devil'. . . . 'You are not
> Eurylochus, but Elpenor, a miserable
> enchanted beast, a filthy swine, accustomed
> to a sordid slavery even under a woman:'
>
> (From *A Defence of the People of England*.)

From the other bank, the Royalist supporters also dehumanized their Puritan enemies, seeing them in turn merely as predatory animals:

> Of all those Monsters which we read
> In Africk, Inde, or Nile,
> None like to those now lately bred
> Within this wretched Isle.
>
> The Cannibal, the Tygre fell,
> Croc'dile and Sycophant;
> The Turk, the Jew, and Infidel,
> Make up an English Saint.[5]

or

> Now as the Martyrs were inforc'd to take
> The shapes of beasts, like hypocrites, at stake,
> I'le bait my *Scot* so; yet not cheat your eyes,
> A *Scot* within a beast is no disguise.
> No more let Ireland brag, her harmlesse Nation
> Fosters no Venome, since the Scots Plantation:
> Nor can our feign'd Antiquitie maintaine;
> Since they came in, England hath Wolves againe . . .
> Nature her selfe doth Scotch-men beasts confesse,
> Making their Country such a wildernesse:[6]

On the whole, however, Royalist polemic concentrated on a
more secular version of the monstrousness of their opponents:
their enemy is not Antichrist, but the hydra-headed mob.
For them it is self-evidently monstrous enough that the rabble
should take up arms against their social superiors. The enemy
is 'The rabble, that fierce beast of ours'[7] and 'Democracy is
but the effect of a Crazy Brain'.[8] Bitterly mocking, anti-
popular sentiment is the central pivot of the Cavalier's attack
on the Roundhead. These two versions of Beast are summed
up in Milton's *Defence of the People of England* when he says
to his adversary Salmasius 'You call the people "A Beast"—
what are you yourself?'

Part 1

The Puritan's Image of the Royalist

3.1 The Cavalier seen as a vain, dissolute rake

(a) First and foremost, as the preceding chapter also illustrated, the Puritan was alienated by the Cavalier's life-style—here mirrored in his dress, at once effeminate and lecherous:

PICTURE OF AN ENGLISH ANTICK

with a list of his ridiculous Habits and apish Gestures

MAIDS, WHERE ARE YOUR HEARTS BECOME?
LOOK YOU WHAT HERE IS!

1. His hat in fashion like a close-stoolepan.
2. Set on the top of his noddle like a coxcombe.
3. Banded with a calves tail, and a bunch of riband.
4. A feather in his hat, hanging down like a Fox taile.
5. Long haire, with ribands tied in it.
6. His face spotted.
7. His beard on the upper lip, compassing his mouth.
8. His chin thrust out, singing as he goes.
9. His band lapping over before.
10. Great band strings, with a ring tied.
11. A long wasted dubblet unbuttoned half way.
12. Little skirts.
13. His sleeves unbuttoned.
14. In one hand a stick, playing with it, in the other his cloke hanging.
15. His breeches unhooked ready to drop off.

16. His shirt hanging out.
17. His codpeece open tied at the top with a great bunch of riband.
18. His belt about his hips.
19. His sword swapping betweene his legs like a Monkeys taile.
20. Many dozen points at knees.
21. Above the points of either side two bunches of riband of severall colours.
22. Boot hose tops, tied about the middle of the Calfe, as long as a paire of shirt sleeves, double at the ends like a ruffe band.
23. The Tops of his boots very large turned down as low as his spurs.
24. A great paire of spurres, gingling like a Morrice dancer.
25. The feet of his boots 2 inches too long.
26. Two horns at each end of his foot, stradling as he goes.

Nov. 18.1646.[9]

(b) From RICHARD BAXTER'S *Autobiography*.

Richard Baxter corroborates this view. Those who took the King's side were:

> The gentry that were not so precise and strict against an oath, or gaming, or plays, or drinking, nor troubled themselves so much about the matters of God and the world to come, and the ministers and people that were for the King's Book, for dancing and recreations on the Lord's-days, and those that made not so great a matter of every sin, but went to church and heard Common Prayer, and were glad to hear a sermon which lashed the Puritans. . . .
>
> An abundance of the ignorant sort of the country, who were civil, did flock in to the parliament, and filled up their armies afterward, merely because they heard men *swear* for the Common Prayer and bishops, and heard others *pray* that were against them; and because they heard the king's soldiers with horrid oaths abuse the name of God, and saw them live in debauchery, and the parliament's soldiers flock to sermons and talking of religion, and praying and singing Psalms together on their guards. And all the sober men that I was acquainted with, who were against the parliament, were wont to say 'The King hath the better cause, but the parliament hath the better men'. . . .

When the war was beginning the parties set names of contempt upon each other, and also took such titles to themselves and their own cause as might be the fittest means for that which they designed. . . .

The parliament's party called the other side commonly by the name of Malignants, as supposing that the generality of the enemies of serious godliness went that way in a desire to destroy the religious out of the land . . . and the soldiers they called Cavaliers, because they took that name to themselves; and afterwards they called them Dammes, because 'God damm me' was become a common curse, and as a byword among them.'[10]

One is reminded of the lords and gentry in Bunyan's Vanity Fair who burned Faithful,—Lord *Carnal Delight*, Lord *Luxurious*, Lord *Desire of Vain Glory*, my old Lord *Lechery*, Mr *Love-lust*, Mr *Live-loose*, Mr *Heady*, Mr *Enmity*, Mr *Cruelty* and Mr *Hate-light*.[11]

3.2 The impact of the massacre of Protestants in Ireland

It is always easiest to dehumanize a *foreign* foe. For almost a century Catholic Spain had embodied the Englishman's idea of alien inhumanity, but in the autumn of 1641 the Catholic Irish supplanted the Spanish as the archetype of devilish cruelty, the enemies of both God and man. The facts of the Irish rebellion against English domination were distorted and the scale of the killings was wildly exaggerated. Protestants were killed, but not *two hundred thousand* of them. But what mattered was what was sincerely believed to have taken place rather than what did take place, and the significance of the *idea* of the huge massacre of Protestants in Ireland cannot be exaggerated. The King and his party were associated with a lukewarm reaction to the perpetrators of the Catholic attack and hence even with complicity in it.

(a) LUCY HUTCHINSON, from *Memoirs of the Life of Colonel Hutchinson.*

While the King was in Scotland, that cursed rebellion in Ireland broke out, wherein above 200,000 were massacred in two-months space, being surpriz'd, and besides the slaine, abundance of poore famelies stript and sent naked away, out of all their possessions: and, had not the providence of God miraculously prevented the surprize of Dublin castle, the night it should have bene seiz'd, there had not bene any remnant of the protestant name left in that country. As soone as this sad newes came to the parliament, they vigorously set themselves to the worke of relieving them, but then the king return'd from Scotland, and being sumptuously welcomed home by the citie tooke courage thereby against the parliament, and obstructed all their proceedings for the effectuall reliefs of Irelande. Long was he before he could be drawne to proclaime these murtherers rebells, and when he did, by speciall command, there were but 40 proclamations printed, and care taken that they should not be much dispers'd; which courses aflicted all the good protestants in England, and confirm'd that the rebellion in Ireland receiv'd countenance from the king and queene of England.[12]

(b) From PETER VERNEY: *The Standard Bearer*.

Sir Ralph Verney wrote to Lady Barrymore, then in Ireland, trying to persuade her to come to England and safety:

Your stay afflicts mee extreamly least you should bee suddainly surprised by thos Barbarous Rebells who (if Fame belye them not) delight in cruelty, and take pleasure in insolency, above and beyond ye worst of infidells. truly maddame though I have never been much in love with Papists, yet I beeleeved them to bee christians, but if they offer violence to you or yours, I shall change my opinion. . . . (2 February 1641).[13]

(c) MILTON, from *The Reason of Church Government Urged against Prelaty*.

Milton reacted to the Irish rebellion in the context of his own attack on the Anglican Episcopacy, holding the English Bishops ultimately responsible for the Catholic Irish excesses and arguing that the best way to avenge the latter was to speed up radical reformation at home rather than delay it on the pretext of the need to maintain the *status quo* in England whilst concentrating on quelling rebellion in Ireland. It is noteworthy that Milton has no moral qualms about the rectitude of the subjugation of Ireland in the first place by England—England is to his mind: 'a right pious, right honest, and right hardy nation':[14]

It is not rebellion that ought to be the hinderance of reformation but it is the want of this which is the cause of that. The prelates which boast themselves the only bridlers of schism, God knows, have been so cold and backward both there and with us to repress heresy and idolatry, that either, through their carelessness, or their craft, all this mischief is befallen. What can the Irish subjects do less in God's just displeasure against us, than revenge upon English bodies the little care that our prelates have had of their souls? Nor hath their negligence been new in this island, but ever notorious in Queen Elizabeth's days, as Camden, their known friend, forbears not to complain. Yet so little are they touched with remorse of these their cruelties, (for these cruelties are theirs, the bloody revenge of those souls which they have famished), that whenas against our brethren the Scots, who, by their upright and loyal deed, have now brought themselves an honourable name to posterity, whatsoever malice by slander could invent, rage in hostility attempt, they greedily attempted; towards these murderous Irish, *the enemies of God and mankind*, a cursed offspring of their own connivance, no man takes notice but that they seem to be calmly and indifferently affected. Where then should we begin to extinguish a rebellion that hath its cause from the misgovernment of the church? Where, but at the church's reformation, and the removal of that government which pursues and wars with all good Christians under the name of schismatics, but maintains and fosters all papists and idolaters as tolerable Christians? . . . But it will here be said, that the reformation is a long work, and the miseries of Ireland are urgent of speedy redress. They be indeed; and how speedy we are, the poor afflicted remnant of our martyred countrymen that sit there on the seashore, counting the hours of our delay with their sighs, and the minutes with their falling tears, perhaps with the distilling of their bloody wounds, if they have not quite by this time cast off, and almost cursed the vain hope of our foundered ships and aids, can best judge how speedy we are to their relief. But let their succours be hasted, as all need and reason is; and let not, therefore, the reformation, which is the chiefest cause of success and victory, be still procrastinated. . . . [We] for our parts, a populous and mighty nation, must needs be fallen into a strange plight either of effeminacy or confusion, if Ireland, that was once the conquest of one single earl with his private forces, and the small assistance of a petty Kernish prince, should now take up all the wisdom and prowess of this potent monarchy, to quell *a barbarous crew of rebels*, whom, if we take but the right course to subdue, that is, beginning at the reformation of our church, *their own horrid murders and rapes* will so fight against them, that the very sutlers and horse-boys of the camp will be able to rout and chase them, without the staining of any noble sword.[15] (my italics)

(d) From RICHARD BAXTER'S *Autobiography*.

Richard Baxter sums up the decisive importance of the alleged Irish atrocities most cogently of all:

. . . but of all the rest there was nothing that with the people wrought so much as the Irish massacre and rebellion. The Irish Papists did, by an unexpected insurrection, rise all over Ireland at once, and seized upon almost all the strengths of the whole land, and Dublin wonderfully excaped (a servant of Sir John Clotworthy's discovering the plot), which was to have been surprised with the rest, Octob. 23, 1641. Two hundred thousand persons they murdered (as you may see in the Earl of Orrery's 'Answer to a Petition' and in Dr. Jones's 'Narrative of the Examinations' and Sir John Temple's 'History', who was one of the resident justices). Men, women and children were most cruelly used, the women ripped up and filthily used when they killed them, and the infants used like toads or vermin. Thousands of those that escaped came stripped and almost famished to Dublin, and afterwards into England to beg their bread. Multitudes of them were driven together into rivers and cast over bridges and drowned. Many witnesses swore before the lords justice that at Portdown Bridge a vision every day appeared to the passengers of naked persons standing up in the middle of the river and crying out, 'Revenge! Revenge!' In a word, scarce any history mentioned the like barbarous cruelty as this was. The French massacre murdered but thirty or forty thousand; but *two hundred thousand* was a number which astonished those that heard it. This filled all England with a fear both of the Irish and of the Papists at home, for they supposed that the priests and the interest of their religion were the cause; insomuch that when the rumour of a plot was occasioned at London the poor people, all the countries over, were ready either to run to arms or hide themselves, thinking that the Papists were ready to rise and cut their throats. And when they saw the English Papists join with the king against the parliament, it was the greatest thing that ever alienated them from the king.

A little later (post-1660) when Baxter is trying to explain why he had sided against the King, he adds:

I freely confess that being astonished at the Irish massacre, and persuaded fully both of the parliament's good endeavours for reformation and of their real danger, my judgment of the main cause much swayed my judgment in the matter of the wars.[16]

(e) From CROMWELL'S *Letters.*

Atrocity begets counter-atrocity. Cromwell, glorying in his devastation of the Irish at Wexford in 1649, feels totally justified as merely the tool of Divine Justice:

... causing *them* to become a prey to the soldier who in their piracies had made preys of so many families, and now with their bloods to answer the cruelties which they had exercised upon the lives of divers poor Protestants! Two 'instances' of which I have been lately acquainted with. About seven or eight score poor Protestants were by them put into an old vessel; which being, as some say, bulged by them, the vessel sank, and they were all presently drowned in the Harbour. The other 'instance' was thus: They put divers poor Protestants into a Chapel (which, since, they have used for a Mass-house, and in which one or more of their priests were now killed) where they were famished to death.[17]

And before Waterford Cromwell wrote that 'these victories and successes are the righteous judgments and mighty works of God. . . . He thus breaks the enemies of His Church in pieces.'[18]

3.3 The Royalist seen as a perpetrator of atrocities in England

Prince Rupert was singled out by many Puritans as a ring-leader in committing outrages on non-combatants:

> Prince Rupert flew about the countries with his body of horse, plundered and did many barbarous things.[19]

> ... the troops under ... Prince *Robert* killed countrey-men that came in with their teemes, and poore women, and children that were with them.[20]

> My fear is most of Prince Rupert, for they say he has little mercy when he comes. ... I have made up some of the doors and piled them so with wood that I believe my house is able to keep out a good many now; if we escape plundering I shall account it a great mercy of God; they are all about us here in such grievous fears that if they see but a gentleman riding they think it is to rob them.[21]

There were also less exalted notorious individuals such as Colonel Thomas Lunsford. He was called a 'baby-eater', a 'cannibal', a 'devourer of children' by the Puritans, and after he had been wrongly reported killed at Edgehill a ballad ran:

> The post that came from Banbury
> Riding in his blue rocket,
> He swore he saw when Lunsford fell
> A child's arm in his pocket

A later caricature purports to quote him:

> I'le helpe to kill, to pillage and destroy
> All the opposers of the Prelacy.
> My fortunes are grown small, my Friends are less
> I'le venter therefore life to have redress
> By picking, stealing, or by cutting throats,
> Although my practice crosse the kingdom's votes.[22]

'Englands Wolfe with eagles clawes, or the cruell Impieties of Bloud-Thirsty Royalists, and blasphemous *Anti-Parliamentarians*, under the command of that inhumane Prince *Rupert*, *Digby* and the rest. . . .'

(Broadsheet 1646. Reproduced in John Ashton, *Humour, Wit and Satire in the Seventeenth Century*.)

Arminian

Diuorcer

Anabaptist

Iefuit

Catalogue of the severall Sects and Opinions in England and other Nations with a briefe Rehearsall of their false and dangerous Tenents. 1646 (reproduced in Ashton, op. cit.).

(We should note the inclusion of the Jesuit on the principle that seditious extremes meet.)

Part 2

The Royalist's Image of the Puritan

3.4 The Puritan seen as a fanatical, seditious sectarian

Clarendon laid the whole blame for the political rebellion on the incitement of the people from the pulpit by demagogic Puritan preachers:

I must not forget, though it cannot be remembered without too much horror, that this strange wildfire among the people was not so much and so furiously kindled by the breath of the parliament, as of the clergy, who both administered fuel, and bloued the coals in the houses too. These men having creeped into, and at last driven all learned and orthodox men from the pulpits, had as is before remembered, from the beginning of this parliament, under the notion of reformation and extirpating of popery, infused seditious inclinations into the hearts of men against the present government of the church, with many libellous invectives against the state too. But since the raising of an army, and rejecting the king's last overture of a treaty, they contained themselves within no bounds; and as freely and without control inveighed against the person of the king, as they had before against the most malignant; profanely and blasphemously applying whatsoever had been spoken and declared by God himself, or the prophets, against the most wicked and impious kings, to increase and stir up the people against their most gracious sovereign.

(From *The History of the Great Rebellion*.)

Cleveland's vituperative poem, 'Hue and Cry after Sir John Presbyter' (1647), seethes with contempt and revulsion at the phenomenon of the militant Presbyterian whom he depicts as half-animal, half-devil:

> With Hair in Characters, and Lugs in text;
> With a splay mouth, and a nose circumflext;
> With a set Ruff of Musket bore, that wears
> Like Cartrages or linen Bandileers,
> Exhausted of their sulpherous Contents
> In Pulpit fire-works, which that Bomball vents;
> The *Negative* and *Covenanting* Oath,
> Like Two Mustachoes issuing from his mouth; . . .
> Madams Confession hanging at his eare,
> Wiredrawne through all the questions, *How and Where*
> Each circumstance so in the hearing Felt
> That when his ears are cropt hee'le count them gelt; . . .
> What zealous Frenzie did the *Senate* seize,
> That tare the *Rotchet* to such Rags as these?
> *Episcopacy* minc't, Reforming *Tweed*
> Hath sent us *Runts*, even of Her Churches breed; . . .
> The Beast at wrong end branded, you may trace
> The Devils foot-steps in his cloven Face.

3.5 The Puritans seen as 'that many Round-headed beast, a self-deified rout'

(a) ANON., from *The Blessed Anarchie.*

That apprentices, street-vendors, tinkers and even women should presume to have opinions on religion and politics, let alone to air them, was ridiculous but also frightening to supporters of the old order. The only possible outcome must be anarchy, to judge from this ballad:

> Now that, thanks to the Powers below,
> We have e'en done our do,

The mitre is down,
And so is the crown,
And with them the coronet too;
Come clowns, and come boys,
Come hober-de-hoys,
    Come females of each degree;
Stretch your throats, bring in your votes,
And make good the Anarchie.
    And thus it shall go, says Alice,
    Nay, thus it shall go, says Amy;
        Nay, thus it shall go, says Taffy, I trow,
        Nay, thus it shall go, says Jamy.

Ah! but the truth, good people all,
The truth is such a thing,
For it would undo, both Church and State too,
And cut the throat of our King;
    Yet not the Spirit, nor the new light,
    Can make this point so clear,
    But thou must bring out, thou deified rout,
        What thing the truth is, and where.
Speak Abraham, speak Kester, speak Judith, speak Hester,

    Speak tag and rag, short coat and long;
Truth's the speall made us rebel,
    And murder and plunder, ding-dong.
        Sure I have the truth, says Numph;
        Nay I ha' the truth, says Reverend Ruth;
        Nay, I ha' the truth, says Nem. . . .

        Neighbours and friends, pray one word more,
        There's something yet behind;
        And wife though you be, you do not well see,
        In which door sits the wind.
            As for poor Religion, to speak right,
                And in the House's sense.
            The matter's all one to have any or none,
                If 'twere not for the pretence:
            But herein doth lurk the key of the work,
                Even to dispose of the crown,
            Dexterously, and as may be
                For your behoof in our own.
                    Then let's ha' King Charles, says George;
                    Nay, let's have his son, says Hugh;

Nay, let's ha' none, says jabbering John;
Nay, let's be all kings, says Prue.

Oh! we shall have (if we go on
In plunder, excise, and blood)
But few folks and poor to dominion o'er,
And that will not be so good:
    Then let's resolve on some new way,
    Some new and happy course;
    The country's grown sad, the city born mad,
        And both Houses are worse.
    The Synod has writ, the General hath—
        And both to like purpose too;
Religion, laws, the truth, the Cause,
        Are talkt of, but nothing we do.
            Come, come, shall's ha' peace, says Nell;
            No, no, but we won't, says Madge;
            But I say we will, says fiery-faced Phill;
            We will and we won't, says Hadge.

Thus from the rout who can expect
Ought but division;
Since Unity doth with Monarchy,
Begin and end in One.

If then when all is thought their own,
    And lies at their behest;
These popular pates reap nought but debates,
    From that many Round-headed beast.
Come Royalists then do you play the men,
    And Cavaliers give the word;
Now let's see, at what you would be,
    And whether you can accord.
    A health to King Charles, says Tom;
        Up with it, says Ralph, like a man;
        God bless him, says Doll; and raise him, says Moll
        And send him his own, says Nan.[23]

(b) MARCHAMONT NEEDHAM, from *The History of the English Rebellion.*

There could be no comparison between the worth of the lives lost on the King's side and that of the low-born rascals fighting against him:

> ... When ev'ry Priest becomes a Pope,
>   Then Tinkers and Sow-gelders
> May, if they can but 'scape the Rope,
>   Be Princes and Lay-Elders.
>
> If once the Kirk-men pitch their Tents
>   With our Assembly-Asses,
> Synods will eat up Parliaments,
>   Courts be devour'd by Classes.
>
> Look to't, ye Gentry, else, be Slaves
>   To Slaves that can't abide ye:
> Though ye have been cow'd down by Knaves,
>   Oh! let not Fools now ride ye.
>
> But sev'n years of a thousand ('tis)
> Our Saints must Rulers be:
> So they shall loose in years of bliss,
>   Nine hundred ninety three.

(c) BISHOP KING, from *Elegy on Sir Charles Lucas and Sir George Lyle.*

This popular element in the Puritan movement was no laughing matter to Bishop Henry King—he saw unmistakable signs of a recurrence of the patricians' nightmare—another *bellum servile*:

> ... to Gull the People, you pretend,
> That Military Justice was Your end;
> As if we still were Blind, not knowing this
> To all your other Virtues suited is;
> Who only Act by your great Grandsires' Law,
> The Butcher Cade, Wat Tyler, and Jack Straw,
> Whose Principle was Murther, and their Sport
> To cut off those they fear'd might do them hurt;
> Nay, in your Actions we compleated find,
> What by those Levellers was but designed, ...

(d) SAMUEL BUTLER, from *Hudibras.*

Finally, in one of the most famous passages in *Hudibras*, Samuel Butler lashed the mingled absurdity and savagery consequent upon 'the rabble' taking it upon themselves to reform Church and State. All that their great new world-order has achieved is the abolition of bear-baiting:

For, if bear-baiting we allow,
What good can reformation do?
The blood and treasure that's laid out
Is thrown away, and goes for nought.
Are these the fruits o' th' protestation,
The prototype of reformation,
Which all the saints and some, since martyrs,
Wore in their hats, like wedding-garters,
When 'twas resolv'd by either House,
Six Members' quarrel to espouse?
Did they, for this draw down the rabble,
With zeal and noises formidable;
And make all cries about the town
Join throats to cry the bishops down?

Who, having round begirt the palace,
(As once a month they do the gallows)
As members gave the sign about,
Set up their throats with hideous shout
When tinkers bawl'd aloud to settle
Church-discipline, for patching kettle;
No sow-gelder did blow his horn
To geld a cat, but cry'd Reform.
The oyster-women lock'd their fish up,
And trudg'd away to cry No Bishop:
The mouse-trap men laid save-alls by,
And 'gainst ev'l counsellors did cry;
Botchers left old cloaths in the lurch,
And fell to turn and patch the church;
Some cry'd the covenant, instead
Of pudding-pies and ginger-bread,
And some for brooms, old boots and shoes,
Bawl'd out to purge the Common-house:
Instead of kitchen-stuff, some cry,
A gospel-preaching ministry
And some for old suits, coats, or cloak,
No surplices nor service-book:
A strange harmonious inclination
Of all degrees to reformation.
And is this all? Is this the end
To which these carry'ngs-on did tend?[24]

3.6 The Puritan seen as a canting Humbug

The Calvinist doctrine of 'the Elect' was naturally vulnerable to 'Saint-baiting'; every Puritan, including Cromwell, was seen by his enemies to be a moral sham. That there could be genuine sanctity, or a genuine struggle to achieve sanctity, was laughed out of court.

(a) ANON., *The Lancashire Puritane*, below, was surely the ancestor of Burns' 'Holy Willie' and the whole company of 'unco Guid':

>   The Puritane for painted show
>   The Pharisee doth farre outgoe;
>   His tedious Praiers of ten miles long,
>   His faith then *Samson* much more strong:
>   Though Looks and Gestures seeme all sprite,
>   Hee's Purus-putus Hypocrite.
>
>   This pure demure, this spottles Swanne
>   Is form'd of purer mould then Man;
>   Hee's dropp't from foorth some falling starre,
>   Which makes him passe vild Earth so faire:
>   Or being above with good St Paul,
>   From Heavens third loft to Earth did fall.
>
>   And well Hee might. Since *Lucifer*
>   For Pride his onely *Signifer*
>   Was hurld from Heaven; In puritanes
>   More Pride then in the Divell remaines:
>   Like Himm Hee can turne Angell bright,
>   Though Purus-putus Hypocrite.
>
>   Hee talks, Hee walks, Hee frames his looke,
>   Hee eates, drinks, sleeps, and all by booke;
>   Offer him Gold Hee doth abhorre itt,
>   Unless You can bring Scripture for itt:
>   In all Hee's more then most Divine,
>   And letts no Fart but under Line.
>
>   For with a Holy Sister meeting,
>   Hee gives her William Thrust's kind greeting;

> And sowes his Holy Seed so fast,
> That faire yong Ears peepe foorth att last;
> > Which what from Sires and Sisters traine
> > May prove a double Puritane.
>
> This *Cumane Asse* in *Lyons* skinne
> His side Ears cannot keepe within;
> Stripp't of his stol'n Plumes glorious show,
> Within there's nought but Aesops Crow;
> > Pluck off his Vizard, view him right,
> > Hee is a bisconted Hypocrite.[25]

(b) BUTLER'S *Roundhead* also had a weakness for surreptitious fornication:

> What's he that, if he chance to hear
> A little piece of *Common-Prayer*,
> > Doth think his conscience wounded;
> Will go five miles to preach and pray,
> And meet a sister by the way?
> > O! such a rogue's a Roundhead.

(c) STRODE'S *The Puritan*, often wrongly ascribed to Cleveland,[26] anticipated the unctuous mannerisms of that later nonconformist minister, Mr Chadband, in *Bleak House*:

> With face and fashion to be known,
> > For one of sure election;
> > With eyes all white, and many a groan,
> > With neck aside to draw in tone,
> With harp in's nose, or he is none;
> > See a new Teacher of the town—
> O the Town, O the Town's new Teacher!
>
> With pate cut shorter than the brow,
> With little ruff starch'd, you know how,
> With cloak like Paul, no cape I trow,
> With surplice none; but lately now
> With hands to thump, no knees to bow;
> > See a new Teacher of the town—
> O the Town, O the Town's new Teacher![27]

(d) SAMUEL BUTLER, from *Hudibras*.

Butler, the archetypal Conservative, could never stomach the fact that the rebels, led by their preachers, destroyed in the name of Reform:

> The Saints in masquerade would have us
> Sit quietly whilst they enslave us;
> And, what is worse, by lies and cants,
> Would trick us to believe 'em saints;
> And though by fines and sequestration
> They've pillaged and destroy'd the nation,
> Yet still they bawl for Reformation.[28]

3.7 The Puritan seen as a Monster of Cruelty in his turn

One paradox that hostile Royalists were very quick to seize on was the spectacle of self-avowed model Christians resorting to a competition in killing in order to establish their preferred model of Church Government.

In this poem Marchamont Needham begins by likening the Presbyterian to the plotting Jesuit:

(a) MARCHAMONT NEEDHAM, from *The History of the English Rebellion*.

> These both agreed to have *no King*;
>   The Scotchman he cries further,
> *No Bishop*: 'tis a godly thing
>   States to reform by Murther ...
>
> No *Sadduces* but must confess,
>   Those Monsters which are told
> In story, are risen now no less
>   *Prodigious* then of old
>
> Both *Cain* and *Judas* back are come,
>   In Vizards most divine:
> GOD bless us from a Pulpit-Drum,
>   And a preaching *Catiline* ...

> *Faith* and *Religion* bleeding lie,
>   And *Liberty* grows faint:
> No Gospel, but pure Treachery,
>   And Treason make the Saint.

(b) SAMUEL BUTLER, *Hudibras* (from Part I, Canto I).

Samuel Butler also, of course, did not let this unchristian militarism go unnoted. His hero's religion was:

> ... Presbyterian true blue, For he was of that
>   stubborn crew
> Of errant saints, whom all men grant To be the
>   true church militant;
> Such as do build their faith upon The holy test
>   of pike and gun;
> Decide all controversies by Infallible artillery;
> And prove their doctrine orthodox By apostolic
>   blows and knocks;
> Call fire and sword, and desolation, A godly
>   thorough reformation.

(c) BISHOP KING, from *Elegy on Sir Charles Lucas and Sir George Lisle*.

Even more bitter was Bishop King's denunciation of the Parliamentarians' blood-lust:

> You never must the Souldier's glory share,
> Since all your Trophies Executions are:
> Not thinking your Successes understood,
> Unless Recorded and Scor'd up in Blood.

He likened the Puritans to devils, to 'scum' and 'vermine', and accused the enemy of many atrocities, including killing men who surrendered under the promise of clemency, the selling of defeated Welsh as slaves to the Plantations, and the shooting of prisoners-of-war too weak to continue their forced march:

> ... this Murth'rous Crew
> All those they could drive on no further, Slew;
> What Bloody Riddle's this? They mercy give,
> Yet those who should enjoy it, must not live.

Indeed we cannot less from such expect,
Who for this Work of Ruine are Elect:
This Scum drawn from the worst, who never knew
The Fruits which from Ingenuous Breeding grew: . . .
Thus 'tis our Fate, I fear to be undone
Like Egypt once with Vermine over-run.[29]

4
THE CAVALIER AND PURITAN SELF-IMAGES

The Cavalier's ethic was individualistic: he valued his personal honour, personal loyalty, and personal enjoyment, thus fusing elements from the traditional ideals of chivalry and Pagan Classicism. As far as he could see his was the only civilized position. All the refining culture of life adorned *his* side. Wit, university learning, the active enjoyment as well as connoisseurship of all the arts, including music, the capacity to fashion exquisite, polished verse, horsemanship—all these were his. The Banqueting Hall designed by Inigo Jones was a memorial to Caroline architectural taste and the Cavalier's own person he adorned equally decoratively in a rich costume combining gorgeousness and elegance. Clarendon's portrait of the Duke of Newcastle is of the typical cultivated aristocrat of the period—obviously a charming man, but with no stamina for a long arduous struggle:

> He was a very fine gentleman, active, and full of courage, and most accomplished in those qualities of horsemanship, dancing and fencing, which accompany a good breeding; in which his delight was. Besides that he was amorous in poetry and music, to which he indulged the greatest part of his time; and nothing could have tempted him out of those paths of pleasure, which he enjoyed in a full and ample fortune, but honour and ambition to serve the king when he saw him in distress. . . .
>
> He liked the pomp and absolute authority of a general well, and preserved the dignity of it to the full; and for the discharge of the outward state, and circumstances of it, in acts of courtesy, affability, bounty, and generosity, he abounded. . . . But the substantial part, and fatigue of a general, he did not in any degree understand, (being utterly unacquainted with

war,) nor could submit to; ... In all actions of the field he was still present, and never absent in any battle; in all which he gave instances of an invincible courage and fearlessness in danger; ... Such articles of action were no sooner over, than he retired to his delightful company, music, or his softer pleasures, to all which he was so indulgent, and to his ease, that he would not be interrupted upon what occasion soever; insomuch as he sometimes denied admission to the chiefest officers of the army, even to general King himself, for two days together; from whence many inconveniences fell out.[1]

After the defeat at Marston Moor, 'utterly tired with a condition and employment so contrary to his humour, ... he transported himself out of the kingdom.'[2]

The Cavalier's *need* of sensuous beauty in all his surroundings is well evoked by the balladist Martin Parker:

> Though for a time we see Whitehall
>   With cobwebs hanging on the wall,
> Instead of silk and silver brave,
>   Which formerly it used to have;
> With rich perfume
>   In every room,
> Delightful to that princely train,
>   Which again you shall see,
>   When the time it shall be,
> That the king enjoys his own again.[3]

And Aubrey tells us that the poet Suckling when 'at his lowest ebbe in gameing ... then would make himselfe most glorious in apparell, and sayd that it exalted his spirits.'[4] He exalted the spirits of his Royalist troops likewise, for they were, '100 very handsome young proper men, whom he clad in white doubletts and scarlett breeches, and scarlet coates, hatts, and feathers, well-horsed, and armed. They say 'twas one of the finest sights in those dayes'.[5] The Cavalier gentry and aristocracy would have applauded Burke's affirmation of the value of nobility: 'Nobility is a graceful ornament to the civil order. It is the Corinthian capital of polished society.'[6]

Part 1

The Cavalier
Self-Image

4.1 The Cavalier's sense of honour

(a) LOVELACE, *To Lucasta, going to the warres*.

This poem, which is the most famous of all Cavalier songs, expresses to perfection the Cavalier's cherished image of himself as a brave knight galloping into the fray, fired by a picturesque chivalric tradition which Shakespeare has shown us to have been outmoded even by Hotspur's time. War is seen as a personal, quasi-erotic adventure; it is a matter of 'I', not 'we' dashing after the *first* Foe in the Field to win individual renown or 'Honour'; but Sword, Horse and Shield were to confront an impregnable phalanx of Roundhead pikemen and musketfire.

> Tell me not, Sweet, I am unkinde,
> That from the Nunnerie
> Of thy chaste breast and quiet minde,
> To Warre and Armes I flie.
>
> True; a new Mistresse now I chase,
> The first Foe in the Field;
> And with a stronger Faith imbrace
> A Sword, a Horse, a Shield.
>
> Yet this Inconstancy is such,
> As you too shall adore;
> I could not love thee, Deare, so much,
> Lov'd I not Honour more.

(b) BISHOP KING, from *Elegy on Sir Charles Lucas and Sir George Lisle.*

In this elegiac panegyric Bishop King gives a more detailed definition of honour in action stressing both the incomparable courage against overwhelming odds and the chivalrous magnanimity to their conquered foes of the two young men who:

> Were for their daring Sallies so much fear'd
> The' Assailants feld them like a frighted Heard; ...
> They, whose bold charge whole Armies did amaze,
> Rendring them faint and heartless at the Gaze,
> To see Resolve and Naked Valour charmes
> Of higher Proof than all their massy Armes:
> They whose bright swords ruffied the proudest Troop
> (As fowl unto the towring Falcon stoop)
> Yet no advantage made of their Success
> Which to the conquer'd spake them merciless;
> (For they, when e'er 'twas begg'd did safety give,
> And oft unasked bid the vanquish'd live; ...) [7]

(c) CLARENDON, *Lord Falkland.*

Clarendon completes the portrait of the ideal Cavalier in his great obituary on *Lord Falkland*, his friend for twenty years. It is characteristic of the supreme value placed on personal relations by the Cavaliers, that to Clarendon the Civil War itself was almost less damnable for its noxious principles than for its causing the death of this one outstanding man. For Viscount Falkland was

> a person of such prodigious parts of learning and knowledge, of that inimitable sweetness and delight in conversation, of so flowing and obliging a humanity and goodness to mankind, and of that primitive simplicity and integrity of life, that if there were no other brand upon this odious and accursed civil war, than that single loss, it must be most infamous, and execrable to all posterity.

Clarendon gives an interesting example of Falkland's gentlemanly sense of honour which directed him in civilian life as the King's secretary even to the detriment of his reputation for efficiency:

> ... two things he could never bring himself to, whilst he

continued in that office. ... The one, employing of spies, or giving any countenance or entertainment to them. I do not mean such emissaries, as with danger would venture to view the enemy's camp, and bring intelligence of their number, or quartering ... but those who by communication of guilt, or dissimulation of manners, would themselves into such trusts and secrets, as enabled them to make discoveries for the benefit of the state. The other, the liberty of opening letters, upon a suspicion that they might contain matter of dangerous consequence. For the first he would say, 'such instruments must be void of all ingenuity, and common honesty, before they could be of use; and afterwards they could never be fit to be credited: and that no single preservation could be worth so general a wound, and corruption of human society, as the cherishing such persons would carry with it.' 'The last', he thought 'such violation of the law of nature, that no qualifications by office could justify a single person in the trespass;' and though he was convinced by the necessity and iniquity of the time, that these advantages of information were not to be declined, and were necessarily to be practised, he found means to shift it from himself; when he confessed he needed excuse and pardon for the omission: so unwilling he was to resign any thing in his nature to an obligation in his office.

On the battlefield he was of course honour personified: in the forefront of the action and yet eager to spare the weak and defeated:

He had a courage of the most clear and keen temper, and so far from fear, that he was not without appetite of danger; and therefore upon any occasion of action, he always engaged his person in those troops, which he thought, by the forewardness of the commanders, to be most likely to be farthest engaged and in all such encounters he had about him a strange cheerfulness and companionableness, without at all affecting the execution that was then principally to be attended, in which he took no delight, but took pains to prevent it, where it was not, by resistance, necessary: insomuch that at Edgehill, when the enemy was routed, he was like to have incurred great peril, by interposing to save those who had thrown away their arms, and against whom, it may be, others were more fierce for their having thrown them away: insomuch as a man might think, he came into the field only out of curiosity to see the face of danger, and charity to prevent the shedding of blood. . . .

When there was any overture or hope of peace, he would be more erect and vigorous, and exceedingly solicitous to press any thing which he thought might promote it; and sitting among his friends, often, after a deep silence and frequent sighs, would, with a shrill and sad accent, ingeminate the word *Peace, Peace*; and would passionately profess, 'that the very agony of the war, and the view of the calamities and desolation the kingdom did and must endure, took his sleep from him, and would shortly break his heart.' This made some think, or pretend to think, 'that he was so much enamoured on peace, that he would have been glad the king should have bought it at any price'; which was a most unreasonable calumny. As if a man, that was himself the most punctual and precise in every circumstance that might reflect upon conscience or honour, could have wished the king to have committed a trespass against either. And yet this senseless scandal made some impression upon him, or at least he used it for an excuse of the daringness of his spirit; for at the leaguer before Gloucester, when his friends passionately reprehended him for exposing his person unnecessarily to danger, (as he delighted to visit the trenches and nearest approaches, and to discover what the enemy did,) as being so much beside the duty of his place, that it might be understood against it, he would say merrily, 'that his office could not take away the privileges of his age; and that a secretary in war might be present at the greatest secret of danger;' but withal alleged seriously, 'that it concerned him to be more active in enterprises of hazard, than other men; that all might see, that his impatiency for peace proceeded not from pusillanimity, or fear to adventure his own person'.

In the morning before the battle, as always upon action, he was very cheerful, and put himself into the first rank of the lord Byron's regiment, who was then advancing upon the enemy, who had lined the hedges on both sides with musketeers; from whence he was shot with a musket in the lower part of the belly, and in the instant falling from his horse, his body was not found till the next morning. . . .[8]

4.2 The Cavalier's over-riding sense of personal loyalty to the King

The Cavaliers were perhaps the last men in England still to feel a feudal bond of allegiance towards their Sovereign—a sense of personal obligation to him that could end only with death. The Scottish Jacobites of course were to continue in this (fatal) devotion to the Stuarts for another century. Not all those fighting for the King in the 1640s would have felt this overpowering loyalty, but there is enough evidence to convince us that the outstanding Cavalier spirits *were* thus motivated. And even the poetasting Duke of Newcastle, as we have seen, felt emotionally driven to forsake his pleasures by 'honour and ambition to serve the king when he saw him in distress, and abandoned by most of those who were in the highest degree obliged to him, and by him'.

(a) STRAFFORD'S last letter to the King, written from the Tower, entreats the King to sign his death-warrant and so avert a collision with Parliament fatal both to King and Kingdom:

> May it please your Sacred Majesty . . . I understand the minds of men are more and more incensed against me, notwithstanding your Majesty hath declared, that in your princely opinion I am not guilty of treason, and that you are not satisfied in your conscience to pass the Bill. . . . This bringeth me in a very great streight, there is before me the ruin of my children and family, . . . here are before me the many ills, which may befall your Sacred Person and the whole kingdom should yourself and Parliament part less satisfied one with the other than is necessary for the preservation both of King and people; they are before me the things most valued, most feared by mortal men, Life or Death.
>
> To say, Sir, that there hath not been a strife in me, were to make less man than, God knoweth, my infirmities make me, and to call a destruction upon myself and my young children may be believed, will find no easy consent from flesh and blood, . . . so now to set your Majesty's conscience at liberty, I do most humbly beseech your Majesty for prevention of evils which may happen by your refusal to pass this Bill. . . .

Sir, my consent shall more acquit you herein to God than all the world can do besides; to a willing man there is no injury done, . . . so Sir, to you, I can give the life of this world with all the cheerfulness imaginable, . . . God long preserve your Majesty. Your Majesty's most faithful and humble subject and servant Strafford.

(b) SIR EDMUND VERNEY.

That the Cavalier could place the demands of loyalty to the King above the dictates of conscience on a matter of principle—a thing impossible to be imagined of a Puritan in his relation to Cromwell—is attested by the conversation Sir Edmund Verney had with Clarendon:

'My condition', said he, 'is much worse than yours, and different, I believe, from any other man's; and will very well justify the melancholic that, I confess to you, possesses me. You have satisfaction in your conscience that you are in the right; that the king ought not to grant what is required of him; and so you do your duty and your business together: but for my part I do not like the quarrel, and do heartily wish that the king would yield and consent to what they desire; so that my conscience is only concerned in honour and in gratitude to follow my master. I have eaten his bread, and served him near thirty years, and will not do so base a thing as to forsake him; and choose rather to lose my life (which I am sure I shall do) to preserve and defend those things which are against my conscience to preserve and defend: for I will deal freely with you, I have no reverence for the bishops, for whom this quarrel [subsists].' It was not a time to dispute; and his affection to the church had never been suspected. He was as good as his word: and was killed, in the battle of Edge-hill, within two months after this discourse.[9]

(c) ALEXANDER BROME, *On the Loss of a Garrison.*

Brome captures the pathos of a frequently defeated and deserted King whom he addresses with increasing intimacy in this disastrous situation, calling him 'My soul' and advising him to trust in God alone:

Another city lost! Alas, poor king!
Still future griefs from former griefs do spring.
The world's a seat of change: kingdoms and kings,

Though glorious, are but sublunary things:
Crosses and blessings kiss; there's none that be
So happy, but they meet with misery.
He that ere while sat center'd to his throne,
And all did homage unto him alone;
Who did the sceptre of his power display
From pole to pole, while all his rule obey,
From stair to stair now tumbles, tumbles down,
And scarce one pillar doth support his crown.
Town after town, field after field,
This turns, and that perfidiously doth yield;
He's banded on the traitorous thought of those
That, Janus like, look to him and his foes.
In vain are bulwarks, and the strongest hold,
If the besiegers' bullets are of gold.
My soul, be not dejected: would'st thou be
From present trouble or from danger free?
Trust not in rampires, nor the strength of walls,
The town that stands to day, to morrow falls;
Trust not in soldiers, though they seem so stout,
Where sin's within, vain is defence without;
Trust not in wealth, for in this lawless time,
Where prey is penalty, there wealth is crime;
Trust not in strength or courage, we all see
The weak'st of times do gain the victory;
Trust not in honour; honour's but a blast,
Quickly begun, and but a while doth last.
They that to day to thee 'Hosanna' cry,
To morrow change their note for 'Crucify'.
Trust not in friends, for friends will soon deceive thee:
They are in nothing sure, but sure to leave thee.
Trust not in wit: who run from place to place,
Changing religion, as chance does her face,
In spite of cunning, and their strength of brain,
They're often catch'd, and all their plots are vain.
Trust not in counsel: potentates, or kings
All are but frail and transitory things.
Since neither soldiers, castles, wealth, or will,
Can keep off harm from thee, or thee from ill
Since neither strength nor honour, friends nor lords,
Nor princes, peace or happiness affords,

    Trust thou in God, ply Him with prayers still,
    Be sure of help: for He both can, and will.[10]

(d) RICHARD LOVELACE, *To Lucasta, From Prison, An Epode.*

Here another poet pledges himself with renewed loyalty to the King, the Sun of his universe, even from prison and when all other ideals—including love and religion—have failed in practice:

> Since then none of these can be
> Fit objects for my Love and me;
> What then remaines, but th' only spring
> Of all our loves and joyes, the KING.
>
> He who, being the whole Ball
> Of Day on Earth, lends it to all;
> When seeking to acclipse his right,
> Blinded, we stand in our owne light.
>
> And now an universall mist
> Of Error is spread or'e each breast
> With such a fury edg'd, as is
> Not found in th' inwards of th' Abysse.
>
> Oh from thy glorious Starry Waine
> Dispense on me one sacred Beame,
> To light me where I soone may see
> How to serve you, and you trust me! '[11]

In Lovelace's better known poem *To Althea from Prison*, the penultimate stanza evokes once more the Cavalier's idealization of his Royal master:

> When (like committed Linnet) I
>   With shriller throat shall sing
> The sweetness, Mercy, Majesty,
>   And glories of my KING:
> When I shall voyce aloud, how Good
>   He is, how Great should be;
> Inlarged Winds that curle the Flood,
>   Know no such Liberty.

4.3 The Cavalier's unashamed enjoyment of this world now

It was a well-documented side of the Cavalier ethos to 'seize the present time' and find life's meaning in self-authenticating moments of erotic, poetic or wine-drunk abandon. In the three following extracts Herrick drinks to Ovid and Catullus, trusting to his good verses to win him immortality once his body is drowned in Lethe, whilst the anonymous poet of *The Secret* claims that he and his mistress have engrossed all the love in the kingdom, thus causing the hate-filled Civil War, and Brome illustrates the more brutish side of Cavalier pleasure-seeking.

(a) HERRICK, 'To live Merrily, and to trust to Good Verses', from *Hesperides* (1648).

> Now is the time for mirth,
> Nor cheek, or tongue be dumbe:
> For with the flowrie earth,
> The golden pomp is come.
>
> The golden Pomp is come;
> For now each tree does weare
> (Made of her Pap and Gum)
> Rich beads of Amber here.
>
> Now raignes the *Rose*, and now
> Th' *Arabian* Dew besmears
> My uncontrolled brow,
> And my retorted haires.
>
> *Homer*, this Health to thee,
> In Sack of such a kind,
> That it would make thee see,
> Though thou were ne'er so blind. . . .
>
> Then this immensive cup
> Of *Aromaticke* wine,
> *Catullus*, I quaffe up
> To that terse Muse of thine.

Wild I am now with heat;
O Bacchus! coole thy Rayes!
Or frantick I shall eate
Thy *Thyrse*, and bite the *Bayes*. . . .

Behold, *Tibullus* lies
Here burnt, whose small return
Of ashes, scarce suffice
To fill a little Urne.

Trust to good Verses then:
They onely will aspire,
When Pyramids, as men,
Are lost, i' th' funerall fire.

And when all Bodies meet
In *Lethe* to be drown'd;
Then onely Numbers sweet,
With endlesse life are crown'd.

(b) ANON., *The Secret* (written at the time of the Civil War).

Hark, Celia, hark! but lay thou close thine ear;
    There's for it a concerning reason:
For I've a secret now to tell my dear,
    And 'tis no less than treason.

Let silly worldlings of their causes prate
    From whence our civil rage begins;
Let wise men talk of errors in our state,
    And churchmen of our sins;

Let others blame the stars' malignancy,
    Others the people's peevish call;
But, dearest, speak not of 't, for thou and I
    Are authors of it all:

We have all love engrossed: in us alone
    All kindness extant doth abide:
Nor have we left the land enough t' atone
    One pair of hearts beside.

When close as men in famines viands do,
    Let us our loves in secret lay:
Such useful treasure should the world but know,
    Alas, they 'd take 't away.

No, Celia, no; our love's transcendent worth
    No force, no injury, can fear;
Then let it stream with all its glory forth,
    And like itself appear:

That when great Charles shall clear our troubled air,
    And crown our orb with peaceful hours,
The nation all may unto us repair,
    And light their loves at ours.[12]

(c) ALEXANDER BROME, *The Mad Lover.*

I have been in love, and in debt, and in drink,
    This many and many a year;
And those three are plagues enough, one would think,
    For one poor mortal to bear.
'Twas drink made me fall into love,
    And love made me run into debt,
And though I have struggled and struggled and strove,
    I cannot get out of them yet.

There's nothing but money can cure me,
    And rid me of all my pain;
        'Twill pay all my debts,
        And remove all my lets,
And my mistress, that cannot endure me,
    Will love me, and love me again:
Then I'll fall to loving and drinking amain.

4.4 The Cavalier's struggle to survive: from the Knyvett Letters (1620–1644)

For every Cavalier who was a devoted servant of the King, or his muse, or his mistress or his wine, or all four, there must have been a hundred, like poor Thomas Knyvett, gentleman of Norfolk, whose one overwhelming preoccupation was *survival* during these times. Hence this record of the Cavaliers' accounts of themselves ends with some of Knyvett's many anxious letters to his wife concerning the fate of their property threatened by Parliamentary sequestration:

My deer   May 30th 1644

Hart', I must be breefe with thee, I am so full of troubled business in my head. I feare I shall doe little in my busines a great while, for nowe I am advised that I must petition the house first & get my case referred to the Committe before that will meddle with it, And when I shall get a motion ther, God knowes. I wish thou weart heer with all my hart, for yor solicitation would doe more in a weeke then I am like to doe in a Quarter. Besides, you are not subiect to some obnox'ius Questions that I am, w^{ch}, if vnsatisfy'd, may turne me into a worss condition. I knowe not wch way to stire my cours. God direct me. But all the freinds that I speake with are absolute of opinion that yor solicitation would prevaile farr beyond mine. . . .

Deer   June 8th 1644

Hart', Hovells arrivall with yor wofull complaints hath struck' me almost dead. I feard the last cruel ordinance would put vs into this sad condition. I have indeavord all meanes & imploy'd all my Industry to have gain'd some com'fort, but yor intercepted letters & yor discoursses amongst you have so inraged m^r Cor^t that I cannot get to be heard. Some letter of yor have come to his hands, besides my Brother Natt^s & Jack'. Nay I was tould this day of some discourse of yor with the Lady Fra: at Norw: was informed heer. Oh' sweet Hart, ist possible you can be guilty of so much indiscretion as to fall into any argum^t in such a place, & going vpon such a busines. Truly I was tould that the Lady showld say she wondred that you showld taulke so, being in such a condition. You may see how dangerous a thing it is to maintaine argumen^t, thoughe you be perswaded of the truth of it. Sr Will. Paston hath profest much love to me, who tould me this morning that he, being at his chamber, found him in a good vaine & fell a mov'ing him for me. He much declaim'd against all our malignancyes, esspetially of my wife & my chilldren, & my Brother, saying he had seene some letters of yor. I hear he hath sent them downe to the Committee at Norw:—a strang' thing. Sr Will: sweetned all his obiections &

extenuated our offences aswell as he could, And tould him, if he would admit me to come & speake with him out of Passion, he doubted not but I would give him satisfaction, wch he intertain'd with a great complem^t, & to morrowe morning I am to performe that servis when I meane to present him thy letter, wch came to me at my cosin Ellsings. Sr W. P. being ther, I shew'd it him, hav'ing had this discourse but littell before. He lik't it exceeding well & doubts not but that it will worke very well with him. Howe I speed to morrowe you shall knowe, for 'till I can make him my freind againe, I strive but like a bird in a Net & more intangle my selfe. S^r W: P: is got his sequestration dischargd. Sr Robt. Kempe the like, with a war^t from the Committee to take his goods that have been plundred that are vnsould wher ever he can find them. I hope I shall not be made the only obiect of Pitty & scorne in the country. The next scean that presents you is from m^r Cor^s: house yesterday & to day from the Committe. I was som'what to ear'ly for m^r Cor: &, after full 3 howers attendance, I was admitted to some discourse. I presented yor letter wch he seem'd to take very kindly, & after many Questions & Answeares he appear'd to be very well satisfy'd & promist me all fayer assistance at the Committee, so came with me in my coach' to Westm^er. I was not a littel proude to be seen with him. . . .

I am vnder the lash' & must induer the scourge with patience. I shall arme my selfe for my defence aswell as I can, for I exspect A Thundring charge from m^r Beadles certificat. God Allmighty, I hope, will protect my Innocency & mollify' ther harts that are so set against me. Ther was no possibility of getting a stay' of the sale of our goods 'till twas heard & determin'd heer, therfore you must vse yor best indevors with Browne. I fear the late newe officer wilbe firce in his execution. You may tell him, if he comes, that I have propounded tearmes of composition to m^r Cor^t for my goods, wch he likes well, & a summ is partly agreed on, if I may have security for the future. I am most troubled for my Farmors that have pay'd ther rents, least ther cattel showld be driven. Tru'ly sweet hart these things wear able to distract a well resolv'd patience, if ther wear not a good God to trust in, & a heavenly Kingdome to exspect. I pray satisfy my best Tenants that thay shalbe no loosers if I be master of my owne. . . .

I knowe not what to doe for mony to go through with my busines. My stocke is very lowe. If I get not off this sequestration we are all undon, for I shall have no means to doe any thing for poor Buss. Faile not to send me a letter howe the . . . in before fryday. So in hast. God looke vpon vs in mercy . . . out of the hands of our enemyes.

Thyne most faithfully in all conditions

June 8. 1644.   K.T.A.T.

Address: For his deer freind m^{is} Katherine Knyvett at Ashwell Thorpe these.

June 27th 1644

Deer Hart,

I came from Petersome this morning. I went thether on saturday, my busines being put of on fryday, & wednesday being the fast day I had no hopes 'till to morrowe, yet against ther custome thay sat on Tu'sday, & disspatch't some causes that wear before mine, so that I hope to morrowe I shall get to be heard. I will once more to m^r Cor^t. Indeed, sweet hart, this busines hath almost broake my hart. I am gladd to reade some comfort in thy letters, yet when I looke backe vpon my owne condition, I am struck blancke againe, seeing my selfe inviron'd with eyes & eares that seek's my vtter ruine. God deliver me out of ther hands. I perceive thou art loath' to come vp, And indeed I am asmuch greev'd to disturbe thy Quiet, but if I cannot get off the sequestration, what shall I doe in the country? I have vsd my vttermost indeavore I can possible. God send me good success. . . . It would be to great a happiness for me to exspect for vs to live altogether Quietly. I will not desspaier, but trust in Gods mercy. Oh' this cruell harted man Cor:, 'tis he vndoes me & obstructs all my happiness in these sad times. To take delighte to insulte vppon adnothers misery is not noble, scarce christian. God turne his hart. . . . I pray God we may live to have a Joy'full meeting. I am in a great steight howe to pay' my Brothers Bill of 50, wch he furnisht the boyes with. Truly I knowe not yet howe to performe it, & the time growes neer, being vpon the 8 of July. . . . I am so loath' to trouble thee as I shall not yet desier thy peremptory com'ing vp. I can spend no longer time nowe, being to goe a solicitting against to morrowe. Therfore I end with my humble prayers to God, for the good success in both our business. Farwell.

Thy faithfull loving freind

Yo^r mothers.   T.K.

June 27. 1644.

My Blessing to my Girles. S[r] W.D., I think', hath left vs at
Petersome. 'Tis a sweet place in summer—so was Thorpe,
but—

Address: For his truly beloved freind m[is] Katherine Knyvett
at her house at Ashwell Thorpe these. Norff.

Leave this at Windham at m[r] Punders to be sent.[13]

Part 2
The Puritan
Self-Image

The Puritan's ethic, in contrast to that of the Cavalier,
transcended the merely personal and despised the merely
ornamental. 'Not what I will, but what Thou wilt' was the
imperative that haunted him. God and the establishment of
the Godly Commonwealth were Absolutes for the good of
which personal wishes (the Puritan's enemy might add even
his personal conscience) must be subordinated. It is a familiar
revolutionary position, and is perhaps most chillingly manifested in Cromwell's abandonment of his old acquaintance
Lord Capel for the good of the Parliamentary cause, as
Clarendon reported the scene of the trial:

> Cromwell, who had known him very well, spoke so much
> good of him, and professed to have so much kindness and
> respect for him, that all men thought he was now safe, when
> he concluded, 'that his affection to the public so much weighed
> down his private friendship, that he could not but tell them
> that the question was now, whether they would preserve the
> most bitter and the most implacable enemy they had; that he
> knew the lord Capel very well, and knew that he would be
> the last man in England that would forsake the royal interest;
> that he had great courage, industry, and generosity; that he
> had many friends who would always adhere to him; that that
> as long as he lived, what condition soever he was in, he would

be a thorn in their sides; and therefore for the good of the commonwealth, he should give his vote against the petition' (i.e. of clemency).[1]

Capel of course was executed. A rather more winning instance of this subjection of the personal to a social and spiritual ideal comes at the end of Milton's *Samson Agonistes*. After the hero's self-sacrificial death, vanquishing the enemies of God and his people, his old father, Manoa, refuses to mourn:

> Come, come, no time for lamentation now,
> Nor much more cause, *Samson* hath quit himself
> Like *Samson* and heroicly hath finish'd
> A life Heroic, on his Enemies
> Fully reveng'd, . . .
> > *To Israel*
> Honour hath left, and freedom, let but them
> Find courage to lay hold on this occasion, . . .
> And which is best and happiest yet, all this
> With God not parted from him, as was feard,
> But favouring and assisting to the end.
> Nothing is here for tears, nothing to wail
> Or knock the breast, no weakness no contempt
> Despraise or blame, nothing but well and fair,
> And what may quiet us in a death so noble.

There were many paradoxes and contradictions in English Puritanism, some at least of which are covered in the conflicting definitions of their world-view given by the Puritans themselves (pp. 108–21 below). One paradox is that although the Puritan was compelled to believe that he *ought* to transcend his personal wants and seek to follow God's lead at every turning, yet he had no way of discovering God's will other than by the rigorous searching of his own heart—aided of course by constant scrutiny of relevant passages in Scripture. The period of the Civil War and Interregnum actually offered a kind of brief escape from this squirrel's treadmill of soul-searching for many Puritans, offering them the opportunity to externalize their conflict, fighting Satan in the world outside rather than forever within themselves. But after the Restoration, Christian could only flee the City of Destruction, putting wax in his ears, ignoring even wife and children, as he struggled to save his own soul. Another obvious source of conflict was in the Puritan's dualistic view of flesh and spirit.

He had to believe in the absolute superiority of the spirit, yet he was also a man of sentient flesh and questioning intellect. Some Puritans attempted to repress and silence their non-spiritual self, but others tried to harness their response to beauty, their happiness in sexual union and their gifts of the mind to their religion, arguing that all these positives came from God and not the Devil.

4.5 Contemporary analyses of the Puritan spirit

(a) HENRY PARKER, from *A Discourse Concerning Puritans* (1641).

Henry Parker (1604–1652) was one of the first Parliamentarians to argue for the sovereignty of Parliament, thus breaking through the shibboleth of the 'balanced polity', so popular with writers from all sides in the period before the Civil War. Parker has sometimes been seen as a rather cold, Erastian observer, but this brilliantly sympathetic analysis of his fellow Puritans in 1641 gives the lie to such a view:[2]

... I cannot but professe it, there is nothing more scandalizes me at this time, than to see Puritans being so few in number, so despicable in condition, so harmless in example, so blameless in opinion, yet sentenced and condemned in judgment, as if they were the greatest Incendiaries, and the only Innovators in the Christian World. ...

... Let us then a little farther search into the mysterious abuse, and misapplication of this word Puritan. Those whom we ordinarily call Puritans are men of strict life, and precise opinions, which cannot be hated for any thing but their singularity in zeale and piety, and certainly the number of such men is too small, and their condition too low, and dejected: *but they* which are the Devils chiefe Artificers in abusing this word, when they please can so stretch and extend the same that scarce any civill honest Protestant which is hearty and true to his Religion can avoid the aspersion of it, and when they list againe, they can so shrink it into a narrow sense, that it shall seem to be aimed at none but monstrous, abominable Heretickes and Miscreants. *Thus* by its latitude it strikes generally, by its contractions it pierces deeply, by its confused application it deceives invisibly. Small scruples first intitle mee to the name of Puritan, and then the Name of Puritan intitles me further to all mischiefs whatsoever. . . .

. . . This detested odious name of Puritan first began in the Church presently after the Reformation, but now it extends itselfe further, and gaining strength as it goes, it diffuses its poysonous ignominy further and being not contented to Gangrene Religion, Ecclesiasticall and Civill policy, it now threatens destruction to all morality also. The honest strict demeanour, and civill conversation which is so eminent in some men, does so upbraid and convince the Antipuritan that even honesty, strictnesse, and civility itselfe must become disgracefull, or else they which are contrary cannot remaine in grace: But because it is too grosse to deride vertue under the name of vertue, therefore other colours are invented, and so the same thing undergoes derision under another name. The zealous man is despised under the name of zealot, the Religious honest man has the vizard of an hypocrite and dissembler put upon him to make him odious.

Puritans by *some are parallelled to Jesuites*, Jesuites are called Popish Puritans, and Puritans, Protestant Jesuites; yet this is not intended disparageable to them: For doubtlesse fiery zeale and rigour were not blameable in Jesuites, were not their very Religion false; as celerity and expedition in a Traveller is not in itselfe faulty, but commendable, though the Traveller being in a wrong path, it causes him to stray the further from his journeys end. . . .

. . . *I have beene a deligent inquirer into Puritans* and have exactly tryed them three wayes. First, in themselves, and so I finde them zealous, at least seeming so outwardly, and distinguisht principally from other men by their remarkable, and singular zeal to God and the Truth: and this to me is no ground of uncharitable censure. Secondly, in those, which in these times thinke and speake charitably of them; and they are so many in number, and of so good quality, that indeed to the Popish and Episcopall faction, all the Kingdome almost seemes Puritanicall; but for this I cannot thinke the worse of them. But thirdly when I consider Puritans, and compare them with their common notorious adversaries, then their goodnesse seemes most evident to me, as if it were legible ingraved in the open wickednesse and scandall of their chiefe opposers. *Nothing* but Truth, Holinesse, and Goodnesse, seemes to me to the cause, that Papists do so implacably abominate them that our proud Hierarchists, Ambidexters, and Neuters in Religion, do so uncessantly pursue their sub version,; that Court-flatterers, and time-serving Projectors, and the revenous Caterpillars of the Realme, doe so virulently prosecute them with defamations and contumelies; that Stage-poets, Minstrels, and the jesting Buffoones of the age, make them the principall subject of derision: lastly, that all the shameless rout of drunkards, lechers, and swearing ruffians; and the scum of the vulgar are so tickled with their reproach, and abuse.

Certainly, nothing but an unappeasable antipathy could be the cause of all this, and no testimony of goodness can be more sure, un-erring, and unanswerable than such antipathy.

(b) LUCY HUTCHINSON (1620–*c.* 1675) wrote the famous memoirs of her husband to vindicate his reputation as man and political figure after he had died in prison without trial, following the Restoration. In the eloquent and ironic extract which follows, she builds up a composite image of the Puritan derived from the abusive and distorting slander to which they were subjected by their enemies:

If any were griev'd at the dishonor of the kingdome or the griping of the poore, or the unjust oppressions of the subject, by a thousand wayes, invented to maintaine the riotts of the courtiers and the swarms of needy Scots, the king had brought in to devoure like locusts the plenty of this land, he was a Puritane: if any, out of mere morallity and civill honesty, discountenanc'd the abominations of these days, he was a Puritane, however he conform'd to their superstitious worship: if any shew'd favour to any godly honest person, kept them company, reliev'd them in want, or protected them against violent or uniust oppression, he was a Puritane: if any gentleman in his country maintain'd the good lawes of the land, or stood up for any publick interest, for good order or government, he was a Puritane: in short, all that crost the viewes of the needie courtiers, the proud encroaching priests, the theevish protectors, the lewd nobillity and gentrie, whoever was zealous for God's glory or worship, could not endure blasphemous oathes, ribbald conversation, prophane scoffes, sabbath breach, derision of the word of God, and the like;

whoever could endure a sermon, modest habitt or conversation, or aniething good, all these were Puritanes; and if Puritanes, then enemies to the King and his government, seditious factious hipocrites, ambitious disturbers of the publick peace, and finally, the pest of the kingdome; such false logick did the children of darknesse use to argue with against the hated children of light, whom they branded besides as an illiterate, morose, melancholly, discontented, craz'd sort of men, not fitt for humane conversation; as such they made them not only the sport of the pulpitt, which was become but a more solemne sort of stage, but every stage, and every table, and every puppett-play, belcht forth prophane scoffes upon them, the drunkards made them their songs, all fidlers and mimicks learnt to abuse them, as finding it the most gamefull way of fooling.[3]

4.6 The Puritans' shared faith and collective purpose during the War and Interregnum

(a) The Scottish Presbyterian influence on the Puritan movement, both in form and content, is clear in the two poems below, whether in the use of lowlands vernacular or the rhythms of the metrical psalms dear to the Covenanters.

LESLEY'S MARCH TO LONG-MARSTON MOOR
1641

March! March! March!
   Why the devil do ye na March!
Stand to your arms, my lads,
   Fight in good order,
Front about, front, ye musketeers all,
   Until ye come to the English border.
   Stand till't, and fight like men,

True Gospel to maintain.
The Parliaments blyth to see us a' coming.

When to the kirk we come,
Wee'l purge it ilka room
Frae Popish relics and a' sic innovation,
That a' the world may see
There's nane in the right but we,
O' the sons of the auld Scotish nation.

Jenny shall wear the hood,
Jockey the sark o' God,
And the kist fu' o' whistles, that mak sic a cleiro
Our pipers braw shall hae them a',
Whate'er comes on it.
Busk up your plaids, my lads,
Cock up your bonnets.
March! March![4]

THE BATTLE OF WORCESTER
1650

The mighty God hath once again
Appear'd from Heaven high,
His people to deliver from
The House of Slavery.

The 'Iron yoke he lately broke,
Which men prepared had
To put upon the neck of saints,
To make their hearts full sad.

The *Northern* waves lift up their voice,
And roar'd so terribly,
That *English* land thereat 'gan quake,
And tremble fearfully.

Of Men and Horses, fierce and stout,
Their Armies were prepared;
Gilial, and Ammon, Amalek,
And Tyre were insnared

To joyn in sinfull leage against
The *Lord*, the *Lord* of might,
And his despised ones, because
They weak appear'd in fight.

Come, let us tread them down (said they)
   Like clay and mire in street;
We'll give them Laws, and Lords, and Kings,
   And all as we think meet.

Our Sword shall teach them what to know
   Of God, what to believe:
To worship him as they think meet,
   No longer will we give.

Their lives upon their knees they shall
   Of us begg and intreat;
The dust o' th' Earth we will compel
   Them to lick at our feet.

These swelling words the Heavens above
   Disdeyned long to hear;
The Stars made ready for to fight,
   Each one out of his sphere.

And God, the holy one of those
   Who thus despised were,
To stop the way 'gainst such rebukes,
   Brought forth both shield and spear.

His Enemies' heart he takes away,
   And gives unto his Friends,
To them the wings of fear for flight:
   To these, a Sword he sends.

To execute his judgement just
   On them that sought their woe,
To teach them violence to hate,
   And righteous things to do.

The Lord, and his, together thus
   Triumphed gloriously:
Thousands by death, yet thousands more
   Fell by captivity.

This mighty work recalls to mind
   The days of ancient date,
When God on high the swelling powers
   Of Egypt did abate,

And when the staff of Midian
  Was by him broke asunder,
Wherewith he smote the innocent,
  And sought to bring them under.

This is a day the Lord hath made
  A day of grace and wonder,
Wherein our prayers from the Heavens
  He answer'd hath in Thunder.

Out of the hands, and bands of those
  Who sought to make us thrall,
He hath deliver'd us by an Hand
  Far higher than them all.

He that hath thus deliver'd us
  Shall be our God for ever;
Him will we love, Him will we serve:
  Forsake us he will never.[5]

(b) MILTON, from *An Apology for Smectymnuus* (1642).

The sense of what would now be called 'revolutionary solid-
arity' is also expressed in Milton's paean of praise to the
Long Parliament for its ideological firmness and accessibility
to popular grievances; we note his early reference to 'the
commonwealth' which was to be a republican rallying-cry
later on.

> With such a majesty had their wisdom begirt itself, that
> whereas others had levied war to subdue a nation that sought
> for peace, they sitting here in peace could so many miles
> extend the force of their single words, as to overawe the
> dissolute stoutness of an armed power, secretly stirred up and
> almost hired against them. And having by a solemn protesta-
> tion vowed themselves and the kingdom anew to God and his
> service, and by a prudent foresight ... prevented the disso-
> lution and frustrating of their designs by an untimely breaking
> up; notwithstanding all the treasonous plots against them,
> all the rumours either of rebellion or invasion, they have not
> been yet brought to change their constant resolution, ever to
> think fearlessly of their own safeties and hopefully of the
> commonwealth: which has gained them such an admiration
> from all good men, that now they hear it as their ordinary

surname, to be saluted the fathers of their country, and sit as gods among daily petitions and public thanks flowing in upon them. Which doth so little yet exalt them in their own thoughts, that, with all gentle affability and courteous acceptance, they both receive and return that tribute of thanks which is tendered them; testifying their zeal and desire to spend themselves as it were piece-meal upon the grievances and wrongs of their distressed nation; insomuch that the meanest artisans and labourers, at other times also women, and often the younger sort of servants assembling with their complaints, and that sometimes in a less humble guise than for petitioners, have gone with confidence, that neither their meanness would be rejected, nor their simplicity contemned; nor yet their urgency distasted either by the dignity, wisdom, or moderation of that supreme senate; nor did they depart unsatisfied.

(c) MILTON, from *Areopagitica* (1644).

Milton's hopeful idealism extended from the House of Commons to the Puritan stronghold of London and even to the whole of England at this time:

> Behold now this vast city, a city of refuge, the mansion-house of liberty encompassed and surrounded with his [God's] protection; the shop of war hath not there more anvils and hammers working, to fashion out the plates and instruments of armed justice in defence of beleagured truth, than there be pens and heads there, sitting by their studious lamps, musing, searching, revolving new notions and ideas wherewith to present, as with their homage and their fealty, the approaching reformation: others as fast reading, trying all things, assenting to the force of reason and convincement.
>
> What could a man require more from a nation so pliant and so prone to seek after knowledge? What wants there to such a towardly and pregnant soil, but wise and faithful labourers, to make a knowing people, a nation of prophets, of sages and worthies? . . .
>
> Methinks I see in my mind a noble and puisant nation rousing herself like a strong man after sleep, and shaking her invincible locks: methinks I see her as an eagle mewing her mighty youth, and kindling her undazzled eyes at the full midday beam; purging and unscaling her long-abused sight at the fountain itself of heavenly radiance; . . .

(d) MILTON, from *Reason of Church Government Urged against Prelaty*.

Milton's faith in the *unity* of the Puritans in the early 1640s was most roundly declared in this challenge to the Anglican establishment. His optimism, of course, was to be unfounded, and he himself later admitted—'New Presbyter is but Old Priest writ large':[6]

> Noise it till ye be hoarse, that a rabble of sects will come in; it will be answered ye, No rabble, sir priest; but an unanimous multitude of good protestants will then join to the church which now, because of you stand separated.

4.7 Three Puritan viewpoints

(a) JOHN MILTON.

The extracts below, taken for the most part from Milton's less familiar work, are chosen to illustrate his 'Puritanism with a human face'. His less human face, as he cast out the unrighteous from him, has already been seen (see above, 2.3). I cannot attempt to summarize either his theological or political development here; what I am concerned with is evoking Milton's changing *emotional* response to the experience of living through some of the most stirring conflicts in English history. My emphasis is on Milton's idealism—his passionate concern for justice, his rapturous sense of beauty, his disciplined self-dedication to the Highest, and his idealistic view both of sexual love and of the free play of intellect. No man has had a clearer or more ardent idea of what human life on earth *ought* to be like. His disappointment was proportional, and his darkening world-view is illustrated in the later passages. But first the youthful high hopes:

> Let us with a gladsom mind
> Praise the Lord, for he is kind,
> For his mercies ay endure,
> Ever faithfull, ever sure. . . .

O let us his praises tell,
That doth the wrathfull tyrants quell.
For his mercies ay endure,
Ever faithfull, ever sure. . . .

In bloody battail he brought down
Kings of prowess and renown.
For his mercies ay endure,
Ever faithfull, ever sure.[7]

Ring out ye Cristall sphears,
Once bless our human ears,
(If ye have power to touch our senses so)
And let your silver chime
Move in melodious time;
And let the Base of Heaven's deep Organ blow,
And with your ninefold harmony
Make up full consort to th' Angelike symphony.

For if such holy Song
Enwrap our fancy long,
Time will run back, and fetch the age of gold,
And speckl'd vanity
Will sicken soon and die,
And leprous sin will melt from earthly mould,
And Hell itself will pass away,
And leave her dolorous mansions to the peering day.

Yea Truth and Justice then
Will down return to men, . . .[8]

How soon hath Time the suttle theef of youth,
Stoln on his wing my three and twentieth yeer!
My hasting dayes flie on with full career,
But my late spring no bud or blossom shew'th.
Perhaps my semblance might deceive the truth,
That I to manhood am arriv'd so near,
And inward ripenes doth much less appear,
That som more timely-happy spirits indu'th,
Yet be it less or more, or soon or slow,
It shall be still in strictest measure eev'n,
To that same lot, however mean, or high,
Toward which Time leads me, and the will of Heav'n;
All is, if I have grace to use it so,
As ever in my great task Masters eye.[9]

I betook me among those lofty fables and romances, which recount in solemn cantos the deeds of knighthood founded by our victorious kings, and from hence had in renown over all Christendom. There I read in it the oath of every knight that he should defend to the expense of his best blood, or of his life, if it so befell him, the honour and chastity of virgin or matron; . . . Only this my mind gave me, that every free and gentle spirit, without that oath, ought to be born a knight, nor needed to expect the gilt spur, or the laying of a sword upon his shoulder to stir him up both by his counsel and his arms, to secure and protect the weakness of any attempted chastity. . . .

Thus, from the laureat fraternity of poets, riper years, and the ceaseless round of study and reading led me to the shady spaces of philosophy; but chiefly to the divine volumes of Plato, and his equal Xenophon: where . . . I learnt of chastity and love, I mean that which is truly so . . . and how the first and chiefest office of love begins and ends in the soul, . . .[10]

Love was the son of Loneliness, begot in Paradise by that sociable and helpful aptitude which God implanted between man and woman toward each other. . . .

Marriage is a covenant, the very being whereof consists not in a forced cohabitation, and counterfeit performance of duties, but in unfeigned love and peace: . . . love in marriage cannot live nor subsist unless it be mutual; . . . And it is less a breach of wedlock to part with wise and quiet consent betimes, than still to soil and profane that mystery of joy and union with a polluting sadness and perpetual distemper: for it is not the outward continuing of marriage that keeps whole that covenant, but whatsoever does most according to peace and love, whether in marriage, or in divorce, he it is that breaks marriage least; it being so often written that 'Love only is the fulfilling of every commandment.'[11]

I cannot praise a fugitive and cloistered virtue unexercised and unbreathed, that never sallies out and seeks her adversary, but slinks out of the race, where that immortal garland is to be run for, not without dust and heat. Assuredly we bring not innocence into the world, we bring impurity rather; that which purifies us is trial, and trial is by what is contrary. . . . And though all the winds of doctrine were let loose to play upon the earth, so truth be in the field, we do injuriously by licensing and prohibiting to misdoubt her strength. Let her and falsehood grapple; who ever knew truth put to the worse, in a free and open encounter?[12]

But the English Revolution was not prepared to sanction either divorce or freedom of the press and Milton turned on the Presbyterian influence in the Long Parliament (whom earlier he had saluted as the Saviours of their people), savage in his disappointment:

> I did but prompt the age to quit their cloggs
>> By the known rules of antient libertie,
>> When strait a barbarous noise environs me
> Of Owles and Cuckoes, Asses, Apes and Doggs.
> As when those Hinds that were transform'd to Froggs
>> Raild at Latona's twin-born progenie
>> Which after held the Sun and Moon in fee.
> But this is got by casting Pearl to Hoggs;
> That bawle for freedom in their senceless mood,
>> And still revolt when truth would set them free.
> Licence they mean when they cry libertie;
> For who loves that, must first be wise and good;
>> But from that mark how far they roave we see
> For all this wast of wealth, and loss of blood.[13]

ON THE NEW FORCERS OF CONSCIENCE UNDER THE LONG PARLIAMENT

> Because you have thrown of your Prelate Lord,
>> And with stiff Vowes renounc'd his Liturgie
>> To seise the widdow'd whore Pluralitie
> From them whose sin ye envi'd, not abhor'd,
> Dare ye for this adjure the Civill Sword
>> To force our Consciences that Christ set free,
>> And ride us with a classic Hierarchy
> Taught ye by meer A.S. and Rotherford?
> Men whose Life, Learning, Faith and pure intent
>> Would have been held in high esteem with Paul
>> Must now be nam'd and printed Hereticks
> By shallow Edwards and Scotch what d'ye call:
>> But we do hope to find out all your tricks,
>> Your plots and packing wors then those of Trent,
>>>> That so the Parliament
> May with their wholsom and preventive Shears

Clip your Phylacteries, though bauk your Ears,
                    And succour our just Fears
When they shall read this clearly in your charge
New Presbyter is but Old Priest writ Large.

It is significant that in 1648 Milton chose to translate Psalm 82 with its fierce call for the speedy implementation of social justice by those who are in power on earth.

PSAL. LXXXII

1 God in the great assembly stands
    Of Kings and lordly States,
  Among the gods on both his hands
    He judges and debates.
2 How long will ye pervert the right
    With judgment false and wrong
  Favouring the wicked by your might,
    Who thence grow bold and strong?
3 Regard the weak and fatherless
    Dispatch the poor mans cause,
  And raise the man in deep distress
    By just and equal Lawes.
4 Defend the poor and desolate,
    And rescue from the hands
  Of wicked men the low estate
    Of him that help demands.
5 They know not nor will understand,
    In darkness they walk on,
  The Earths foundations all are mov'd
    And out of order gon.
6 I said that ye were Gods, yea all
    The Sons of God most high
7 But ye shall die like men, and fall
    As other Princes die.
8 Rise God, judge thou the earth in might,
    This wicked earth redress,
  For thou art he who shalt by right
    The Nations all possess.

As the years passed and there were ominous signs that England was not going to fulfil God's and Milton's plan for her—even under Cromwell, Milton clearly had doubts as to the way things were tending (see below, **6.2**)—a growing sense of isolation is perceptible in his verse. Already in 1653 he chose to translate the first Psalm, contrasting the fate of the just single man with that of the wicked. But there was as yet no indication that the wicked might not only be much more numerous but also actually victorious.

> Bless'd is the man who hath not walk'd astray
> In counsel of the wicked, and ith'way
> Of sinners hath not stood, and in the seat
> Of scorners hath not sate. But in the great
> Jehovahs Law is ever his delight,
> And in his Law he studies day and night.
> He shall be as a tree which planted grows
> By watry streams, and in his season knows
> To yield his fruit, and his leaf shall not fall,
> And what he takes in hand shall prosper all.
> Not so the wicked, but as chaff which fann'd
> The wind drives, so the wicked shall not stand
> In judgment, or abide their tryal then,
> Nor sinners in th'assembly of just men.
> For the Lord knows th'upright way of the just,
> And the way of bad men to ruine must.[14]

After 1660 it was abundantly clear that bad men *could* 'stand in judgement'; Milton never acknowledged that he had been mistaken in his great hopes; he would only admit that his fellow men were neither desirous nor capable of using liberty; they were 'a misguided and abused multitude'. All that was now left for Milton to believe, since England was clearly not going to be the new Jerusalem, was that one or two good men could still survive even in a bad society, and achieve their inner freedom of the spirit. The 'Paradise within thee happier farr' which the Angel Michael told Adam to struggle to achieve, is not unlike Wordsworth's faith in the spiritual dignity of individual man with which he comforted himself after the failure of *his* revolutionary hopes. And the immense demands made by the mental fight necessary to achieve this Promethean victory of the spirit is made clear in Adam's chastened words in Book 12 of *Paradise Lost*:

> Henceforth I learne, that to obey is best,
> And love with fears the onely God, to walk

As in his presence, ever to observe
His providence, and on him sole depend,
Merciful over all his works, with good
Still overcoming evil, and by small
Accomplishing great things, by things deemd weak
Subverting worldly strong, and worldly wise
By simply meek: that suffering for Truths sake
Is fortitude to highest victorie,
And to the faithful Death, the Gate of Life;

(b) LUCY HUTCHINSON, from *Memoirs of the Life of Colonel Hutchinson*.

Colonel John Hutchinson, Puritan and Regicide, opponent of Cromwell and until his death in 1664 of Charles II, is here remembered by his devoted wife: there is no better example of the need to create an idealized self-image on the Puritan side. From his wife's account he emerges as the complete anti-type of the Butler-Cleveland-King stereotype of the Puritan. In fact there *was* one dark shadow over the Colonel—he escaped the regicides' fate of hanging, drawing and quartering by repudiating his republicanism, petitioning the Commons and the Lords for clemency and promising future loyalty to Charles II. But Lucy Hutchinson makes her husband out to be a far more steadfast figure, utterly committed to the Parliamentary cause. He *was* a man with a genuine searching conscience and he was haunted ever after by his sense of guilt for having succumbed to the wish to survive (see below, Chapter 9).

He was of a middle stature, of a slender and exactly well-proportion'd shape in all parts, his complexion fair, his hayre of light browne, very thick sett in his youth, softer then the finest silke, curling into loose greate rings att the ends, his eies of a lively grey, well shaped and full of life and vigour, graced with many becoming motions, his visage thinne, his mouth well made, and his lipps very ruddy and gracefull, his teeth were even and white as the purest ivory, his chin was something long and the mold of his face, his forehead was not very high, his nose was rays'd and sharpe, but withall he had a most amiable countenance, which carried in it something of magnanimity and majesty mixt with sweetenesse, that at the same time bespoke love and awe in all that saw him; his skin was smooth and white, his legs and feete excellently well made, he was quick in his pace and turnes, nimble and active and gracefull in all his motions, he was apt for any bodily exercise, and any that he did became him, he could dance admirably well, but neither in youth nor riper yeares made any practise of it, he had skill in fencing such as became a gentleman, he had a greate love to musick, and often diverted himselfe with a violl, on which he play'd masterly, he had an exact eare and judgement in other musick, he shott excellently in bowes and gunns, and much us'd them for his exercise, he had greate judgment in paintings, graving, sculpture, and all liberal arts, and had many curiosities of value in all kinds, he tooke greate delight in perspective glasses, and for his other rarities was not so much affected with the antiquity as the merit of the worke—he tooke much pleasure in emproovement of grounds, in planting groves and walkes, and fruite-trees, in opening springs and making fish-ponds; of country recreations he lov'd none but hawking, and in that was very eager and much delighted for the time he us'd it, but soone left it of; he was wonderful neate, cleanly and gentile in his habitt, and had a very good fancy in it, but he left off very early the wearing of aniething that was costly, yett in his plainest negligent habitt appear'd very much a gentleman; he had more addresse than force of body, yet the courage of his soule so supplied his members that he never wanted strength when he found occasion to employ it; his conversation was very pleasant for he was naturally chearfull, had a ready witt and apprehension; he was eager in everything he did, earnest in dispute, but withall very rationall, so that he was seldome overcome, every thing that it was necessary for him to doe he did with delight, free and unconstrain'd, he hated ceremonious complement, but yet had a naturall civillity and complaisance to all people. . . . He hated persecution for religion, and was allwayes a champion for all religious people against all their greate oppressors. He detested all scoffs at any practise of worship though such a one as he was not persuaded of. Whatever he practis'd in religion was neither for faction nor for advantage, but contrary to it, and purely for conscience sake. As he hated outsides in religion so could he worse endure, those apostacies and those denialls of the Lord and base compliances with his adversaries, which timorous men practise under the name of prudent and just condescensions to avoid persecution. . . . Never fearing aniething he could suffer for the truth, he never at any time would refreine a true or give a

false witnesse; he lov'd truth so much that he hated even
sportive lies and gulleries. . . . Of all lies he most hated
hipocrisie in religion, either to complie with changing govern-
ments or persons, without a reall persuasion of conscience, or to
practise holy things to get the applause of men or any advantage.

(c) JOHN BUNYAN from *Grace Abounding to the Chief of Sinners*
(1666).

John Bunyan (1628–1688), itinerant Baptist preacher and
writer, imprisoned for twelve years after the Restoration, is
the greatest example of the *inwardness* of one side of English
Puritanism.

But the same day, as I was in the midst of a game at cat,
and having struck it one blow from the hole, just as I was
about to strike it the second time, a voice did suddenly dart
from heaven into my soul, which said, Wilt thou leave thy
sins and go to heaven, or have thy sins and go to hell? At this
I was put to an exceeding maze; wherefore leaving my cat
upon the ground, I looked up to heaven, and was, as if I had,
with the eyes of my understanding, seen the Lord Jesus
looking down upon me, as being very hotly displeased with
me, and as if he did severely threaten me with some grievous
punishment for these and other my ungodly practices.

Now, you must know, that before this I had taken much
delight in ringing, but my conscience beginning to be tender,
I thought such practice was but vain, and therefore forced
myself to leave it, yet my mind hankered; wherefore I should
go to the steeple house, and look on it, though I durst not
ring. But I thought this did not become religion neither, yet I
forced myself, and would look on still; but quickly after, I
began to think, How, if one of the bells should fall? Then I
chose to stand under a main beam, that lay overthwart the
steeple, from side to side, thinking there I might stand sure,
but when I should think again, should the bell fall with a
swing, it might first hit the wall, and then rebounding upon
me, might kill me for all this beam. This made me stand in the
steeple door; and now, thought I, I am safe enough; for, if a
bell should then fall, I can slip out behind these thick walls,
and so be preserved notwithstanding.

So, after this, I would yet go to see them ring, but would not
go farther than the steeple door; but then it came into my head,

How, if the steeple itself should fall? And this thought, it may fall for aught I know, when I stood and looked on, did continually so shake my mind, that I durst not stand at the steeple door any longer, but was forced to flee, for fear the steeple should fall upon my head.

Another thing was my dancing; I was a full year before I could quite leave that; but all this while, when I thought I kept this or that commandment, or did, by word or deed, anything that I thought was good, I had great peace in my conscience; and should think with myself, God cannot choose but be now pleased with me; yea, to relate it in mine own way, I thought no man in England could please God better than I.

But poor wretch as I was, I was all this while ignorant of Jesus Christ, and going about to establish my own righteousness; and had perished therein, had not God, in mercy, showed me more of my state of nature.

But upon a day, the good providence of God did cast me to Bedford, to work on my calling; and in one of the streets of that town, I came where there were three or four poor women sitting at a door in the sun, and talking about the things of God; and being now willing to hear them discourse, I drew near to hear what they said, for I was now a brisk talker also myself in the matters of religion, but now I may say, I heard, but I understood not; for they were far above, out of my reach; for their talk was about a new birth, the work of God on their hearts, also how they were convinced of their miserable state by nature; they talked how God had visited their souls with his love in the Lord Jesus, and with what words and promises they had been refreshed, comforted, and supported against the temptations of the devil. Moreover, they reasoned of the suggestions and temptations of Satan in particular; and told to each other by which they had been afflicted, and how they were borne up under his assaults. They also discoursed of their own wretchedness of heart, of their unbelief; and did contemn, slight, and abhor their own righteousness, as filthy and insufficient to do them any good.

By these things my mind was now so turned, that it lay like a horse leech at the vein, still crying out, Give, give (Prov. xxx. 15); yea, it was so fixed on eternity, and on the things about the kingdom of heaven, that is, so far as I knew, though as yet, God knows, I knew but little; that neither pleasures, nor profits, nor persuasions, nor threats, could loosen it, or makei t let go his hold; and though I may speak it with shame, yet it is in very deed a certain truth, it would then have been as difficult for me to have taken my mind from heaven to earth, as I have found it often since to get it again from earth to heaven.

While I was thus afflicted with the fears of my own damnation, there were two things would make me wonder; the one was, when I saw old people hunting after the things of this life, as if they should live here always; the other was, when I found professors much distressed and cast down, when they met with outward losses; as of husband, wife, child, etc. Lord, thought I, what ado is here about such little things as these! What seeking after carnal things by some, and what grief in others for the loss of them! If they so much labour after, and spend so many tears for the things of this present life, how am I to be bemoaned, pitied, and prayed for! My soul is dying, my soul is damning. Were my soul but in a good condition, and were I but sure of it, oh! how rich should I esteem myself, though blessed but with bread and water; I should count those but small afflictions, and should bear them as little burdens. 'A wounded spirit who can bear?'

But to be brief, one morning, as I did lie in my bed, I was, as at other times, most fiercely assaulted with this temptation, to sell and part with Christ; the wicked suggestion still running in my mind, Sell him, sell him, sell him, sell him, sell him, as fast as a man could speak; against which also, in my mind, as at other times, I answered, No, no, not for thousands, thousands, thousands, at least twenty times together. But at last, after much striving, even until I was almost out of breath, I felt this thought pass through my heart, Let him go, if he will! and I thought also, that I felt my heart freely consent thereto. Oh, the diligence of Satan! Oh, the desperateness of man's heart!

Now was the battle won, and down fell I, as a bird that is shot from the top of a tree, into great guilt, and fearful despair. Thus getting out of my bed, I went moping into the field; but God knows, with as heavy a heart as mortal man, I think, could bear; where, for the space of two hours, I was like a man bereft of life, and as now past all recovery, and bound over to eternal punishment.

I feared therefore that this wicked sin of mine might be that sin unpardonable, of which he there thus speaketh, 'But he that shall blaspheme against the Holy Ghost hath never forgiveness, but is in danger of eternal damnation' (Mark iii.

29). And I did the rather give credit to this, because of that sentence in the Hebrews, 'For ye know, how that afterward, when he would have inherited the blessing, he was rejected; for he found no place of repentance, though he sought it carefully with tears.' And this stuck always with me.

And now was I both a burden and a terror to myself, nor did I ever so know, as now, what it was to be weary of my life, and yet afraid to die. Oh, how gladly now would I have been anybody but myself! Anything but a man! and in any condition but mine own! for there was nothing did pass more frequently over my mind, than that it was impossible for me to be forgiven my transgression, and to be saved from wrath to come.

What, thought I, is there but one sin that is unpardonable? But one sin that layeth the soul without the reach of God's mercy; and must I be guilty of that? Must it needs be that? Is there but one sin among so many millions of sins, for which there is no forgiveness; and must I commit this? Oh, unhappy sin! Oh, unhappy man! These things would so break and confound my spirit, that I could not tell what to do; I thought, at times, they would have broke my wits; and still, to aggravate my misery, that would run in my mind, 'Ye know how that afterward, when he would have inherited the blessing, he was rejected.' Oh! none knows the terrors of those days but myself.

Once as I was walking to and fro in a good man's shop, bemoaning of myself in my sad and doleful state, afflicting myself with self-abhorrence for this wicked and ungodly thought; lamenting, also, this hard hap of mine, for that I should commit so great a sin, greatly fearing I should not be pardoned; praying also, in my heart, that if this sin of mine did differ from that against the Holy Ghost, the Lord would show it me. And being now ready to sink with fear, suddenly there was, as if there had rushed in at the window, the noise of wind upon me, but very pleasant, and as if I heard a voice speaking, Didst ever refuse to be justified by the blood of Christ? And, withal my whole life and profession past was, in a moment, opened to me, wherein I was made to see that designedly I had not; so my heart answered groaningly, No. Then fell, with power, that word of God upon me, 'See that ye refuse not him that speaketh' (Heb. xii. 25). This made a strange seizure upon my spirit; it brought light with it, and commanded a silence in my heart of all those tumultous thoughts that before did use, like masterless hell-hounds, to roar and bellow, and make a hideous noise within me. It showed me, also, that Jesus Christ had yet a word of grace and mercy for me, that he had not, as I had feared, quite forsaken and cast off my soul; yea, this was a kind of a chide for my proneness to desperation; a kind of a threatening me if I did not, notwithstanding my sins and the heinousness of them, venture my salvation upon the Son of God. But as to my determining about this strange dispensation, what it was I knew not; or from whence it came I know not. I have not yet, in twenty years' time, been able to make a judgment of it; I thought then what here I shall be loath to speak. But verily, that sudden rushing wind was as if an angel had come upon me; but both it and the salvation I will leave until the day of judgment; only this I say, it commanded a great calm in my soul, it persuaded me there might be hope; it showed me, as I thought, what the sin unpardonable was, and that my soul had yet the blessed privilege to flee to Jesus Christ for mercy. But, I say, concerning this dispensation, I know not what yet to say unto it; which was, also, in truth, the cause that, at first, I did not speak of it in the book; I do now, also, leave it to be thought on by men of sound judgment. I lay not the stress of my salvation thereupon, but upon the Lord Jesus, in the promise; yet, seeing I am here unfolding of my secret things, I thought it might not be altogether inexpedient to let this also show itself, though I cannot now relate the matter as there I did experience it. This lasted, in the savour of it, for about three or four days, and then I began to mistrust and to despair again.

This scripture did also most sweetly visit my soul, 'And him that cometh to me I will in no wise cast out' (John vi. 37). Oh, the comfort that I have had from this word, 'in no wise'! as who should say, by no means, for no thing, whatever he hath done. But Satan would greatly labour to pull this promise from me, telling of me that Christ did not mean me, such as I, but sinners of a lower rank, that had not done as I had done. But I should answer him again, Satan, here is in this word no such exception; but 'him that comes,' HIM, any him; 'him that cometh to me I will in no wise cast out.' And this I well remember still, that of all the sleights that Satan used to take this scripture from me, yet he never did so much as put this question, But do you come aright? And I have thought the reason was, because he thought I knew full well what coming aright was; for I saw that to come aright was to come as I was, a vile and ungodly sinner, and to cast myself at the feet of mercy, condemning myself for sin. If ever Satan and I did strive for any word of God in all my life, it was for this good word of Christ; he at one end and I at the other. Oh what work did we make! It was for this in John, I say, that we did so tug and strive; he pulled and I pulled; but, God be praised, I got the better of him, I got some sweetness from it.

5
CHARLES I:
ROYAL MARTYR OR
'POPISH FAVOURITE'?

The past three chapters have shown the growth of two nations. The execution of the King on 30 January 1649 is the logical end of that division. The regicide was, for Clarendon, the most execrable crime since the murder of Christ, whereas, for Milton, the slaying of the tyrant was 'an extraordinary great action' (5.6). Both points of view will be found in the extracts of poems with which we conclude this chapter (5.7). But we have chosen to begin our chapter with extracts from contemporaries who did not see the issues in such a clear-cut way: Cromwell, Downes, Hutchinson and Josselin.

Our choice is deliberate. The reactions after the event—important as they are—must be distinguished from the mood which led up to it. In his devious negotiations of 1647 and 1648 Charles I had won the distrust of many men who were monarchist in sympathy. If they found it hard to see him as a Christ figure, it did not follow—as Milton would have it—that they were leafing through the pages of Calvin, Beza, Knox and Buchanan in readiness to justify the killing of the tyrant. For many, judgment on the individual was separable from their feelings about monarchy as an institution. Indeed, the decision to abolish the office was taken a week *after*, not *before*, the death of the man.

The point at which individuals decided that action had to be taken against the man varied from person to person, as did the choice of the action to be taken. Cromwell comes down to us in history textbooks as the incarnation of revolution: the man who bullied Downes, who shouted down a judge at the trial, who held down Ingoldsby's hand to enforce his signature on Charles I's death warrant. Cromwell was in reality much more confused: witness the tortuous letter to Hammond on 25 November 1648 (5.1). Professor Underdown's researches have established Cromwell as the reluctant accomplice of Pride's Purge, and not its architect.[1] As late as 23 December 1648 he was still working through the Earl of Denbigh as a go-between for reconciliation with the King. Only after that date did he despair of compromise, and his decisive actions belong to the period of five weeks before the death of the King. His son-in-law Ireton had reached that decision two months earlier. But his too was a pragmatic judgment on the man rather than a doctrinaire rejection of the office: it was not to be supposed that Ireton, who had been the principal opponent of Leveller demands at Putney a year earlier, had become convinced by November 1648 that monarchy was incompatible with human dignity. Mrs Hutchinson's account of the trial—with its reference to Charles's 'disdainfull smiles'—makes it appear that her husband had thought along those very lines (5.4); his recantation at the Restoration would suggest the opposite. Probably neither exaltation nor contrition is the key to his mood *at the time*: for him, as for Purefoy, the Purge was probably a more revolutionary and interesting act than the regicide. Others like Heveningham would support both the Purge and the regicide in order to keep power in civilian rather than military hands. Downes could support the Purge but not the trial (5.3.) Josselin's misgivings about both were tempered by a curious excitement at the prospect of great things to come (5.5). The mistake would be to dismiss Josselin's tears on reading of the King's death (5.2) as crocodile tears. The tears which he shed for monarchy were as genuine as were the millenarian dreams of his diary, and for him, as for Baxter, a respect for monarchy was compatible with a lively interest in the Book of Revelation. Cromwell's pursuit of both in his Protectorate later is then less of a paradox than it is sometimes made out to be.

There were others at this time—a minority, but an important minority—who found in the Book of Revelation the promise of a future millennium, and for whom the regicide was welcomed as a step towards the fulfilment of their programme: whether it was Leveller, Digger, Ranter, Fifth Monarchist, or Anabaptist in inspiration.[2] It is important that others, like Baxter, Cromwell and Josselin, who did not agree with their solutions, were nevertheless not cut off wholly in sympathy from the source of their aspirations, and could even from time to time share the excitement that they felt.

Charles I was not executed in a millenarian spasm, but moderates like Josselin made their pragmatic judgments on the man against the background of expectation that 'the Lord hath some great things to doe' which they shared with immoderate colleagues. Perhaps the greatest burden that the monarchy had to carry were the apocalyptic expectations of its admirers. If only Josselin's tears had been feigned, the respect for the King a mask, how much easier Charles's lot might have been! This was a point that Roger Williams had already grasped: those who were ready to give so much power to the civil magistrate were also the most ruthless in 'cutting off his skirts' when he disappointed their hopes.[3]

Imperial Protestants had had a number of years to come to terms with the sombre historical fact that Charles I was no second Constantine. Even when the Civil War had started many had failed to do so: Henrietta Maria, Archbishop Laud and Strafford were the convenient scapegoats. Nobody sustained the myth with more heroic tenacity than William Prynne; yet by 1643 and 1644 even his fidelity had snapped. With the interception of Charles's private correspondence, it was impossible to pretend that he had only been misled by evil counsellors. Out of the bitterness of that betrayal came Prynne's savage *The Popish Royall Favourite*: his new term for the Christian Emperor. By the late 1640s it was a different story. Prynne, like other imperial Protestants, alarmed at egalitarian noises in the Army, sought to reassure colleagues that Charles was genuine in the concessions he was now ready to make at the Isle of Wight. But Prynne had already given cogent reasons why Charles could not be trusted, as opponents were not slow to point out. Pointless for Prynne now to protest at the Purge, the trial, the regicide: he had earlier provided the ammunition for all three. This is the merciless logic of a pamphlet like *Prynne against Prin*.[4] Against this, what had Prynne to offer? Only an absurd story that Henrietta Maria's chaplain was present at the King's execution and was seen to wave his sword in triumph when the King's head was cut off. But the point of the story was that the regicide could be represented as a Jesuit triumph. Charles I had expiated earlier faults by his martyrdom at the hands of Papists. That this farrago of nonsense should be taken up seriously by many of the most moderate and serious Protestants of the day[5] is more than a comment on human credulity—as a despairing Catholic controversialist pointed out—and stands as a testimony to the abiding force of the imperial myth.

Yet those who believed in the imperial myth were prepared to 'cut off the skirts' of the magistrate who betrayed the cause for which he had been set up. Prynne's pamphlets of 1643 and 1644 provide the same grounds for the repudiation of a 'Popish Royall Favourite' on the English throne as were offered by the apologists for the Glorious Revolution of 1688, even though by 1648 Prynne no longer saw Charles I in that light. But if he didn't, others did, and there is no reason to assume that they were less sincere than he in their attachment to monarchy.

Clarendon and Milton saw 1649 in too dramatic terms. For both, it was a drastic break with the past: deplored by one as a collective bout of madness; welcomed by the other as the fashioning of a new revolutionary will. Both underrated the continuity of the Protestant imperial tradition. Probably the most influential pamphleteer on the Parliamentarian side was Thomas Bilson. He had several disadvantages: he had been a bishop, he was dead, and the pamphlet that he wrote dated from 1585. But why he continued to be quoted, and read, was that he abhorred 'Unchristian Rebellion' and yet— memories invoked of Mary Tudor and the martyrs in Foxe— insisted that 'Christian Subjection' had its limits. Those limits were clearly set when a Protestant sovereign could not be trusted to carry out his imperial mandate against Rome. No wonder the able anonymous pamphleteer of 1689 would blow the dust off Bilson, and use him again to defend Protestant action against another 'Popish Royall Favourite'.[6]

There was probably no single action by which Charles I lost the trust of the bulk of his Protestant subjects. The breaking point for individuals varied with political circumstances; it was rarely reached without agonies of scruple; for some the breach was permanent, for others—like Prynne—only temporary. But all *could* draw—and some *did* draw—when that breaking point came, upon an ideology that was neither new nor imported from abroad, which combined respect for the institution of monarchy with retribution on the individual who violated its principles: in other words, the Protestant imperial tradition of Foxe and Jewel and Bilson.

5.1 Oliver Cromwell: Robert Hammond, 25 November 1648

From *Oliver Cromwell's Letters and Speeches*, (ed. T. Carlyle, London, 1897)

Oliver Cromwell (1599–1658) was writing to his cousin Robert Hammond (1621–1654) at a critical time for both of them: the attempt to tease out the meaning of 'providences' was no academic exercise when Hammond was custodian of Charles I as Governor of the Isle of Wight, and Cromwell was on the threshold of Pride's Purge. Since by the time he received the letter Hammond's caution had cost him his Governorship, whereas two months later Cromwell was bullying the hapless John Downes into acceptance of regicide (5.3), it would seem as if the two men were talking across a gulf. Recent research, however, has minimized the distance between them.[7] Cromwell might distrust King and Treaty but his actions up to 23 December support the argument that he was sincere in his earlier letter to Hammond (6 November), when he said that he preferred Presbyterianism to episcopacy, was ready to co-operate with the Presbyterians provided that they put severe restrictions on the King's power, and wanted a dissolution with elections rather than a purge. While Cromwell, as he says in this letter to Hammond, was with his Northern Army 'in a waiting posture; desiring to see what the Lord would lead us to', Ireton was acting.

... Dear Robin, our fleshly reasonings ensnare us. These make us say, 'heavy', 'sad', 'pleasant', 'easy'. Was there not a little of this when Robert Hammond, through dissatisfaction too, desired retirement from the Army, and thought of quiet in the Isle of Wight? Did not God find him out there? I believe he will never forget this.—And now I perceive he is to seek again; partly through his sad and heavy burden, and partly through his dissatisfaction with friends' actings.

Dear Robin, thou and I were never worthy to be door-keepers in this Service. If thou wilt seek, seek to know the mind of God and all that chain of Providence, whereby God brought thee thither, and that Person to thee: how, before and since, God has ordered him, and affairs concerning him: and then tell me, whether there be not some glorious and high meaning in all this, above what thou hast yet attained? And laying aside thy fleshly reason, seek of the Lord to teach thee what that is: and He will do it. I dare be positive to say, It is not that the wicked should be exalted, that God should so appear as indeed He hath done. For there is no peace to them. No, it is set upon the hearts of such as fear the Lord, and we have witness upon witness, That it shall go ill with them and their partakers. I say again, seek that spirit to teach thee; which is the spirit of counsel and might, of wisdom and of the fear of the Lord. That spirit will close thine eyes and stop thine ears, so that thou shall not judge by them; but thou shalt judge for the meek of the Earth, and thou shalt be made able to do accordingly. The Lord direct thee to that which is well-pleasing in his eyesight.

As to thy dissatisfaction with friends' actings upon that supposed principle, wonder not at that. If a man take not his own burden well, he shall hardly others', especially if involved by so near a relation of love and Christian brotherhood as thou art. I shall not take upon me to satisfy, but I hold myself bound to lay my thoughts before so dear a friend. The Lord do His own will.

You say: 'God hath appointed authorities among the nations, to which active or passive obedience is to be yielded. This resides in England in the Parliament. Therefore active or passive resistance' etc.

Authorities and powers are the ordinance of God. This or that species is of human constitution and limited, some with larger, others with stricter bands, each one according to its constitution. But I do not therefore think the Authorities say do anything, and yet such obedience be due. All agree that there are cases in which it is lawful to resist. If so, your ground fails, and so likewise the inference. Indeed, dear Robin, not to multiply words, the query is, Whether ours be such a case? This ingeniously is the true question.

To this I shall say nothing, though I could say very much, but only desire thee to see what thou feelest in thy own heart to two or three plain considerations. First, Whether *Salus Populi* be a sound position. Secondly, Whether in the way in hand, really and before the Lord, before whom conscience has to stand, this be provided for;—or if the whole fruit of the War is not like to be frustrated, and all most like to turn to what it was, and worse? And this, contrary to Engagements, explicit Covenants with those who ventured their lives upon those Covenants and Engagements, without whom perhaps, in equity, relaxation ought not to be? Thirdly, Whether this

Army be not a lawful Power, called by God to oppose and fight against the King upon some stated grounds; and being in power to such ends, may not oppose one Name of Authority, for those ends, as well as another Name—since it was not the outward Authority summoning them that by its power made the quarrel lawful, but the quarrel was lawful in itself? If so, it may be, acting will be fortified *in foro humano*—But truly this kind of reasonings may be but fleshly, either with or against: only it is good to try what truth may be in them. And the Lord teach us.

My dear Friend, let us look into providences, surely they mean somewhat. They hang so together; have been so constant, so clear, unclouded. Malice, sworn malice against God's people, now called 'Saints' to root-out their name;—and yet they, 'these poor Saints', getting arms, and therein blessed with defence and more!—I desire, he that is for a principle of suffering would not too much slight this. I slight not him who is so minded: but let us beware lest fleshly reasoning see more safety in making use of this principle than in acting! Who acts, if he resolve not through God to be willing to part with all? Our hearts are very deceitful, on the right and on the left. . . .

5.2 *King Charles his Speech* (London, 1649)

This anonymous narrative of 1649 was typical of many that appeared at this time in response to the public interest in the execution of Charles I. We know that on the actual day of the execution advance copies of *Eikon Basilike* were already circulating. This book—purporting to be Charles I's reflections on his reign and most probably written by John Gauden, Bishop of Worcester—had gone into twenty editions within a month and a half of Charles's death. But supporters of the regicide had not only to deal with conscious political propaganda—as *Eikon Basilike* was swiftly recognized to be—but had to counter the effects of straightforward political reporting, as in this extract. Certainly if this writer has a bias it is not a pronounced Cavalier one: a reference to the scaffold inspires a marginal reference to its nearness to 'the very place where the first blood in the beginning of the late troubles was shed when the King's Cavaliers fell upon the Citizens, killed one, and wounded about 50 others.' But then there were many Army and Parliament stalwarts—the unfortunate Downes (5.3) and the irresolute Fairfax among them—who could accept Cavalier war guilt without accepting the regicide inference from it. To such people the deliberately low-key non-partisan narrative of the events in the last hours of Charles I's life—with full accounts of his speeches—must have been intensely moving and prepared the climate for a sympathetic reception to *Eikon Basilike*.[8]

KING CHARLS
HIS
SPEECH

MADE UPON THE SCAFFOLD AT WHITEHALL GATE
IMMEDIATELY BEFORE HIS EXECUTION

Tuesday, January 30.

About ten in the Morning the King was brought from St James's, walking on foot through the Park, with a Regiment of Foot, part before and part behinde him, with Colours flying, Drums beating, his private guard of Partizans, with some of his Gentlemen before, and some behinde bareheaded, Dr Juxon next behinde him, and Col. Thomlinson (who had the charge of him) talking with the King bareheaded from the Park, up the stairs into the Gallery, and so into the Cabinet Chamber,* where he used to lie, where he continued at his Devotion, refusing to dine (having before taken the sacrament) only about an hour before he came forth, he drank a glass of Claret wine, and eat a piece of bread about twelve at noon.

From thence he was accompanied by Dr Juxon, Colonel Thomlinson, and other officers, formerly appointed to attend him, and the private Guard of Partizans, with Musketiers on each side, through the Banqueting-house adjoyning to which the Scaffold † was erected between Whitehall Gate, and the

* It is observed The King desired to have the use of the Cabinet, and the little room next it, where there was a Trap-door.

† It was near (if not in) the very place where the first blood in the beginning of the late troubles was shed when the Kings Cavaliers fell upon the Citizens, killed one, and wounded about 50 others.

Gate leading into the Gallery from St James's: The Scaffold
was hung round with black and the floor covered with black,
and the Ax and Block laid in the middle of the Scaffold. There
were divers Companies of Foot, and Troops of Horse placed
on the one side the Scaffold towards Kings-Street, and on the
other side towards Charing-Cross, and the multitudes of
people that came to be Spectators, very great.

The King being come upon the Scaffold, look'd very
earnestly on the Block, and asked Col. Hacker if there were
no higher; and then spake thus (directing his Speech chiefly
to Colonel Thomlinson).

King. I shall be very little heard of any body here, I shall
therefore speak a word unto you here: Indeed I could hold
my peace very well, if I did not think that holding my peace
would make some men think, that I did submit to the guilt,
as well as to the punishment; but I think it is my duty to God
first, and to my Countrey, for to clear myself both as an honest
man, and a good King, and a good Christian. I shall begin
first with my Innocency, In troth I think it not very needful
for me to insist long upon this, for all the world knows that I
never did begin a war with the two Houses of Parliament,
and I call God to witnes to whom I must shortly make an
account, That I never did intend for to incroach upon their
Priviledges, they began upon me, it is the Militia they began
upon, they confest that the Militia was mine, but they thought
it fit for to have it from me; and to be short, if anybody will
look to the dates of Commissions, of their Commissions and
mine, and likewise to the Declarations, will see clearly that
they began these unhappy Troubles, not I; so that the guilt of
these enormous crimes that are laid against me, I hope in God
that God will clear me of it, I will not, I am in charity; God
forbid that I should lay it upon the two Houses of Parliment,
there is no necessity of either, I hope they are free of this
guilt; for I do believe that ill instruments between them and
me, has been the chief cause of all this bloodshed; so that by
way of speaking, as I finde my self clear of this, I hope (and
pray God) that they may too; yet for all this, God forbid that
I should be so ill a Christian, as not to say that Gods Judge-
ments are just upon me: Many times he does pay Justice
by an unjust Sentence, that is ordinary; I will onely say this,
That an unjust Sentence * that I suffered for to take effect, is

* Strafford.

punished now, by an unjust Sentence upon me; that is, so far
I have said, to shew you that I am an innocent man.

Now for to shew you that I am a good Christian: I hope
there is * a good man what will bear me witness, that I have
forgiven all the world, and even those in particular that have
been the chief causers of my death; who they are, God knows,
I do not desire to know, I pray God forgive them. But this is
not all, my Charity must go farther, I wish that they may
repent, for indeed they have committed a great sin in that
particular; I pray God with St Stephen, That this be not
laid to their charge; nay, not onely so, but that they may take
the right way to the Peace of the Kingdom, for my Charity
commands me not onely to forgive particular men, but my
Charity commands me to endeavor to the last gasp the Peace
of the Kingdom: So (Sirs) I do wish with all my soul, and I
do hope (there is † some here will carry it further) that they
may endeavor the Peace of the Kingdom.

Now (Sirs) I must shew you both how you are out of the
way, and will put you in a way: First, you are out of the way,
for certainly all the way you ever have had yet, as I could
finde by anything, is in the way of Conquest; certainly this is
an ill way, for Conquest (Sir) in my opinion is never just,
except there be a good just Cause, either for matter of Wrong
or just Title, and then if you go beyond it, the first quarrel
that you have to it, that makes it unjust at the end, that was
just at first; But if it be only matter of Conquest, then it is a
great Robbery; as a Pirat said to Alexander, that He was the
great Robber, he was but a petty Robber; and so, Sir, I do
think the way that you are in, is much out of the way: Now
Sir, for to put you in the way, believe it you will never do
right, nor God will never prosper you, until you give God his
due, the King his due (that is, my Successors) and the People
their due; I am as much for them as any of you: You must give
God his due by regulating rightly his Church (according to his
Scripture) which is now out of order: For to set you in a way
particularly now I cannot, but onely this, A National Synod
freely called, freely debating among themselves, must settle
this, when that every Opinion is freely and clearly heard.

For the King, indeed I will not (then turning to a Gentleman that touched the Ax, said, Hurt not the Ax, that may

---

* Pointing to Dr Juxon.
† Turning to some Gentlemen that wrote.

hurt me.* For the King) the Laws of the Land will clearly instruct you for that; therefore because it concerns my own particular, I only give you a touch of it.

For the People: And truly I desire their Liberty and Freedom as much as anybody whomsoever, but I must tell you That their Liberty and their Freedom, consists in having of Government; those Laws, by which their Life and their Goods may be most their own. It is not for having share in Government (Sir) that is nothing pertaining to them; A Subject and a Soveraign are clean different things, and therefore until they do that, I mean That you do put the People in that Liberty as I say, certainly they will never enjoy themselves.

Sirs, It was for this that now I am come here: If I would have given away to an Arbitrary way, for to have all Laws changed according to the power of the Sword, I needed not to have come here; and therefore I tell you (and I pray God it be not laid to your charge) That I am the Martyr of the People.

In troth Sirs I shall not hold you much longer, for I will onely say this to you, That in truth I could have desired some little time longer, because that I would have put this that I have said in a little more order, and a little better digested than I have done, and therefore I hope you will excuse me.

I have delivered my Conscience, I pray God that you do take those courses that are best for the good of the Kingdom, and your own salvations.

Doctor Juxon. Will your Majesty (though it may be very well known your Majesty's affections to Religion, yet it may be expected that you should) say somewhat for the worlds satisfaction.

King. I thank you very heartily (my Lord) for that I had almost forgotten it. In troth Sirs, My Conscience in Religion I think is very well known to all the world and therefore I declare before you all, That I dye a Christian, according to the profession of the Church of England, as I found it left me by my Father, and this honest man † I think I will witness it. Then turning to the Officers said, Sirs, excuse me for this same, I have a good cause, and I have a gracious God, I will say no more. Then turning to Colonel Hacker, he said, Take care that they do not put me to pain, and Sir this, and it please you; But then a Gentleman coming near the Ax, the

---

* Meaning if he did blunt the edge.
† Pointing to Dr Juxon.

King said, Take heed of the Ax, pray take heed of the Ax. Then the King speaking to the Executioner, said, I shall say but very short prayers, and when I thrust out my hands—. Then the King called to Dr Juxon for his Night-cap and having put it on, he said to the Executioner, Does my hair trouble you? who desired him to put it all under his Cap, which the King did accordingly, by the help of the Executioner and the Bishop: Then the King turning to Dr Juxon, said, I have good Cause, and a gracious God on my side.

Doctor Juxon. There is but one Stage more. This Stage is turbulent and troublesome; it is a short one; But you may consider, it will soon carry you a very great way: it will carry you from Earth to Heaven; and there you shall find a great deal of cordial joy and comfort.

King. I go from a corruptible to an incorruptible Crown; where no disturbance can be, no disturbance in the world.

Doctor Juxon. You are exchanged from a temporal to an eternal Crown, a good exchange.

The King then said to the Executioner, is my hair well? Then the King took off his cloak and his George, giving his George to the Doctor Juxon, saying, Remember *—Then the King put of his Dublet, and being in his Wastcoat, put his Cloak on again, then looking upon the Block, said to the Executioner, You must set it fast.

Executioner. It is fast Sir.

King. It might have been a little higher.

Executioner. It can be no higher Sir.

King. When I put out my hands this way,† then——After that having said two or three words (as he stood) to Himself with hands and eyes lift up; Immediately stooping down, laid his Neck upon the Block: And then the Executioner again putting his Hair under his Cap, the King said Stay for the sign.

Executioner. Yes I will and it please your Majesty. And after a very little pawse, the King stretching forth his hands, The Executioner at one blow severed his head from his body.

That when the Kings head was cut off, the Executioner held it up, and shewed it to the Spectators.

---

* It is thought for to give it to the Prince.
† Stretching them out.

And his Body was put in a coffin covered with Black Velvet for that purpose.

The King's Body now lies in his lodging Chamber in Whitehall.

Sic transit gloria mundi.
FINIS.

5.3 'Extract from the Narrative of John Downes'
(R. Lockyer ed., from *The Trial of Charles I*, London, 1959, Appendix B)

This extract comes from an account by John Downes, after the Restoration, when he was about to stand trial for regicide. He was condemned but afterwards reprieved and kept a close prisoner in Newgate and then the Tower of London. Downes was a heroic waverer: it took courage on 27 January to succeed in temporarily adjourning the Court. If Cromwell (a belated but now enthusiastic convert to regicide) had not kept his nerve, Downes's action might have even saved the King. Downes had been a regular attender of the Commons since Pride's Purge and had been one of the first to dissent from further negotiations with Charles I on 5 December 1648; in the event, after some fierce conversations behind the scenes, Downes was persuaded to sign the death-warrant. His bleak retrospective self-analysis impresses by its accuracy as well as by its lack of special pleading: 'I was single, I was alone; only I ought not to have been there at all.'

Then the King, not in passion, but with the greatest earnestness of affection, desired the Court that they would once more consider of it; 'For' said He, 'you may live to repent of such a Sentence', and therefore desired they would withdraw but for half an hour. 'Or' said He 'if that be too much trouble for you, I will withdraw' (and passionately moved his body).

The President was not affected with all this, but commanded the Clerk to read the Sentence. God knows I lie not, my heart was ready to burst within me. And as it fell out, sitting on the seat next to Cromwell, he perceived some discomposure in me, and turned to me and said, 'What ails thee? Art thou mad? Canst thou not sit still and be quiet?' I answered 'Quiet! No Sir, I cannot be quiet', and then presently I stood up, and with an audible voice said: 'My Lord President, I am not satisfied to give my consent to this Sentence, but have reasons to offer to you against it, and therefore I desire the Court may adjourn to hear me.' Then the President stood up and said, 'Nay, if any Member of the Court be unsatisfied, then the Court must adjourn.' And accordingly they did adjourn into the inner Court of Wards. . . .

And as this relation shows, I am but a weak imprudent man, yet I did what I could. I did my best, I could do no more. I was single, I was alone; only I ought not to have been there at all.

5.4 Lucy Hutchinson, from *Memoirs of the Life of Colonel Hutchinson*

Lucy Hutchinson disingenuously comments here that her husband knew that the regicide 'might one day come to be again disputed among men'. What she fails to make clear is that the Restoration was the time for concentrating men's minds wonderfully upon the rightness of the King's execution and that, if Hutchinson escaped Tyburn, this was because of an abject repentance in 1660 for the 'seduced judgment' which had led him to oppose the King (see below **8.7**, p. 229).

In January 1648, the court sat, the king was brought to his trial, and a charge drawn up against him for levying war against the parliament and people of England, for betraying the public trust reposed in him, and for being an implacable enemy to the commonwealth. But the king refused to plead, disowning the authority of the court, and after three several days persisting in contempt thereof, he was sentenced to suffer death. One thing was remarked in him by many of the court, that when the blood spilt in many of the battles where he was in his own person, and had caused it to be shed by his own command, was laid to his charge, he heard it with disdainful smiles, and looks and gestures which rather expressed sorrow that all the opposite party to him were not cut off, than that any were: and he stuck not to declare in words, that no man's blood spilt in this quarrel troubled him except one, meaning the Earl of Strafford. The gentlemen that were appointed his judges, and divers others, saw in him a disposition so bent on the ruin of all that opposed him, and of all the righteous and just things they had contended for, that it was upon the consciences of many of them, that if they did not execute justice upon him, God would require at their hands all the blood and desolation which should ensue by their suffering him to escape, when God had brought him into their hands. Although the malice of the malignant party and their apostate brethren seemed to threaten them, yet they thought they ought to cast themselves upon God, while they acted with a good conscience for him and for their country. Some of them afterwards, for excuse, belied themselves, and said they were under the awe of the army, and overpersuaded by Cromwell, and the like; but it is certain that all men herein were left to their free liberty of acting, neither persuaded nor compelled; and as there were some nominated in the commission who never sat, and others who sat at first, but durst not hold on, so all the rest might have declined it if they would, when it is apparent they would have suffered nothing by so doing. For those who then declined were afterwards, when they offered themselves, received in again, and had places of more trust and benefit than those who ran the utmost hazard; which they deserved not, for I know upon certain knowledge that many, yea the most of them, retreated, not for conscience, but from fear and worldly prudence, foreseeing that the insolency of the army might grow to that height as to ruin the cause, and reduce the kingdom into the hands of the enemy; and then those who had been most courageous in their country's cause would be given up as victims. These poor men did privately animate those who appeared most publicly, and I knew several of them in whom I lived to see that saying of Christ fulfilled, 'He that will save his life shall lose it, and he that for my sake will lose his life shall save it;' when afterwards it fell out that all their prudent declensions saved not the lives of some nor the estates of others. As for Mr Hutchinson, although he was very much confirmed in his judgment concerning the cause, yet herein being called to an extraordinary action, whereof many were of several minds, he addressed himself to God by prayer; desiring the Lord that, if through any human frailty he were led into any error or false opinion in these great transactions, he would open his eyes, and not suffer him to proceed, but that he would confirm his spirit in the truth, and lead him by a right enlightened conscience; and finding no check, but a confirmation in his conscience that it was his duty to act as he did, he, upon serious debate, both privately and in his addresses to God, and in conferences with conscientious, upright, unbiassed persons, proceeded to sign the sentence against the king. Although he did not then believe but that it might one day come to be again disputed among men, yet both he and others thought they could not refuse it without giving up the people of God, whom they had led forth and engaged themselves unto by the oath of God, into the hands of God's and their own enemies; and therefore he cast himself upon God's protection, acting according to the dictates of a conscience which he had sought the Lord to guide, and accordingly the Lord did signalise his favour afterwards to him.

5.5 From Ralph Josselin's *Diary*
(ed. E. Hockliffe, London, 1908, Camden Third Series XV)

Ralph Josselin's diary in the Interregnum is as important a source for our understanding of politics at this time as Roger Lowe's is for a slightly later period in the seventeenth century, and for the same reason. It has been said that historians are too often confronted with the extraordinary: Lowe's and Josselin's *ordinariness* gives their testimony a special value.[9] A great deal of interesting material has been drawn from Josselin's diary by the application of techniques from other disciplines and it has been found that something like a third of the original has been omitted from the Essex Record Office transcript.[10] Much of this missing material reflects an apocalyptic interest which, however, as the extracts show, did little to comfort him in the belief that regicide was right. Nor is this now surprising to us, since we recognize that the Apocalypse and the civil magistrate were intertwined in the minds of many seventeenth-century Protestants. Thus it is not coincidental that on Queen Elizabeth's Accession Day, 17 November 1650, Josselin's thoughts should be 'much that God was beginning to raise the kingdom of the earth, and bringing Christ's kingdom in'.

61, 63 Jan. 4. 1649	This day 7 yeares King Charles came to demand the 5 members, and it was thought with an intention to have offered violence to the house; this day the Commons of themselves ordered the tryall of the King; many men cry out of this worke that it will ruin the kingdome, the army, religion, etc. For my part I conceive it strange, extraordinary, and that it will occasion very much trouble betwixt the prince, and his friends, and the joyners in the new representative, but if the worke bee of God it will prosper, if not it will come to nothing. . . .
Feb. 4. 1649	I was much troubled with the blacke providence of putting the King to death; my teares were not restrained at the passages about his death; the Lord in mercy lay it not as sinne to the charge of the kingdome, but doe in mercy do us good by the same; the small pox on some familyes of the towne but spreadeth not, to God be the glory thereof: this weeke I could doe nothing neither in my Hebrew, nor in my reconciler. The death of the king talked much of; very many men of the weaker sort of Christians in divers places passionate concerning it, but so ungroundedly, that it would make any to bleed to observe it; the Lord hath some great things to doe; fear and tremble at it, oh England.

5.6 John Milton, from *The Tenure of Kings and Magistrates* (London, 1649)

John Milton (1608–1674) wrote this pamphlet in response to the arguments of some Presbyterian ministers in *A Serious and Faith-*

ful Representation, which they had addressed 'to the General and his Council of War' on the day before the King's trial. The ministers had defended the right of Parliament to continue negotiations with the King against the Army's resolve to punish him. Milton did not altogether eschew arguments through legality: he argued that the trial was legal by referring to the parliamentary authority through which the Court of Justice had been established. But he went beyond such cavils to the primary argument: the right of a people to alter government 'as they shall judge most conducing to the public good'. The extracts show two interesting consequences from this position. Milton now uses the Book of Revelation not as a Foxeian support for the civil magistrate but as a warning against tyranny; if he retains from Foxe the concept of England as an Elect Nation, that mission is now given a radical twist: not to *honour* precedents but to *create* them.

Therefore kingdom and magistracy, whether supreme or subordinate, is called 'a human ordinance,' (1 Pet ii. 13, &c.,) which we are there taught is the will of God we should submit to, so far as for the punishment of evil-doers, and the encouragement of them that do well. 'Submit,' saith he, 'as free men.' 'But to any civil power unaccountable, unquestionable, and not to be resisted, no, not in wickedness, and violent actions, how can we submit as free men?' 'There is no power but of God,' saith Paul; (Rom. xiii.;) as much as to say, God put it into man's heart to find out that way at first for common peace and preservation, approving the exercise thereof; else it contradicts Peter, who calls the same authority an ordinance of man. It must be also understood of lawful and just power, else we read of great power in the affairs and kingdoms of the world permitted to the devil: for saith he to Christ, (Luke, iv. 6,) 'All this power will I give thee, and the glory of them, for it is delivered to me, and to whomsoever I will, I give it:' neither did he lie, or Christ gainsay what he affirmed; for in the thirteenth of the Revelation, we read how the dragon gave to the beast his power, his seat, and great authority: which beast so authorized most expound to be the tyrannical powers and kingdoms of the earth. Therefore Saint Paul in the forecited chapter tells us, that such magistrates he means, as are not a terror to the good, but to the evil; such as bear not the sword in vain, but to punish offenders, and to encourage the good.

If such only be mentioned here as powers to be obeyed,

and our submission to them only required, then doubtless those powers that do the contrary are no powers ordained of God; and by consequence no obligation laid upon us to obey or not to resist them. And it may be well observed, that both these apostles, whenever they give this precept, express it in terms not concrete, but abstract, as logicians are wont to speak; that is, they mention the ordinance, the power, the authority, before the persons that execute it; and what that power is, lest we should be deceived, they describe exactly. So that if the power be not such, or the person execute not such power, neither the one nor the other is of God, but of the devil, and by consequence to be resisted. From this exposition Chrysostom also, on the same place, dissents not; explaining that these words were not written in behalf of a tyrant. And this is verified by David, himself a king, and likeliest to be author of the Psalm (xciv. 20) which saith, 'Shall the throne of iniquity have fellowship with thee?' And it were worth the knowing, since kings in these days, and that by Scripture, boast the justness of their title, by holding it immediately of God, yet cannot shew the time when God ever set on the throne them or their forefathers, but only when the people chose them; why by the same reason, since God ascribes as oft to himself the casting down of princes from the throne, it should not be thought as lawful, and as much from God, when none are seen to do it but the people, and that for just causes. For if it needs must be a sin in them to depose, it may as likely be a sin to have elected. And contrary, if the people's act in election be pleaded by a king, as the act of God, and the most just title to enthrone him, why may not the people's act of rejection be as well pleaded by the people as the act of God, and the most just reason to depose him? So that we see the title and just right of reigning or deposing, in reference to God, is found in Scripture to be all one; visible only in the people, and depending merely upon justice and demerit. Thus far hath been considered chiefly the power of kings and magistrates; how it was and is originally the people's, and by them conferred in trust only to be employed to the common peace and benefit; with liberty therefore and right remaining in them, to reassume it to themselves, if by kings or magistrates it be abused; or to dispose of it by any alteration, as they shall judge most conducing to the public good.

... How much more justly then may they fling off tyranny, or tyrants; who being once deposed can be no more than private men, as subject to the reach of justice and arraignment as any other transgressors? And certainly if men, not to speak of heathen, both wise and religious, have done justice upon tyrants what way they could soonest, how much more mild and humane then is it, to give them fair and open trial; to teach lawless kings, and all who so much adore them, that not mortal man, or his imperious will, but justice, is the only true sovereign and supreme majesty upon earth? Let men cease therefore, out of faction and hypocrisy, to make outcries and horrid things of things so just and honourable. Though perhaps till now, no protestant state or kingdom can be alleged to have openly put to death their king, which lately some have written, and imputed to their great glory; much mistaking the matter. It is not, neither ought to be, the glory of a protestant state never to have put their king to death; it is the glory of a protestant king never to have deserved death. And if the parliament and military council do what they do without precedent, if it appear their duty, it argues the more wisdom, virtue, and magnanimity, that they know themselves able to be a precedent to others; who perhaps in future ages, if they prove not too degenerate, will look up with honour, and aspire towards these exemplary and matchless deeds of their ancestors, as to the highest top of their civil glory and emulation; which heretofore, in the pursuance of fame and foreign dominion, spent itself vaingloriously abroad; but henceforth may learn a better fortitude, to dare execute highest justice on them that shall by force of arms endeavour the oppressing and bereaving of religion and their liberty at home. That no unbridled potentate or tyrant, but to his sorrow, for the future may presume such high and irresponsible licence over mankind, to havoc and turn upside down whole kingdoms of men, as though they were no more in respect of his perverse will than a nation of pismires.

5.7 Reactions to the Execution of Charles I

We have already seen (above, 4.2) that many Royalists felt a quasi-religious veneration for the King. Their sense of outrage at the open enmity manifested towards him was consequently proportionate. The humour in the following anonymous diatribe ('Printed in a Hollow-tree for the good of the State 22 Feb. 1647') does not diminish its savagery, and the writer's recourse to 'cursing like a drab' indicates the desperation of the Royalists by the late 1640s.

AN EXECRATION TO ALL THAT HATE KING CHARLES

May God forſake ye, may the Devil take ye, may diſease eat up your bones, conſume your rotten members, may the palſie ſhake your hands and heads, and bloody viſions haunt your beds; all Egypt's plagues, and two times more, wait on you all at either door; may all your wives turn arrant jades, and you live upon their trades; may the gout be in your toes, and no end be to your woes; may no ſurgeon hear your moans, and all your joys be ſighs and groans; may the running of the reins, or the quinzy ſeize your brains; may the toothache and the fever, to plague you ſtill do their endeavour; may the ſtrangullion be your beſt friend, and ne'er forſake you till your end; may you be the People's ſcorn, and curſe the hour that you were born; May Bedlam or Bridewell be all the houſe you have to dwell; may your children's children beg from door to door, and all their kindred, may they ſtill be poor; may a guilty conſcience ſtill affright ye, and no earthly joys delight ye; may you have aches in your rotten bones, gravel in your kidneys, as well as ſtones; may your daughters turn out bad, and their fathers go clean mad; may they never ſleep in quiet, and fear poiſon in their diet; may they never ſorrow lack, and ſo the Pedlar ſhuts his Pack. Only when they die ('cauſe they were never true), when that their ſouls depart, Devil claim thy due![11]

The actual beheading of the King was received with stunned horror. As C. V. Wedgwood said: 'Many, if not most, thinking men then in England felt the earth shake under them when a king was executed on a public scaffold.'[12] Clarendon summed up the Royalist attitude in his *History of the Great Rebellion*, asserting that Charles I was the 'most innocent person in the world'; that his execution was therefore 'the most execrable murder that was ever committed since that of our blessed Saviour', and that he met his death with 'the saint-like behaviour of a blessed martyr'. This view that Charles's execution was a *religious* martyrdom second only to the Crucifixion was reiterated in poem after poem, often having to be circulated in manuscript since the censorship made their printing impossible.[13]

KING CHARLES HIS SPEECH, AND LAST FAREWELL TO THE WORLD, MADE UPON THE SCAFFOLD AT WHITE-HALL-GATE, ON TUESDAY, JANUARY 30, 1648

To the Tune of, Weladay.

1 Faire Englands joy is fled,
    Weladay, weladay,
  Our Noble King is dead,
    Sweet Prince of love;
  This heavy news so bad,
  Hath made three Kingdoms sad,
  No comfort to be had,
    But from above.

2 On Tuesday last his Grace,
    Chearfully, chearfully,
  Went to his dying place,
    to end all strife,
  Where many a weeping eye
  With groans unto the skie,
  To see his Majesty
    there end his life.

3 His Foes he did forgive,
    Graciously, graciously,
  And wisht we all might live
    in quiet peace.
  He wisht what ere was past,
  That he might be the last,
  No sorrow we might taste,
    but wars might cease.

4 Theres nothing griev'd him so,
    Weladay, weladay,
  As when he thought that woe
    might light on all.
  The tears stood in his eyes
  To heare the people cries,
  And think what miscarries
    on us should fall.

5 Upon the Scaffold then,
    Weladay, weladay,
In hearing of all men
    this he made knowne,
That Hee was innocent
of all the blood was spent,
He strove with Parliament
    but for his owne.

6 Quoth he, themselves confest,
    Weladay, weladay,
And thus much have exprest
    in mine owne hearing,
The Militia in mine hand
was granted by the land
To be at my command,
    none with me sharing.

7 The keeping of the same,
    Weladay, weladay,
I know not who to blame,
    they did desire.
Which made us disagree,
The fault's now laid on me,
This all the world may see
    set all on fire.

LINES ON THE DEATH OF CHARLES I
(attributed to Montrose)

Great, good and just, could I but rate,
My grief and thy too rigid fate,
I'd weep the world in such a strain,
As it should deluge once again:
But since thy loud tongued blood demands supplies
More from Briareus hands than Argus eyes
I'll tune thy elegies to trumpet sounds
And write thy epitaph with blood and wounds.

ABRAHAM COWLEY, from *A Discourse by way of Vision concerning the Government of Oliver Cromwell.* (*Essays, Plays* and *Verses*, ed. A. R. Waller, Cambridge, 1906, pp. 343–4.)

Yet mighty God, yet yet, we humbly crave,
This floating Isle from shipwrack save;

And though to wash that Bloud which does it stain,
It well deserves to sink into the Main;
Yet for the Royal Martyr's prayer
(The Royal Martyr prays we know)
This guilty, perishing Vessel spare;
Hear but his Soul above, and not his bloud below . . .
Come rather Pestilence and reap us down;
Come Gods sword, rather than our own.
Let rather *Roman* come again,
Or *Saxon, Norman,* or the *Dane,*
In all the bonds we ever bore,
We griev'd, we sigh'd, we wept; we never blusht before.

MARCHAMONT NEEDHAM, from *History of the English Rebellion.*

The Adjutators stern and proud,
Said, He should have no Quarter
Because he is a King; and vow'd
To make the Saint a Martyr.

Their Officers cry'd, Hail, O King;
The rest made mocks and scorns;
The Houses vinegar did bring;
And all did plat the thorns.

Thus crucifi'd, Great Charles did live
As dead, is gone away:
For Resurrection, God will give
A new Cor'nation day. . . .

BISHOP HENRY KING, from *A Deepe Groane, fetch'd at the Funerall of that incomparable and Glorious Monarch, Charles the First, On whose Sacred Person was acted that execrable, horrid & prodigious Murther, by a trayterous Crew and bloudy Combination at Westminster, January the 30. 1648.*

. . . Alas! our Ruines are cast up, and sped
In that black Totall—Charles is Murthered.
Rebellious Gyant hands have broake that Pole,
On which our Orbe did long in Glory roule.
That Roman Monster's wish in Act we see,
Three Kingdoms' necks have felt the Axe in Thee.
The Butchery is such, as when by Caine,
The fourth Division of the world was slaine.

The mangled Church is on the shambles lay'd,
Her Massacre is on thy Blocke display'd.
Thine is Thy people's epidemicke Tombe:
Thy Sacrifice a num'rous Hecatombe.
The Powder-mine's now fir'd; we were not freed,
But respited by Traytours thus to bleed.
November's plots are brew'd and broach't in worse,
And January now compleats the Curse.
Our Lives, Estates, Lawes, and Religion, All
Lye crush'd, and gasping at this dismall fall.

Accursed Day that blotted'st out our Light!
May'st Thou be ever muffled up in Night.
At Thy returne may sables hang the skie;
And teares, not beames, distill from Heaven's Eye.
Curs'd be that smile that guilds a Face on Thee,
The Mother of prodigious Villanie.
Let not a breath be wafted, but in moanes;
And all our words be but articulate groanes.
May all Thy Rubrick be this dismall Brand:
Now comes the miscreant Doomes-day of the Land.
Good-Friday wretchedly transcrib'd; and such
As Horrour brings alike, though not so much.
May Dread still fill Thy minutes, and we sit
Frighted to thinke, what others durst commit. . . .

. . . Hellish Complotment! which a League renewes,
Lesse with the men, then th'Actions of the Jewes.
Such was their Bedlam Rabble, and the Cry
Of Justice now, 'mongst them was Crucifie:
Pilate's Consent is Bradshaw's Sentence here;
The Judgement-hall's remov'd to Westminster.
Hayle to the Reeden Scepter; th' Head, and knee
Act o're againe that Cursed Pageantrie.
The Caitiffe crew in solemne pompe guard on
Mock'd Majesty as not to th'Block, but Throne. . . .

. . . Bloud-thirsty Tygars! could no streame suffice
T'allay that Hell within your Breasts but This? . . .

. . . For such a Varlot-brood to teare all downe,
And make a common Foot-ball of the Crowne;
T'insult on wounded Majesty, and broach
The bloud of Honour by their vile reproach;

What Royall Eye but Thine could sober see,
Bowing so Low, yet bearing up so high?
What an unbroken sweetnesse grac'd Thy Soule
Beyond the World's proud conquest, or controule?
Maugre grim cruelty, thou kept'st Thy Hold;
Thy Thorny Crowne was still a Crowne of Gold. . . .

. . . Thus Thou our Martyr died'st: but Oh! we stand
A Ransome for anoother Charles his Hand;
One that will write Thy Chronicle in Red,
And dip His Pen in what Thy Foes have bled;
Shall Treas'nous Heads in purple Caldrons drench,
And with such veines the Flames of Kingdomes quench.
Then Thou at last at Westminster shal't be
Fil'd in the Pompous List of Majestie.
Thy Mausoloeum shall in Glory rise,
And Teares and wonder force from Nephews' Eyes.
Till when (though black-mouth'd Miscreants engrave
No Epitaph, but Tyrant, on Thy Grave)
A Vault of Loyalty shall keep Thy Name,
An orient, and bright Olibian flame.
On which, when times succeeding foot shall tread,
Such Characters as these shall there be read.

Here Charles the best of Monarchs butcher'd lies;
The Glory of all Martyrologies.
Bulwarke of Law; the Churche's Cittadell;
In whom they triumph'd once, with whom they fell:
An English Salomon, a Constantine;
Pandect of Knowledge, Humane and Divine.
Meeke ev'n to wonder, yet of stoutest Grace,
To sweeten Majesty, but not debase.
So whole made up to Clemencie, the Throne
And Mercy-seat, to Him were alwaies one.
Inviting Treason with a pardoning looke,
Instead of Gratitude, a Stab He tooke.
With passion lov'd, that when He murd'red lay,
Heav'n conquered seem'd, and Hell to bear the sway.
A Prince so richly good, so blest a Reigne,..
The World ne're saw but once, nor can againe. . . .

After reading expressions of such wild grief it becomes almost impossible to believe that the execution could ever have been allowed to happen. We have to remind ourselves that other men saw Charles very differently. Milton, for one, fiercely attacked the worship 'of a god of flesh and blood'. To him 'this man was a tyrant', the enemy of his people, whose execution was 'an extraordinary great action' and whose Judge, John Bradshaw, was 'the friend whom I most revere'.

Andrew Marvell's attitude in 1650 was far more complex and is still the subject of argument. The following stanzas from the *Horatian Ode* seem to be an attempt to do justice to two conflicting truths, the personal and the political. Charles was the victim of 'angry Heaven', of 'Fate' and of 'Nature', all of which called for the utilization of that 'greater spirit', Cromwell, as their instrument at this particular moment. The execution was, however, also a personal tragedy, since the King was a 'comely' man without spite. Nevertheless, the poet hopes that this bloody act will prove to be the necessary price paid for great social achievements in the future, both in England and abroad. The Commonwealth, born out of the execution of the king, promises to be a second, liberating Republican Rome.

> 'Tis madness to resist or blame
> The face of angry Heaven's flame;
>   And if we would speak true,
>   Much to the man is due,
>
> Who would his private gardens, where
> He lived reserve'd and austere,
>   (As if his highest plot
>   To plant the bergamot;)
>
> Could by industrious valour climb
> To ruin the great work of Time,
>   And cast the kingdoms old,
>   Into another mould;
>
> Though Justice against Fate complain,
> And plead the ancient rights in vain;
>   (But those do hold or break,
>   As men are strong or weak.)
>
> Nature that hateth emptiness,
> Allows of penetration less,
>   And therefore must make room
>   Where greater spirits come.

What field of all the civil war,
Where his were not the deepest scar?
   And Hampton shows what part
   He had of wiser art;

Where, twining subtle fears with hope,
He wove a net of such a scope
   That Charles himself might chase
   To Caresbrooke's narrow case,

That thence the royal actor borne,
The tragic scaffold might adorn
   While round the arme'd bands
   Did clap their bloody hands.

He nothing common did, or mean,
Upon that memorable scene,
   But with his keener eye
   The axe's edge did try:

Nor called the gods with vulgar spite
To vindicate his helpless right;
   But bowed his comely head
   Down, as upon a bed.

This was that memorable hour,
Which first assured the force'd power;
   So, when they did design
   The Capitol's first line,

A bleeding head, where they begun,
Did fright the architects to run
   And yet in that the state
   Foresaw its happy fate. . . .

As Caesar, he [i.e. Cromwell], ere long, to Gaul,
To Italy and Hannibal,
   And to all states not free,
   Shall climacteric be.

Finally, we refer back to Lucy Hutchinson's account of the trial and condemnation of Charles (see above, pp. 135–6). Was it these 'disdainefull smiles, and looks and gestures', which eventually convinced some of his judges at least that Charles was not merely a tyrant, but that, in Milton's word in his *Defence of the People of England*, he was '*incurable*'?

6
CROMWELL:
FOR AND AGAINST

At the end of the nineteenth century Flora Thompson would recall in her Oxfordshire village that 'some of the older mothers and grandmothers still threatened naughty children with the name of Cromwell. "If you aren't a good gal, Old Oliver Cromwell'll have 'ee," they would say, or "Here comes old Cromwell!"'.[1] After the Restoration they remembered him in a different way. Pepys could write in his diary: 'Everybody do now-a days reflect upon Oliver and commend him, what brave things he did and made all the neighbour princes fear him.' A few months later Slingsby Bethel challenged this view: his *critique* of Cromwell's foreign policy was launched with the modest title of *The World's Mistake in Oliver Cromwell* (6.4).

Cromwell, a figure from demonology: Cromwell, a figure from hagiography. Two retrospective judgments on the man: for and against in their most extreme form. We have included at the end of this chapter excerpts from verse of the time which echo these judgments (6.8). But—as in the previous chapter— we have also included more ambivalent responses from men who felt, with Bethel, that the world had made a mistake about Cromwell and were anxious to present *their* Cromwell.

We begin with a famous assault on Cromwell from the Left (6.1): only two months after the regicide, the five Leveller soldiers launched their broadside at the betrayer of radical hopes. The Levellers were the romantics, the Diggers the realists. Disappointment with Cromwell would take Levellers like Sexby, Lilburne and Wildman into the *Royalist* camp. Winstanley, on the other hand, saw Cromwell as a useful instrument for his designs and—it is now clear with the recent discovery of his pamphlet, *England's Spirit Un-foulded*—he could out-Hobbes Hobbes in pragmatic acceptance of *de facto* rule.[2] Although Milton's eulogy of Cromwell in 1654 has a Stalinist ring, this is misleading (6.2). Perhaps the relationship is more that of Gorky to Lenin: admiring, watchful, conditional. Like Winstanley, Milton had a programme for Cromwell—the abolition of tithes, freedom of divorce and religious toleration—and the pamphlet was specifically designed for Cromwell's ear. It is fascinating that the work has no reference to the Kingdom of Christ (the Fifth Monarchists were troubling the Protector at the time) or to the disadvantage of monarchy (there was a prospect then that Cromwell would accept the throne). This may be, as one commentator has suggested, a unique instance of Milton's 'suppressing ideas for politic reasons',[3] and if so would show the seriousness of his commitment to the task of persuading Oliver. But compromise had its limits: his hostility to monarchy is clear in the names which he commends to Cromwell; nor does he join many of Cromwell's supporters in a frontal attack on the millenarians.

Criticism of Cromwell is weak in documentation. Prynne called him a Richard III revived, but his only recorded clash with him was in a dream. According to Prynne, the night before he died, Cromwell appeared to him in a dream pleading for forgiveness. Prynne answered that there would be none until he restored Parliament's liberties. Cromwell was speechless; and a day later was dead. A conjunction of events which staggered Prynne as well as several news-journals.[4] And when Cromwell's non-dreaming critics have a point to make against him, it is frequently a contradictory one. Compare, for instance, Clarendon's and Baxter's judgments on how Cromwell dealt with Presbyterians (6.3 and 5). Part of the problem lay in his reserve: no English ruler ever *listened* more. His willingness to submit himself to harangues from men like George Fox, Colonel Biscoe and John Rogers shows a refreshingly untotalitarian cast of mind. Perhaps, however, these encounters left the listeners with the delusion that he was of their mind: silence meant consent. Perhaps, again, Cromwell intended them to leave with such an impression.

And so we have the phenomenon of a chorus of agreement from very opposite political wings that Cromwell was two-faced, with very little to substantiate it. What were the primary grounds for this sly reputation?

Probably they derived less from his specific actions than from a combination of things, trivial in themselves, but in their cumulative effect deadly. We may isolate a few of them.

The 'five small Beagles' found it hard to reconcile the unctuous language with the manipulative skills of the successful politician. But Cromwell belonged to a generation that had 'the name of God and of Christ in their mouths': the same accusation could have been applied (and was) to many of his contemporaries. At the Putney Debates nothing seems odder to a modern eye than the convoluted wranglings about men's motives in calling on a morning of prayer. But Cromwell's emphasis on 'waiting for Providences' gave the accusation a particular cutting edge, when applied to himself. Christopher Hill pointed out that no suggestion roused Cromwell to greater fury than the one that 'waiting for Providences' was a mask for waiting upon the favourable political moment.[5]

Clarendon and Baxter were irritated by another pose in Cromwell: that of the simple homespun country gentleman. As in eighteenth-century politics, 'country' was identified with a freedom from the corruption of Court and synonymous with a claim to virtue: even in the parodying by the younger Strafford of his own lack of Court sophistication one can see a groping after this identification (see above, 1.8). But Cromwell may have suffered here more from his admirers' pretensions than from his own: there was a tendency, as in Sir Philip Warwick's reference to his 'plain cloth suit', to magnify his later achievements by an absurd emphasis on his earlier uncouthness. Marvell's *Horatian Ode* is itself one contribution to this myth.

Cromwell's temperament gave more ammunition to his critics: there is an almost manic-depressive volatility about his actions—the troughs of the 1630s giving way to the Marston Moor peaks of the 1640s; the agony of indecision over the monarchy in December 1648 giving way to the throwing of ink over Henry Marten's face when signing Charles I's death warrant. Christopher Hill comments that he 'was always liable to be ill in a crisis'.[6] Again this was not unique in an age that seemed to live on its nerves: one thinks of the shrewd judgment by his biographer on a contemporary Puritan schoolmaster, the Reverend Thomas Hall, who 'when his work decreased (as at Vacation times when the children went home) there usually he was aguish and sick'. Hall's biographer adds: 'the Christian Holy dayes were his worst dayes'.[7] With Cromwell there was the added point: *his* worst days seemed to coincide with his political needs (one thinks again of his absence from the scene at the big crises like Cornet Joyce's seizure of the King and Pride's Purge of Parliament).

Cromwell's prose gives us a clue to his reputation for two-facedness. His letters have a protean quality. He could write marvellous sentences of comfort to Colonel Walton on his son's death that are crisp, economical, muscular (7.4); he could write vividly and feelingly to his beloved 'Robin' Hammond (see above, 5.1); or he could entangle himself in those labyrinthine sentences (often when addressing the Commons) which are the despair of all his admirers, with the single intrepid exception of Carlyle. Thus he could seem to be all things to all men.

With such a reputation even his most generous impulses were open to question. A good example here is Lucy Hutchinson's description of Cromwell's conciliatory approach to Colonel Rich: on the face of it a magnanimous gesture but which Mrs Hutchinson deplores as a trick to make Rich his creature (6.7). But the most recent student of Cromwell's religious policy has pointed out how slow many Puritans were to honour the freedom which they won in the Protectorate.[8] When we look at Richard Baxter we can see why. It was not only that Baxter did not *trust* Cromwell: he could not *acknowledge* him. Charles II was the legitimate ruler: Cromwell was stained with the crime of regicide. But his son was not, and we see during the brief interlude of Richard Cromwell's rule Baxter moving towards a compromise position which would be politically embarrassing for him at the Restoration. We have included a letter from John Durie—that tireless worker for Church unity—to Baxter at this time, precisely because it shows the charm to liberal-minded men of compromise with the Cromwellian Establishment. Durie was referring to Richard, not Oliver, and this was politically more palatable to Baxter. But the general point holds good for both: men who were straining to promote religious freedom knew that they had a powerful friend at Court.

Oliver Cromwell boasted in 1655 that his greatest achievement had been that he had 'not been unhappy in hindering any one Religion to impose upon another'.[9] Under such a dispensation Cromwell the sly, Cromwell the usurper, allowed Baxter's Worcestershire Association to flourish, and gave Baxter and his co-religionists a freedom which they would lose at the Restoration under their rightful King. Baxter never wholly resolved that paradox. Cromwell had struck at the accepted wisdom of the century: that religious pluralism spelled anarchy. Even in theory, and with reservations, only a handful of writers—Milton, Roger Williams and Jeremy Taylor among them—had advocated the sort of freedom for Jews, Quakers, Presbyterians, Anglicans (who were not involved in political conspiracies) and Catholics (in England, but not in Ireland) which they were given in the Commonwealth. These gains seemed to have been cancelled out in the bitterness of Cavalier revenge at the Restoration. In the next chapter we examine the roots of that vindictiveness, when we look at the traumatic effects of war upon that generation of Englishmen. But in our final chapter we shall nevertheless argue that, although in the short term the religious toleration secured during the Protectorate was emphatically reversed, in the long term Cromwell's achievement was irreversible. He had destroyed the myth of *one* Church of England, held as strongly by Presbyterians and Independents in the past as by their Anglican rivals. The world's mistake in Oliver Cromwell was not to give that achievement its proper recognition.

6.1 From *The Hunting of the Foxes . . . by Five Small Beagles* (London, 1649)

This classic denunciation of Cromwell as the Lost Leader of the Left appeared on 21 March 1649; almost a month earlier another Leveller spokesman, John Lilburne, had launched a similar attack on Cromwell in his *England's New Chains Discovered*. Cromwell's reaction seemed to vindicate their case: Lilburne's eavesdropping on Cromwell's harangue to the Council of State on the need to break the Levellers before the Levellers broke them; the Army mutiny over pay and service in Ireland, leading to the execution of Robert Lockyer; the brutal suppression in May of the Leveller revolt at Burford.

. . . Dear countreymen and fellow souldiers, you that by your adventurous hazards and bloud have purchased a precedency

in your natural and just rights, consider and weigh these
things in your harts; for surely none are more deeply concerned than yourselves, none are more highly infringed of their
rights than you. You are not so much as suffered (how op-
pressed or abused yourselves, how sensible of the miseries of
the publike soever,) to represent your desires or apprehensions
to the parliament. While you are souldiers, you (in their account) are no freemen, neither have an equal right in the
commonwealth with other of your fellow-members therein.
The general now tells us, if we will petition, we must lay down
our swords. These were his own words unto us. It seems he
hath forgot the contest of the army (in which he concurred)
with Stapleton and Hollis, about their right of petitioning as
soldiers. Why then (if this must be their received maxime)
did he and the general councel (as by usurpation they call it)
present their petition, since we presented ours, and not lay
down their swords and their high places, and petition as
private commoners? We are confident it would be an happy
day for England, would they but practise that doctrine they
preach unto others. But alas! dear friends it is but in this
case with them as in all others: They condemned Stapleton
and Hollis, because they were not the Stapletons and Hollis's
themselves. They condemned private correspondencies with
the king, because they were not the correspondents themselves. They condemned the force offered to the parliament by
the tumult of apprentises, etc. because they were not the
forces themselves. They condemned that monstrous declaration of the parliament against the souldiers petitioning; they
condemned the imprisioning petitioners and burning petitions, because they were not the declarers, imprisoners and
burners themselves: as who, that doth but consider their
waies, may not plainly discern? ... Was there ever a generation of men so apostate, so false, and so perjured, as these?
Did ever men pretend an higher degree of holinesse, religion
and zeal to God and their country than these? These preach,
these fast, these pray, these have nothing more frequent than
the sentences of sacred Scripture, the name of God and of
Christ in their mouthes. You shall scarce speak to Crumwell
about any thing, but he will lay his hand on his breast, elevate
his eyes, and call God to record. He will weep, howl, and repent,
even while he doth smite you under the first rib.

6.2 John Milton, from *The Second Defence of the People of England* (London, 1654)

Milton's confidence in the people was strong in 1649 when he wtote *The Tenure of Kings and Magistrates* (see above, **5.6**), but the success of *Eikon Basilike* in propagating the cult of the Royal Martyr, and the failure of the Commonwealth to win over Leveller, Fifth Monarchist and Presbyterian, drove him to the rueful recognition that democracy could mean the return of the Tsar. The failure of the Rump justified rule by the worthy—in this case the Protector. Cromwell's credentials for the job were that he had rejected Kingship and accepted self-discipline. But he was still very much on trial.

A profound peace ensued; when we found, though indeed not then for the first time, that you was as wise in the cabinet as valiant in the field. It was your constant endeavour in the senate either to induce them to adhere to those treaties which they had entered into with the enemy, or speedily to adjust others which promised to be beneficial to the country. But when you saw that the business was artfully procrastinated, that every one was more intent on his own selfish interest than on the public good, that the people complained of the disappointments which they had experienced, and the fallacious promises by which they had been gulled, that they were the dupes of a few overbearing individuals, you put an end to their domination. A new parliament is summoned; and the right of election given to those to whom it was expedient. They meet; but do nothing; and, after having wearied themselves by their mutual dissensions, and fully exposed their incapacity to the observation of the country, they consent to a voluntary dissolution. In this state of desolation, to which we were reduced, you, O Cromwell! alone remained to conduct the government, and to save the country. We all willingly yield the palm of sovereignty to your unrivalled ability and virtue, except the few among us, who, either ambitious of honours which they have not the capacity to sustain, or who envy those which are conferred on one more worthy than themselves, or else who do not know that nothing in the world is more pleasing to God, more agreeable to reason, more politically just, or more generally useful, than that the supreme power should be vested in the best and the wisest of men. Such, O Cromwell, all acknowledge you to be; such are the services which you have rendered, as the leader of our councils, the general of our armies, and the father of your country. For this is the tender appellation by which all the good among us salute you from the very soul. Other names you neither have nor could endure; and you deservedly reject that pomp of title which attracts the gaze and admiration of the multitude. For what is a title but a certain definite mode of dignity; but actions such as yours surpass, not only the bounds of our admiration, but our titles; and, like the points of pyramids, which are lost in the clouds, they soar above the possibilities of titular commendation. But since, though it be not fit, it may be expedient, that the highest pitch of virtue should be circumscribed within the bounds of some human appellation, you endured to receive, for the public good, a title most like to that of the father of your country; not to exalt, but rather to bring you nearer to the level of ordinary men; the title of king was unworthy the transcendent majesty of your character. For if you had been captivated by a name over which, as a private man, you had so completely triumphed and crumbled into dust, you would have been doing the same thing as if, after having subdued some idolatrous nation by the help of the true God, you should afterwards fall down and worship the gods which you had vanquished. Do you then, sir, continue your course with the same unrivalled magnanimity; it sits well upon you;—to you our country owes its liberties; nor can you sustain a character at once more momentous and more august than that of the author, the guardian, and the preserver of our liberties; and hence you have not only eclipsed the achievements of all our kings, but even those which have been fabled of our heroes. Often reflect what a dear pledge the beloved land of your nativity has entrusted to your care; and that liberty which she once expected only from the chosen flower of her talents and her virtues, she now expects from you only, and by you only hopes to obtain. Revere the fond expectations which we cherish, the solicitudes of your anxious country; revere the looks and the wounds of your brave companions in arms, who, under your banners, have so strenuously fought for liberty; revere the shades of those who perished in the contest; revere also the opinions and the hopes which

foreign states entertain concerning us, who promise to themselves so many advantages from that liberty which we have
so bravely acquired, from the establishment of that new
government which has begun to shed its splendour on the
world, which, if it be suffered to vanish like a dream, would
involve us in the deepest abyss of shame; and lastly, revere
yourself; and, after having endured so many sufferings and
encountered so many perils for the sake of liberty, do not
suffer it, now it is obtained, either to be violated by yourself,
or in any one instance impaired by others. You cannot be
truly free unless we are free too; for such is the nature of
things, that he who entrenches on the liberty of others, is the
first to lose his own and become a slave. But if you, who
have hitherto been the patron and tutelary genius of liberty,
if you, who are exceeded by no one in justice, in piety, and
goodness, should hereafter invade that liberty which you have
defended, your conduct must be fatally operative, not only
against the cause of liberty, but the general interests of piety
and virtue. Your integrity and virtue will appear to have
evaporated, your faith in religion to have been small; your
character with posterity will dwindle into insignificance, by
which a most destructive blow will be levelled against the
happiness of mankind. The work which you have undertaken
is of incalculable moment, which will thoroughly sift and expose every principle and sensation of your heart, which will
fully display the vigour and genius of your character, which
will evince whether you really possess those great qualities of
piety, fidelity, justice, and self-denial, which made us believe
that you were elevated by the special direction of the Deity to
the highest pinnacle of power. At once wisely and discreetly
to hold the sceptre over three powerful nations, to persuade
people to relinquish inveterate and corrupt for new and more
beneficial maxims and institutions, to penetrate into the
remotest parts of the country, to have the mind present and
operative in every quarter, to watch against surprise, to provide
against danger, to reject the blandishments of pleasure and
pomp of power;—these are exertions compared with which the
labour of war is mere pastime; which will require every energy
and employ every faculty that you possess; which demand a
man supported from above, and almost instructed by immediate inspiration. These and more than these are, no
doubt, the objects which occupy your attention and engross
your soul; as well as the means by which you may accomplish

these important ends, and render our liberty at once more ample and more secure. And this you can, in my opinion, in no other way so readily effect, as by associating in your councils the companions of your dangers and your toils; men of exemplary modesty, integrity, and courage; whose hearts have not been hardened in cruelty and rendered insensible to pity by the sight of so much ravage and so much death, but whom it has rather inspired with the love of justice, with a respect for religion, and with the feeling of compassion, and who are more zealously interested in the preservation of liberty, in proportion as they have encountered more perils in its defence. They are not strangers or foreigners, a hireling rout scraped together from the dregs of the people, but, for the most part, men of the better conditions in life, of families not disgraced if not ennobled, of fortunes either ample or moderate; and what if some among them are recommended by their poverty? for it was not the lust of ravage which brought them into the field; it was the calamitous aspect of the times, which, in the most critical circumstances, and often amid the most disastrous turn of fortune, roused them to attempt the deliverance of their country from the fangs of despotism. They were men prepared, not only to debate, but to fight; not only to argue in the senate, but to engage the enemy in the field. But unless we will continually cherish indefinite and illusory expectations, I see not in whom we can place any confidence, if not in these men and such as these. We have the surest and most indubitable pledge of their fidelity in this, that they have already exposed themselves to death in the service of their country; of their piety in this, that they have been always wont to ascribe the whole glory of their successes to the favour of the Deity, whose help they have so suppliantly implored, and so conspicuously obtained; of their justice in this, that they even brought the king to trial, and when his guilt was proved, refused to save his life; of their moderation in our own uniform experience of its effects, and because, if by any outrage, they should disturb the peace which they have procured, they themselves will be the first to feel the miseries which it will occasion, the first to meet the havoc of the sword, and the first again to risk their lives for all those comforts and distinctions which they have so happily acquired; and lastly, of their fortitude in this, that there is no instance of any people who ever recovered their liberty with so much courage and success; and therefore let us not suppose, that there can be any persons who will be more zealous in preserving it. . . .

6.3 Clarendon, from *Selections*
(ed. G. Huehns, Oxford, 1953)

True to the theme that is being argued in this section, Clarendon was more admiring of Cromwell than he liked to acknowledge: we know that he admired the discipline which Cromwell imposed on his troops not only in contrast to the generalship of his opponents but also to that of his predecessors, Essex and Waller; he admired the conciliatory skill with which Cromwell set up his Protectorship; he admired the intellectual achievements of Cromwell's Oxford. Cromwell's greatest achievement was, however, hardest of all for Clarendon to honour. The undoctrinaire Erastianism of the Cromwellian religious settlement chimed not only with Clarendon's earlier political philosophy as the Man of Great Tew[10] but also—as we know now—with his own *post-Restoration* political philosophy.[11]

Cromwell, though the greatest dissembler living, always made his hypocrisy of singular use and benefit to him; and never did any thing, how ungracious or imprudent soever it seemed to be, but what was necessary to the design; even his roughness and unpolishedness, which, in the beginning of the parliament, he affected to the smoothness and complacency, which his cousin and bosom friend, Mr Hambden, practised towards all men, was necessary; and his first public declaration, in the beginning of the war, to his troop when it was first mustered, 'that he would not deceive or cozen them by the perplexed and involved expressions in his commission, to fight for king and parliament'; and therefore told them, 'that if the king chanced to be in the body of the enemy that he was to charge, he would as soon discharge his pistol upon him, as any other private person; and if their conscience would not permit them to do the like, he advised them not to list themselves in his troop, or under his command'; which was generally looked upon as imprudent and malicious, and might, by the professions the parliament then made, have proved dangerous to him; yet served his turn, and severed from others, and united among themselves, all the furious and incensed men against the government, whether ecclesiastical or civil, to look upon him as a man for their turn, upon whom they might depend, as one who would go through his work that he undertook. And his strict and unsociable humour in not keeping company with the other officers of the army in their jollities and excesses, to which most of the superior officers under the Earl of Essex were inclined, and by which he often made himself ridiculous or contemptible, drew all those of the like sour or reserved natures to his society and conversation, and gave him opportunity to form their understandings, inclinations, and resolutions, to his own model. By this he grew to have a wonderful interest in the common soldiers, out of which, as his authority increased, he made all his officers, well instructed how to live in the same manner with their soldiers, that they might be able to apply them to their own purposes: whilst he looked upon the presbyterian humour as the best incentive to rebellion, no man more a presbyterian; he sung all psalms with them to their tunes, and loved the longest sermons as much as they; but when he discovered that they would prescribe some limits and bounds to their rebellion, that it was not well breathed, and would expire as soon as some few particulars were granted to them in religion, which he cared not for; and then that the government must run still in the same channel; it concerned him to make it believed 'that the state had been more delinquent than the church, and that the people suffered more by the civil than by the ecclesiastical power; and therefore that the change of one would give them little ease, if there were not as great an alteration in the other, and if the whole government in both were not reformed and altered'; which though it made him generally odious (at first), and irreconciled many of his old friends to him; yet it made those who remained more cordial and firm: he could better compute his own strength, and upon whom he might depend. This discovery made him continue the (new) model of the army; which was the must unpopular act, and disobliged all those who first contrived the rebellion, and who were the very soul of it; and yet, if he had not brought that to pass, and changed a general, who, though not very sharp-sighted, would never be governed, nor applied to any thing he did not like, for another who had no eyes, and so would be willing to be led, all his designs must have come to nothing, and he remained a private colonel of horse, not considerable enough to be in any figure upon an advantageous composition.

6.4 Slingsby Bethel, from *The World's Mistake in Oliver Cromwell* (London, 1668)

This is an attack on Cromwell's foreign policy by an admirer of the Rump. Slingsby Bethel (1617–1697) argued in 1668 that Cromwell's foreign policy took a decisive wrong turn when he abandoned the anti-Dutch commercial foreign policy of the Rump for a quixotic alliance with France against Spain that prepared the way for Louis XIV's ascendancy in Europe. It has been convincingly established that there was much more continuity in the policies between Commonwealth and Protectorate than critics like Bethel were prepared to recognize.[12] The extract is less interesting as an analysis of what Cromwell achieved in 1653 than as a symptom of what men of 1668 *thought* that he had achieved in 1653.

Of all the Sins, that the Children of Men are guilty of, there is none, that our corrupt Natures are more inclinable unto, than of Idolatry, a Sin, that may be towards Men, so well as other Creatures and things; For, as that which a Man unmeasurably relyes, and setts his Heart upon, is Called his GOD, even as that which he falls down before, and worshippeth: so when one hath the Person of another in an excess of admiration, whether for Greatness or Richness, etc. which we are subject to adore, we are said to Idolize him; and therefore the wise Venetians who, of all men, are most Jealous of their Liberty, Considering that as the nature of Man is not prone to any thing more than the Adoration of Men, So nothing is more destructive to Freedom, hath, for preventing the Mischiefs of it, made it unlawfull, even so much as to mourn for the Duke at his death; Intimating thereby, that their Felicity and Safety depends not upon the uncertain Thred of any one Man's life; but upon the Vertue of their good Laws, and Orders, well executed, and that they can never want vertuous Persons to succeed: and how do such Principles in men, lead by little more than Moralitie, reprove those, who have a great measure of Gospel-light, for their senseless excess, in their adoring the remembrance of Cromwell. For as the Objects of Idolatry are mistaken Creatures, or things, proceeding some times from self-love, so well as other Causes, so the undeserved approbation, and applause, that Cromwell's memory seems to have with his Adherents, amounting to little less, than the Idolizing of him appears to me, to be the product of an excessive Veneration of Greatness, and a selfish Partiality towards him; for that the more honour is given to him, the more prayse they think will consequently redound to them, who were his Favourites; and they fortifie themselves herein, with the Credit they say he hath abroad, though there is little in that, because the opinion that Strangers have of him, may well be put upon the accompt of their ignorance, in the Affairs of England, which Travellers do finde, to be so great, even amongst Ministers of State, as is to be admired. And now as this Error in Idolizing Oliver hath two moral Evils in it (besides the sin in it self:) The one, a reflection upon the present times, as if the former were better than these; And the other, the unjust defrauding the Long Parliament of that which is due to them, to give it Idolatrously to him, to whom it doth not belong; I esteem it a Duty incumbent upon me, to discover the Mistake. I am not insensible, that I shall by this, draw the envye of those upon me, who, being Jealous of their Honour, will be angry for touching them in their Diana; but knowing my self clear, from the Vices of envying Vertue in any how contrary soever he may be to me in Judgment, so well, as from being unwilling to allow every one their due Commendations, I will cast my self upon Providence, for the success of this Paper; And in reference to Cromwell's Government, and the present times, make some Observations relating to both, and in order thereunto, shew,

First, That the original cause of the low condition that we are now (in relation to Trade) reduced unto, had its beginning in Oliver's time, and the foundations of it, layed, either, by his ignorant mistaking the Interest of this Kingdome, or wilfully doing it, for the advancement of his own particular Interest.

Secondly, That his time, for the short continuation, had as much of oppression, and injustice, as any former times. Thirdly and lastly, That he never in his later dayes, valued either honour or honesty, when they stood in the way of his ambition, and that there is nothing to be admired in him (though so much Idolized) but that the partiality of the world, should make him so great a favorite of ignorance, and forget-fullness, as he seems to be.

6.5 From Richard Baxter's *Autobiography*
(Everyman's Library, revised by N. H. Keeble, 1974)

This and the following extract illustrate the muddle that Baxter— and many other moderates in the Interregnum—got into when they tried to define their attitude to Oliver Cromwell as Lord Protector. In his *Autobiography* Baxter can with coolness, in retrospect, analyse the Machiavellian intriguer. As a usurper and a regicide, Cromwell had no claims upon the loyalty of his people. Baxter was, however, troubled in 1659 by a Presbyterian corre-spondent who wondered whether Calvin would have approved of actively resisting 'even a meer possessory power'.[13] This is itself an interesting gloss on the thesis, discussed in my opening introduction, that Calvinism is the creed of rebels. And Baxter's hostility to Cromwell could not blind him to the value of his religious settlement in improving morality and strengthening unity.

Having thus forced his conscience to justify all his cause (the cutting off the king, the setting up himself and his adherents, the pulling down the parliament and the Scots), he thinketh that the end being good and necessary, the necessary means cannot be bad. And accordingly he giveth his interest and cause leave to tell him how far sects shall be tolerated and com-mended, and how far not; and how far the ministry shall be owned and supported and how far not; yea, and how far professions, promises and vows shall be kept or broken; and therefore the Covenant he could not away with, nor the ministers, further than they yielded to his ends or did not openly resist them. He seemed exceedingly open-hearted, by a familiar rustic-affected carriage (especially to his soldiers in

sporting with them); but he thought secrecy a virtue and dissimulation no vice, and simulation—that is, in plain English,
a lie—or perfidiousness to be a tolerable fault in a case of
necessity; being of the same opinion with the Lord Bacon
(who was not so precise as learned) that 'the best composition
and temperature is to have openness in fame and opinion,
secrecy in habit, dissimulation in reasonable use, and a power
to feign if there by no remedy' (Essay vi, p. 31). Therefore
he kept fair with all, saving his open or unreconcilable enemies.
He carried it with such dissimulation that Anabaptists, Independents and Antinomians did all think that he was one of
them. But he never endeavoured to persuade the Presbyterians that he was one of them, but only that he would do
them justice and preserve them, and that he honoured their
worth and piety; for he knew that they were not so easily
deceived. In a word, he did as our prelates have done, begin
low and rise higher in his resolutions as his condition rose,
and the praises which he made is the lower condition he used
as the interest of his higher following condition did require,
and kept up as much honesty and godliness in the main as his
cause and interest would allow (but there they left him).
And his name standeth as a monitory monument or pillar to
posterity. . . .

6.6 From *Baxter Mss* (Doctor Williams's Library)

Baxter's correspondence with his fellow ecumenist John Durie
reveals his awareness of the debt to Cromwell which could be
easier paid to the son than to the regicide father. Hence Baxter's
dedication of two books to *Richard* Cromwell as Lord Protector:
an action that was to provide fodder for his enemies at the
Restoration. It was generally only after the Restoration that
Puritans appreciated the freedom which they had enjoyed between 1646 and 1660: of none is this more true than Richard
Baxter.

JOHN DURIE: Richard Baxter, 20 December 1658.
. . . I have not as yet made any application to my Lord
Protector about my business; because I will have things

ripened a little more before I lay it before him, and then I shall desire a reference from him to some of the Counsell whom I shall name who may consider upon the Information which I shall give them what may bee fitter for him to doe in it? how farre he appeare for the encouragement of the worke? in what way hee should assist it at home and abroad? how farre to owne me, or without taking notice of mee (which I think more expedient) to owne the business so we may not give any state Jealousie to those that will bee startled at the full appearance of a reall unitie amongst us (59/1, f. 96v–97).

6.7 Lucy Hutchinson, from *Memoirs of the Life of Colonel Hutchinson*

This priggish denunciation of Cromwell the time-server jars when one knows that Hutchinson saved his own life, to the profound disgust of Ludlow, by selling out on his radical ideals (see above, 5.4). Ironically the bitterness of his hostility to Cromwell, albeit from a radical standpoint, was a marked point in his favour at the Restoration, when his life hung in the balance. After his release in 1660 he spent three years in retirement; was arrested for a suspected part in a 1663 rising; would not submit a second time and died in prison on 11 September 1664.

But now had the poison of ambition so ulcerated Cromwell's heart, that the effects of it became more apparent than before; and while as yet Fairfax stood an empty name, he was moulding the army to his mind, weeding out the godly and upright-hearted men, both officers and soldiers, and filling up their rooms with rascally turn-coat cavaliers, and pitiful sottish beasts of his own alliance, and other such as would swallow all things, and make no questions for conscience' sake. Yet this he did not directly nor in tumult, but by such degrees that it was unperceived by all that were not of very penetrating eyes; and those that made the loudest outcries against him lifted up their voices with such apparent envy and malice that, in that mist, they rather hid than discovered his ambitious minings. Among these, Colonel Rich and Commissary Staines and Watson had made a design even against his life, and the business was brought to the examination of the council of state. Before the hearing of it, Colonel Rich came to Colonel Hutchinson and implored his assistance with tears, affirming all the crimes of Cromwell, but not daring to justify his accusations, although the colonel advised him if they were true to stand boldly to it, if false to acknowledge his own iniquity. The latter course he took, and the council had resolved upon the just punishment of the men, when Cromwell, having only thus in a private council vindicated himself from their malice, and laid open what pitiful sneaking poor knaves they were, how ungrateful to him, and how treacherous and cowardly to themselves, became their advocate, and made it his suit that they might be no farther published or punished. This being permitted him, and they thus rendered contemptible to others, they became beasts and slaves to him, who knew how to serve himself by them without trusting them. This generosity, for indeed he carried himself with the greatest bravery that is imaginable herein, much advanced his glory, and cleared him in the eyes of superficial beholders; but others saw he creeped on, and could not stop him, while fortune itself seemed to prepare his way on sundry occasions. All this while he carried to Mr Hutchinson the most open face, and made the most obliging professions of friendship imaginable; but the colonel saw through him, and forbore not often to tell him what was suspected of his ambition, what dissimulations of his were remarked, and how dishonourable to the name of God and the profession of religion, and destructive to the most glorious cause, and dangerous in overthrowing all our triumphs, these things which were suspected of him, would be, if true. He would seem to receive these cautions and admonitions as the greatest demonstrations of integrity and friendship that could be made, and embrace the colonel in his arms, and make serious lying professions to him, and often inquire men's opinions concerning him, which the colonel never forbore to tell him plainly, although he knew he resented it not as he made show, yet it pleased him so to discharge his own thoughts.

6.8 Reactions to Cromwell in Verse

The seventeenth-century literary response to Cromwell, whether in the form of a coarse ballad attack or a poetic eulogy, was somewhat crude. There is no contemporary writer who gets anywhere near to recreating the whole complex, earthy, spiritual, confident, uncertain, ruthless, tender, clumsy and inspired man who emerges from his own prayers, letters and speeches. What the writers do give us is for the most part a simple response to him, either of hatred or of love. Abraham Cowley is an exception to this pattern.[14]

(a) BALLAD MATERIAL

Most ballads, just because they were *ballads*, hawked outside ale-houses, sold as drinking songs and often containing dirty jokes, were necessarily composed by anti-Puritan wits. So it is not surprising that most of the relevant ballad and chap-book material enjoys making a butt of 'Oliver':

OLIVERUS

> One writ *Olivarius*
> Instead of *Oliverus*,
> In *Oliver's* time; 'twas his will,
>   And his reason was good,
>   If well understood,
> 'Cause he varies from *verus* still.[15]

or there is the mock-creed, January 1647:

I Beleeve in CROMWELL, the Father of all Schisme, Sedition, Heresy and Rebellion, and in his onely Son *Ireton*, our Saviour, begotten by the Spirit in a hole, born of a winching Mare, suffered under a house of Office at *Brainford*, he deserves to be drawn hang'd and quartered, and to remain unburied: for he descended into *Hull*, the third day he rose up in Rebellion against the KING, and now sitteth at the right hand of the Gods at Westminster. He beleeves there is no Holy Ghost, nor Catholique Church, nor forgiveness of sins, but the Communion of Sisters, the resurrection of his Members, and Parliament everlasting. AMEN.[16]

Most popular balladists saw Cromwell as an untrustworthy
bully-boy, a ruthless *arriviste*, whose reign would be as disastrous as that of the other religiously inspired radical leader,
John of Leyden, in Munster.

> ... Then rail no more at *Antichrist*,
>   But learn ye to be *civil*:
> And since ye have King *Cromwel* kist,
>   Shake hands too with the *Devil*. ...
>
> Then *John-a-Leyden*, *Nol*, and all
>   Their goblin ghostly *Train*,
> (Brave *Rebel Saints* triumphant) shall
>   Begin their second *Reign*. ...
>
> 'Tis *Nol's* own *Brew-house* now, I swear;
>   The *Speaker's* but his *Skinker*:
> Their *Members* are, like th' *Council* of War,
>   *Car-men*, *Pedlers*, and *Tinkers*.[17]

Cromwell's family connections with brewing and his red
nose were themes for endless merriment. Another example of
popular mockery is the rollicking, ironic *O Brave Oliver*:

From *O Brave Oliver*

1 The army is come vp, hay hoe,
    The army is come vp, hay hoe!
        to London it is brought,
        and who would haue thought
    It euer would haud proued soe?
        for the indipendants
        ar superindendants
    Ouer kingdome and Cyty also.
    Then O fine Olliver, O braue, O rare Olliver, O,
    Dainty Olliver, O gallant Olliver, O!

3 For Olliver is all in all,
    For Olliver is all in all,
        and Olliver is here,
        and Olliver is there,
    And Olliver is at whitehall.
        And Olliver notes all,
        and Olliver voats all,
    And claps his hand vpon his bilboe.
    Then O fine Olliver, O braue Olliver, &c.

Now Olliver must be he,
Now Olliver must be he,
  for Olliver's nose
  is the Lancaster rose,
And thence comes his souerainety.
  For Olliver teaches,
  and Olliver preaches,
And prayeth vpon his tip-toe.
Then O fine Olliver, O rare Olliver, &c.

6 But doe you not heare? what news?
  But doe you not heare? what news?
    The Prince they say
    will come thys way,
  And the Scots will him not refuse.
    I wish he may enter
    this Land to the Center,
  And winne it, and giue a right blow.
  Then O base Olliver, O s—— Olliver, O,
  Stinking Olliver, O Trayter Olliver, O,
  Damned Olliver, O ! [18]

(b) EXAMPLES OF POETIC EULOGY

Can flattery of a dictator (or a 'Lord Protector') ever be
sincere? How may one tell? And is it very much more morally
acceptable if it *is* sincere? In some instances the poet's own
history as a political weathercock, combined with the very
fulsomeness of his adulation, is a strong indication that he is
merely writing to please whomsoever is in power. Edmund
Waller, for example, whose effusions to Charles and Henrietta
Maria were printed above (see **1.10**), if he feels anything, seems
to feel a happy intoxication at the idea of being one with
whosoever is dominant at the time. This includes a simple-
minded relish at being British and so one of the 'Lords of the
world's great waste, the ocean'. Edmund Waller's *Panegyric
to My Lord Protector* boasts with premature complacency of
England's imperial destiny:

Your drooping country, torn with civil hate,
Restored by you, is made a glorious state;
The seat of empire, where the Irish come,
And the unwilling Scotch, to fetch their doom.

> The sea's our own; and now all nations greet,
> With bending sails, each vessel of our fleet;
> Your power extends as far as winds can blow,
> Or swelling sails upon the globe may go.
>
> Heaven (that has placed this island to give law,
> To balance Europe, and her states to awe),
> In this conjunction does on Britain smile;
> The greatest leader, and the greatest isle.[19]

Although Milton and Marvell also had at certain times high *hopes* of England's destiny to be a new and greater Rome, they were never so swollen with nationalistic pride that they mistook what might be for what in fact was. However, Waller does speak more sympathetically in one stanza; when he alludes to Cromwell's active belief in toleration and the strength which allowed him to protect the weak:

> Hither the oppressed shall henceforth resort,
> Justice to crave, and succour, at your court;
> And then your Highness, not for ours alone,
> But for the world's protector shall be known.

Marvell's long poem, *The First Anniversary of the Government under His Highness The Lord Protector*, begins by contrasting Cromwell, who 'in one year the work of ages acts', with the long line of *fainéant* hereditary monarchs who were merely strong in the oppression of their own subjects. Their religion had been mere superstitious fear, whereas Cromwell directs his whole personal and political life by his lofty Christian faith, tuning 'this lower to that higher sphere'. *The First Anniversary* continues the dialectical approach of the *Horatian Ode* and seems to express an argument going on within the poet's mind. Marvell does not merely assert, he tries to argue the necessity for, and hence the rightness of, the phenomenon of a Cromwell being Lord Protector of England. But in this poem the opposing forces are not Cromwell and Charles, the future versus the past, but Cromwell and the English—that light-minded multitude who, in Milton's words, 'bawl for freedom in their senceless mood,/And still revolt when truth would set them free'. Just because England consists of so many conflicting power-hungry ideological factions, there must be a strong man with a controlling spirit to keep the equipoise steady. Cromwell is therefore seen by Marvell as Amphion, the inspired architect, who frames and roofs a voluntary Commonwealth:

> All other matter yields, and may be ruled,
> But who the minds of stubborn men can build?
> No quarry bears a stone so hardly wrought,
> Nor with such labour from its centre brought:
> None to be sunk in the foundation bends,
> Each in the house the highest place contends;
> And each the hand that lays him will direct,
> And some fall back upon the architect;
> Yet all, composed by his attractive song,
> Into the animated city throng.
>
> The Commonwealth does through their centres all
> Draw the circumference of the public wall;
> The crossest spirits here do take their part,
> Fastening the contignation which they thwart:
> And they whose nature leads them to divide,
> Uphold, this one, and that the other side:
> But the most equal still sustain the height,
> And they, as pillars, keep the work upright,
> While the resistance of opposed minds
> The fabric, as with arches, stronger binds;
> Which, on the basis of a senate free,
> Knit by the roof's protecting weight, agree.

But Marvell fears that although God has sent England her great leader at this crucial point in history—'If these the times, then this must be the man;'—yet the English will be too slow to follow his ardent lead and the great opportunity to build the New Jerusalem will be wasted:

> Hence oft I think, if in some happy hour
> High grace should meet in one with highest power,
> And then a seasonable people still
> Should bend to his, as he to Heaven's will,
> What we might hope, what wonderful effect
> From such a wished conjuncture might reflect!
> Sure, the mysterious work, where none withstand,
> Would forthwith finish under such a hand;

> Foreshortened time its useless course would stay,
> And soon precipitate the latest day:
> But a thick cloud about that morning lies,
> And intercepts the beams to mortal eyes;
> That 'tis the most which we determine can,
> If these the times, then this must be the man;
> And well he therefore does, and well has guessed,
> Who in his age has always forward pressed,
> And knowing not where Heaven's choice may light,
> Girds yet his sword, and ready stands to fight.
> But men, alas! as if they nothing cared,
> Look on, all unconcerned, or unprepared;
> And stars still fall, and still the dragon's tail
> Swinges the volumes of its horrid flail;
> For the great justice that did first suspend
> The world by sin, does by the same extend.
> Hence that blest day still counterpoised wastes,
> The ill delaying, what the elected hastes;
> Hence, landing, Nature to new seas is tossed,
> And good designs still with their authors lost.

Next Marvell stresses Cromwell's long-standing unwilling-ness to rule the country. Is he as anxious as Milton was (6.2) that Cromwell should not merely descend on to a throne? 'For to be Cromwell was a greater thing/Than aught below, or yet above, a king.' Marvell insists that Cromwell was *not* ambitious —''Twas Heaven would not that his power should cease.' Cromwell had *had* to curb other men's will and power to dominate; he is the experienced first mate who grabs the helm from the steersman who was mistakenly making for the rocks in a storm:

> What though awhile they grumble, discontent?
> Saving himself, he does their loss prevent.
> 'Tis not a freedom that, where all command,
> Nor tyranny, where one does them withstand;
> But who of both the bounders knows to lay,
> Him as their father, must the State obey.

Cromwell is like that other reverend father of his people, Noah, the exceptional man who saved his family from the all-destroying Flood; but the English are the shameless sons of Ham, rejoicing in their Noah's weakness (epilepsy), not realizing that the real fatal weakness is their own crazed need for frantic libertarian excesses—

> That sober liberty which men may have,
> That they enjoy, but more they vainly crave;
> And such as to their parent's tents do press,
> May show their own, not see his nakedness.

Nevertheless, the poem ends triumphantly. Cromwell has survived both illness and the attacks of all his enemies at home and abroad, miraculously uniting the nation and firing it with his spiritual energy—'his one soul/Moves the great bulk, and animates the whole'.

Perhaps the one all-important difference between the poems by Milton and Marvell praising Cromwell, and the examples of sycophantic adulation of the King and Queen by the Court Poets (see above, 1.10) is that Milton and Marvell address Cromwell not as some God-figure before whom all must grovel, but always as a *man*—however exceptional, Heaven-sent, or even 'angelic' as in Marvell's *The First Anniversary*, 'Angelic Cromwell, who outwings the wind,/And in dark nights, and in cold days, alone/Pursues the monster thorough every throne'. We should remember Milton's sonnet of 1652 in which he salutes Cromwell as Cromwell, our chief of *men*' (my italics), and then goes on to address him with advice offered in the imperative mood. Similarly, in his *Second Defence of the People of England*, he praises Cromwell for having chosen the title of Protector 'not to exalt, but rather to bring you nearer to the level of ordinary men'; and Marvell has his reluctantly admiring foreign ambassador say in *The First Anniversary*: 'Abroad a king he seems, and something more,/At home a subject on the equal floor.' This insistence that Cromwell is a fellow human being, not a God—whether Jove or Christ—to be worshipped uncritically, makes the poet himself seem more of a man and his praise correspondingly more worth having.

7
THE WRETCHEDNESS
OF WAR

> Oh thou, that dear and happy isle,
> The garden of the world erewhile,
> Thou Paradise of the four seas,
> Which Heaven planted us to please,
> But, to exclude the world, did guard
> With watery, if not flaming sword,—
> What luckless apple did we taste,
> To make us mortal, and thee waste?
>
> Marvell, *On Nun Appleton House*

The English Civil War has so often been discussed in terms of its causation, the principles animating the participants and its socio-political consequences, that the reality of the *suffering* then experienced has rather been overlooked. For many of those who lived through those times, it was a phenomenon of almost incredible horror. That fellow Englishmen, neighbours, even brothers or fathers and sons, should be hacking at each other's heads and limbs, or starving each other during sieges, or blowing each other's bodies to pieces with musket-balls, all out of devotion to God, or King, or English liberty, was hardly to be credited, even when witnessed. Thomas Knyvett wrote to his wife:

> Suerly this History to after Ages will seeme rather a Romancy, a faigned thing then a matter really Acted; And, in my opinion, twilbe much more for the credit of the Nation to have it so constred then cleer'ly beleev'd, for the best excuse that can be made for us must be a fit of Lunacy. The Lord God Allmighty open all our eyes.[1]

A little later he tried to reassure his wife concerning the safety of their son Jack who had joined Lord Craven's regiment, in the Prince of Orange's campaign against the Spanish in the Low Countries:

You seeme much troubled for the course Jack 'hath taken. I cannot blame thy feares in respect of thy motherly affection, but when you are rightly Inform'd in yo[r] Judgm[t], I know yo[r] discretion will correct yo[r] Passion. Ther is no such danger of his Life ther for matter of fight'ing as you App[r]hend, ther warr & ours being farr different in ther nature, the one being altogether by beseed'ging in a slowe pace; ours heer so malitious 'as we fight any way, And Glory in nothing more than killing.[2]

For most of the poets then alive, war in itself was anathema. Marvell, Vaughan, Alexander Brome, Shirley and the anonymous poet of 'The Dominion of the Sword' emerge as essentially pacifist in their response, appalled by the destruction of irreplaceable life. This view is expressed evocatively in the plaint of Marvell's Nymph:

> The wanton Troopers riding by
> Have shot my Faun and it will dye.[3]

Only Milton and a few of the Cavalier poets believed that the war was justified by their respective causes, and Milton himself was well aware that the only justification for the fighting would be the achievement of a more free and just society living at peace—

> For what can Warr but endless Warr still breed,
> Till Truth and Right from Violence be freed.[4]

The 'victories' of peace are even more vital than those of war, for:

War has made many great whom peace makes small. If after being released from the toils of war, you neglect the arts of peace, if your peace and your *liberty be a state of war fare*, if war be your only virtue, the summit of your praise, you will, believe me, soon find peace the most adverse to your interests. Your peace will only be a more distressing war; and that which you imagined liberty will prove the worst of slavery. . . . For if you think that it is a more grand, a more beneficial, or a more wise policy, to invent subtle expedients for increasing the revenue, to multiply our naval and military force, to rival in craft the ambassadors of foreign states, to form skilful treaties and alliances, than to administer unpolluted justice to the people, to redress the injured, and to succour the distressed, and speedily to restore to everyone his own, you are involved in a cloud of error; and too late will you perceive, . . . that in neglecting these, which you now think inferior considerations, you have only been precipitating your own ruin and despair.[5]

The following documents which treat of the miseries of the war itself are in chronological order and illustrate the family divisions caused by the war, personal bereavement in the loss of children or friends, the atrocities perpetrated especially during sieges, the inhumanity towards prisoners and the desperate straits of the unpaid soldiers both during campaigns and after the wars needed them no longer. There is a final section consisting of poems written in this period deploring the misery and futility of the war in general terms.

7.1 Two Examples of Family Divisions in the Civil War

(a) THE D'EWES BROTHERS, from Simonds D'Ewes, *Autobiography and Correspondence*, ed. Halliwell, 1845.

Simonds D'Ewes (1602–1650), antiquarian, barrister and M.P. for Sudbury in the Long Parliament, in the correspondence below explains to his brother Richard why he cannot accept his invitation to join him on the King's side in 1642. It is a remarkable tribute to the power of the hunger for an ethical reformation at this time that it could overcome, in this case, the scruples of a man whose conservative pedantry was later to lead to his opposing the fortification of a town, threatened by royalist troops, on the grounds that it was illegal:

RICHARD D'EWES TO SIR SIMONDS D'EWES

Dear Brother,

I was in good hopes to have seene you heere before the arrival of these will come to your hands: but I should think this or any other paines well awarded, if I could bee the happie inducement to bring you hither. I dayly understand how you stand affected, and what your opinions are, and out of that sincere affection I bear you, I heartily wish you fortunate in their continuance.

If your other occasions will dispense and give place to my hopes, I can in some measure accommodate you with horses for your journey. 'Tis but sending a note under your hand to Sir Hen. Newton for a grey geldinge and a bay mare to be left at his house Salisbury-court, Fleete-street, and he will very soon let you receive them. By this last post I have nothing, so as I confidently beleeve them to be yett in his hands with ye saddles, etc.

I wrote a letter to you some six weeks past about the Prince Elector, but received no answer.

'Tis worth your journey to bee an eyewitness of the justice and equity of the King's Proceedings.

Sir, if you bee affected to this journey, I have said enough: if your time and business permitt nott, then I shall but trouble you. I wish you all health and your own desires, and am,

Your affectionate brother and servant,

D'EWES.

If you send I shall not faile of your returns by the post without any further direction.

York, June 17, 1642.

SIR SIMONDS D'EWES TO RICHARD D'EWES

Dear Brother,

I DID long since receive your letter touching the Prince Elector Palatine, and though I have since remained silent to you, yet upon Thursday, the 12th day of May last past, I did faithfullie vindicate his innocence, there being just occasion offered for my interposition. For mine owne parte I have often repented my being of this Parliament; having not only been much interrupted in my pretious studies by it, but might otherwise in humane reason have been as happie in that inestimable wife I had, as I am now miserable and desolate in her losse.

But now, being called to it by his Majestie's witt, I have noe other resolution but to continue heere wheere I shall persist, as I have done hitherto, *procul amore, procul livore, procul partium studio*, to discharge my duties to God, his sacred Majestie, and the kingdome, without feare or favour.

I have said or done nothing for vindication of the King's just rights, or the upholding of that reverence due to him, but what my conscience dictated to mee to speake in respect of that little knowledge I have in the municipal lawes and ancient records of this State, and, therefore, there is no service of mine that deserves either to be taken notice of in the least measure by his Majestie or any at Yorke.

'Tis true I might, perhaps, have escaped some unjust censures by an unseasonable silence: but I blesse that higher Providence that gave mee courage to speake freelie, and if mine own heart deceive mee not, I could bee willing to re-deeme the re-union of his Majestie and the Two Houses with my dearest bloud; that soe religion might be established in that power and puritie amongst us, and preaching soe settled in those places wheere atheism, profaneness, and ignorance now raignes, as that all men might know their duties to God and the King, soe as his Majestie might raigne many and many years over us with much honour and grace. For, doubtles, by a civil warre hee will bee the greates loser, whosoever gaines; that being true which Gaspar, Earle of Schomberg told Henry the Fourth of France, that the people who weere slaine weere his people, the townes and cities which weere burnt weere his cities and townes, and the kingdome which was harrassed was his kingdome. Let your prayers and en-deavours bee, as mine are, for peace, in which resolution you shall ever oblige,

Your affectionate brother, SIMONDS D'EWES.

Westminster, June 21, 1642.

(b) THE VERNEY FAMILY

Sir Edmund Verney, the King's standard-bearer (see above, 4.2) was wretched to learn that his eldest son Ralph, after conscientious deliberation, had sided with Parliament. Lady Sussex, a family friend, here reports to Ralph Verney on his father's reactions to this situation in a recent letter to her:

It was a very sade [one] and his worde was this of you; 'madam he hath ever lane near my hart and truly he is ther still'; that he hade many afflictyons uppon him, and that you hade usede him unkaindly; this was the effect of itt; The paper you sent of is [his] letter to you i bornt presently; i shall never open my lipes of that nor any thinge else you trust me with; he is passynate, and much troublede i belive that you declarede yourselfe for the parlyment: a littill time will digest all I am confident. . . . Now lett me intrete you as a frende that loves you most hartily, not to right passynatly to your father, but ovour com him with kaindnes; good man I see hee is infinetly malincoly, for many other thinges i belive besides the difference betwist you.

5th September 1644

I see you to much appryhende this unhapye diffirence betwixt your father and selfe; i am very confident a littill time will make all will agane and his affecyon to you ase deare and harty as ever. i pray bee not sade; that will doo you a great dell of hurt i am suer. If it ples God your father retorne, i hope one discorse or to, will make all well agane betwixt you. If Mrs. Sidham [Sydenham] and the rest of your frindes with him be not harty in doinge all good offeses betwixt you, the are most file unworthy pepell. If you hade falede in any thinge of duty or love to him it hade bene some jost case of exceptyon, but in goinge the way your consince telles you to be right, i hope he hath more goodnes and religone then to continue in displesuer with you for it.

9th September 1644

The younger son of Sir Edmund, Mun Verney, was a Cavalier and he was disgusted by his brother Ralph's disloyalty:

Brother, what I feared is proovd too true, which is your being against the king: give me leave to tell you in my opinion tis most unhandsomely done, and it grieves my hearte to thinke that my father allready and I, who soe dearly love and esteeme you, should be bound in consequence (because in duty to our king) to be your enemy. I heare tis a greate greife to my father. . . . I am soe much troubled to think of your being of the syde you are that I can write no more, only I shall pray for peace with all my hearte, but if God grant not that, yet that He will be pleased to turne your hearte that you may soe expresse your duty to your king that my father may still have cause to rejoice in you.

When Ralph did not reply, Mun wrote in gentler terms assuring him that their painful difference in allegiance could not destroy his love:

I beseeche you let not our unfortunate silence breede the least distrust of each other's affections, although I would willingly

lose my right hand that you had gone the other way, yet I
will never consent that this dispute shall make a quarrel
between us, there be too many to fight with besides ourselves.
I pray God grant a suddaine and firme peace that we may
safely meete in persone as well as in affection. Though I am
tooth and nayle for the King's cause, and endure soe to the
death, whatsoever his fortune be, yet sweete brother, let not
this my opinion (for it is guyded by my conscience), nor any
report which you can heare of me, cause a diffidence of my true
love to you.[6]

7.2 The Fate of a Women's Peace Demonstration

(From *The Knyvett Letters*, ed. Bertram
Schofield)

On 8 August 1643 a crowd of women, with white ribbons in their
hats, made a demonstration in favour of peace near the approaches to the House of Commons. The following day they
returned in greater force with the intention of throwing Pym,
Strode and other Roundheads into the river. In the course of the
mêlée two men in the crowd were killed, women were cut down
by a body of Waller's horse, and finally a young woman, crossing
Palace Yard, was accidentally shot.

Deer

Hart, this day's tragedy makes me at my witts end what
to advise thee concerning com'ing vp. We had faier hopes on
saturday last of some overture for Peace, 6 propositions
drawne vp by the Lo[s] sent downe to the house of commons,
very honorab[li]. The consideration of them, after a great
debate, was voted to be referrd 'till Munday. Munday morn-
ning being come, ther came downe a great concourse of people
out of the citty, & filld all passages, crying to the Lo[s] &
commons 'No Peace', 'remember ther late oath & covenant',
'wee'l dye in the cause' & such like acclamations, that would
have made any honest peac'able spirrit hart have bledd. That
night it was carried by the Maior vote against these propositions. Tu'sday morn' A multitude of weomen came &

made an outcry for Peace. Some verball satisfaction thay had, & no hurt done that day. This day thay came againe in a farr greater number, & fell to be more vnruly, wch occasiond A sadder spectacle, divers men & weomen being slaine by the traind gaurd. Such a cumbustion hath been to day, & lik'ly to be worss, y^t, aswell as I love thee, I cannot wish thee heer yet. I rather wish my selfe with thee, or in some other place out of this towne; therfore, I prethe, stirr not 'till I write againe. Y^r last letters, wch I heer wear brought to towne, I have not yet receiv'd. I lighted on this messenger by chance. My distractions are so great as I can say no more at present, but pray to my good God to continue his gratious protection to vs in all hazards, who never failes them that trust in him. I knowe thou wilt doe the like for

Thy poore disconsolate husband

T. K.

7.3 The Muddle and Brutality of the Fighting

(a) *The Taking of Marlborough, Wiltshire, by the Royalists, 5 December 1642.*

In the 1630s Bishop Mathew Wren had deplored the fact that Englishmen had forgotten how to fight. He detected a consequent weakening of the nation's moral fibre. Only a few years later, however, the following scenes were enacted in England and war could no longer be invoked as a morally educative experience:

... Having thus won the town they set fire to it in two other places so that there were four fires blazing at once, and the soldiers fell to pillaging the houses and shops, all the wearing apparel, plate and money they took away and all the horses and carts that were in the town. ... On the Tuesday they carried away the prisoners being in number between 100 and 120, marching on foot, tied two and two together, before the cannon to Oxford. ... There were 53 houses burnt and the damage sustained by the town (besides the value of these houses) in goods, money and ware, was computed to amount to near 50,000£. (from John Rushworth, *Historical Collections 1659–1701* (1721) vol. v, pp. 82–3).

(b) LADY HUTCHINSON, *Memoirs of the Life of Colonel Hutchinson.*

Here follows a vivid account of the attempted Royalist attack on Nottingham Castle, and the later Roundhead storming of Shelford:

the governor's men chased them from streete to streete, till they had cleared the town of them, who runne away confusedly: the first that went out shot their pistolls into the thatcht houses to have fired them, but by the mercy of God neither that, nor other endeavours they shew'd to have fired the towne, as they were commanded, tooke effect. Betweene thirty and forty of them were kill'd in the streetes, fourscore were taken prisoners, and abundance of armes were gather'd up, which the men flung away in hast, as they run; ... Many of them died in their returne, and were found dead in the woods and in the townes thay past through. Many of them, discourag'd with this service, ran away, and many of their horses were quite spoyl'd: for two miles thay left a greate track of blood, which froze as it fell upon the snow, for it was such bitter weather that the foote had waded almost to the middle in snow as they came, and were so numbed with cold when they came into the town, that they were faine to be rubbed to get life in them, and in that conditions, were more eager of fires and warme meate then of plunder ...

[Col. Hutchinson's] men found many difficulties more then they expected, for after they had fill'd up the ditches with faggots, and pitcht the scaling ladders, they were twenty staves too short, and the enemie, from the top of the workes, threw downe loggs of wood, which would sweep of a whole ladder-full of men at once: the lieftenant-collonell himselfe was once or twice so beaten downe. The governor had order'd other musketeers to beate of those men that stood upon the top of the workes, which they fail'd of by shooting without good ayme, but the governor directed them better, and the Nottingham horse dismounting, and assailing with their pistols and headpieces, helpt the foote to beate them downe from the top of the worke, all except one stout man, who stood alone, and did wonders in beating downe the assailants, which the governor being angrie at, fetcht two of his owne musketeers and made them shoot, and he immediately fell, to the greate discouragement of his fellows. Then the governor himselfe first enter'd, and the rest of his men came in as fast as they could. But while his regiment was entering on this side, the Londoners were beaten of on the other side, and the maine force of the garrison turn'd upon him. The cavaliers had halfe moones within, which were as good a defence to them as their first workes; into these the souldiers that were of the queene's regiment were gotten, and they in the house shott out of all the windores. The governor's men, assoone as they gott in, had taken the stables and all their horses, but the governor him-selfe was fighting with the captaine of the papists and some others, who, by advantage of the halfe moone and the house, might have prevail'd to cutt of him and those that were with him, which were not many. The enemie being strengthen'd by the addition of those who had beaten of the assailants on the other side, were now trying their utmost to vanquish those that were within. The lieftenant-collonell, seeing his brother in hazard, made haste to open the drawbridge, that Poyntz might come in with his horse, which he did, but not before the governor had kill'd that gentleman who was fighting with him, at whose fall his men gave way. Poyntz seeing them shoote from the house, and apprehending the king might come to their reliefe, when he came in, order'd that no quarter should be given. And here the governor was in greater danger then before, for the strangers hearing him call'd governor, were advancing to have kill'd him, but that the lieftenant-collonell, who was very watchful to preserve him all that day, came in to his rescue, and scarcely could persuade them that it was the governor of Nottingham, because he, at the beginning of the storme, had put off a very good suite of armor that he had, which being muskett proof, was so heavie that it heated him, and so he would not be persuaded by his friends to weare aniething but his buffe coate. . . .

. . . The governor of Shelford, after all his bravadoes, came but meanely of: 'tis sayd he sate in his chamber, wrapt up in his cloake, and came not forth that day; but that avail'd him not, for how, or by whom, it is not known, but he was wounded and stript, and flung upon a dunghill. The lieftenant-collonell, after the house was master'd, seeing the disorder by which our men were readie to murther one another, upon the command Poyntz had issued to give no quarter, desir'd

Poyntz to cause the slaughter to cease, which was presently obey'd, and about seven score prisoners sav'd. While he was thus busied, enquiring what was become of the governor, he was shewn him naked upon the dunghill; whereupon the lieftenant-collonell call'd for his owne cloake and cast it over him, and sent him to a bed in his owne quarters, and procur'd him a surgeon. Upon his desire he had a little priest, who had bene his father's chaplaine, and was one of the committee faction; but the man was such a pittifull comforter, that the governor (Col. Hutchinson) who was come to visitt him, was forc'd to undertake that office: but though he had all the supplies they could all wayes give him, he died the next day . . .

(c) THE STARVATION OF NON-COMBATANTS UNDER SIEGE.

From the Leagure before Colchester, August 6. 1648.
If it be wondered why Colchester is not taken, we give Answer; We can take it when we please by Storm in few Hours warning. But seeing we are in very good hopes to take it by starving shortly, I see no Reason (to satisfie Men's humours) to cast away our Men by Storm. If Relief comes by Sea or Land, we can draw off 2000 old soldiers and fight them; or if the Relief be too strong, upon few Hours warning storm the town and carry it. We know their Condition within, and every Day adds to their weakness; near 200 are lately run from them, and every Day (as they get Opportunity) they come out. Let them eat Horseflesh and Maggots till the Flux (already among them) increase their Diseases: They do us no hurt, but rather a Courtesie; they keep us from Diseases and healthful, by causing our Men to be in continual Action. This Day, we had 35 Prisoners come out in Exchange for so many sent in Yesterday, which are all but one or two Prisoners they have of ours, tho' we have many of theirs. The middle Mill (which we fired a Week since) is spoiled by our Cannon, that it cannot be serviceable. . . .

Saturday August 19th 1648.
From the Leagure before Colchester, August 18. The last Night Five Soldiers came from the Enemy, and swam before the River, Three of them being Townsmen, who did express, that the Cries of Women and Children, and the poorest sort, are such as would grieve any heart to hear them: that if they be not permitted to come out they must Starve. Three of these

Men left their Arms behind them, pretending they came to let us know the Certainty of the Condition of the Town; we hope that Hunger will necessitate the People to something which may occasion the Soldiers to join with them, which may facilitate our Work in gaining the Town; the Honest and Well-Affected People that are there, we very much pity their Condition; and could we single them out from the rest, they might have Passes from the General; but Goring will let no Well-affected come out, unless some that are Ill-affected, may come out with them.

Yesterday there came out a Woman and five Children, one sucking at her Breast; she fell down at our Guards, beseeching them to pass beyond the Line; the People in the Town looking to see if they had admittance, resolving to follow them; but the Guards were necessitated to turn them back again, or otherwise Hundreds will come out, which would much prejudice the Service.

The Soldiers and the Women said, *That could they get but Dogs and Cats to eat, it were happy for them, but all the Dogs and Cats, and most of the Horses are near eaten already:* Some sad thing of necessity must befall the Town suddenly.

Just now our Trumpeter is come from the Enemy in Colchester, desiring leave to send to know whether they may have Relief, or not, and if they see no hopes of any, within 20 days, then to Treat. By this you may guess the necessity of their Condition; and what a few days may produce. My Lord General returned Answer: *That he cannot give way to their Desire, etc. That he doubts not but within less time than 20 days to have the Town without Terms.* They have this day refused to exchange the Earl of Cleveland, etc. for any of the Committee, which is a sign they reserve the Committee to serve themselves. A mother is stoll'n out of Town, who saith, That this day the Women and Children were at the Lord Goring's Door for Bread; That he told them, *They must eat their Children if they wanted*; the Women Reviled his Lordship, told him, *They would pull out his Eyes rather than starve*, and were in a High Discontent; and that all the Inhabitants set the Women on, and some Soldiers dislike it not.

Heith—Suburbs, Colchester.

August 18 1648   Your Servant,
                                                    W.C.

(from John Rushworth, *Historical Collections the Fourth and Last Part*) (1721, vol. vii, p. 1217.)

(d) CRUELTY TO PRISONERS (see also 3/7).

> ... The Parliament are selling the Scots common prisoners
> to the Barbadoes and other plantations, which I conceive to
> be abouve 12,000 or 14,000 men, and article the merchants
> for their not returning. I think they mean to transplant the
> whole nation of the Scots. . . .
>
> (Edmund Verney to Sir Ralph Verney, 14 September 1648)

7.4 Examples of Personal Bereavement

(a) RALPH VERNEY on the death of his father, Sir Edmund,
at Edgehill, writing to Lady Sussex, 29 October 1642:

> Maddam, I never lov'd to bee the messenger of ill newes:
> therfore I forbore to send you this; which is the saddest and
> deepest affliction that ever befell any poore distressed man . . ..
> God's will bee donn, and give mee patience, to support mee in
> this extremity. there is noe absolute certainty of his Death,
> that I can yet learne but sure tis too true. I have sent 3 mes-
> sengers to both armies to bie informed. On Satterday I expect
> on of them Back, in the meantime I am forced to make dilligent
> enquiries after that which (if it proove true) will make mee
> most unhappy . . . for if hee is gon, I have no freind in this
> world but your self. . . . Last night I had a servant from my
> Lord of Essex Army, that tells mee there is noe possibility of
> finding my Deare father's Body, for my Lord Generall, my
> Lord Brooke, my Lord Grey, Sr Sam Luke and twenty others
> of my acquaintance assured him hee was never taken prisiner,
> neither were any of them ever possessed of his Body; but that
> hee was slaine by an Ordinary trooper. Upon this my man went
> to all the ministers of severall parishes, that buried the dead
> that were slaine in the battle, and none of them can give him
> any information of the body. One of them told him my Lord
> Aubigny was like to have been buried in the feilds, but that
> on came by chance that knew him and tooke him into a church,
> and there laid him in the ground without soe much as a sheete
> about him, and soe divers of good quallity were buried: the

ministers kept Tallies of all that were buried, and they amount to neare 4,000.[7]

(b) *Cromwell to Colonel Valentine Walton, on the death of both their sons*

Dear Sir,

It's our duty to sympathise in all mercies, that we may praise the Lord together in chastisements or trials, that so we may sorrow together.

Truly England and the Church of God hath had a great favour from the Lord, in this great victory given unto us, such as the like never was since this war began. It had all the evidences of an absolute victory obtained by the Lord's blessing upon the godly party principally. We never charged but we routed the enemy. The left wing, which I commanded, being our own horse, saving a few Scots in the rear, beat all the Princes horse. God made them as stubble to our swords, we charged their regiments of foot with our horse, routed all we charged. The particulars I cannot relate now, but I believe, of twenty-thousand the Prince hath not four-thousand left. Give glory, all the glory, to God.

Sir, God hath taken away your eldest son by a cannon-shot. It brake his leg. We were necessitated to have it cut off, whereof he died.

Sir, you know my trials this way; but the Lord supported me with this: that the Lord took me into the happiness we all pant after and live for. There is your precious child full of glory, to know sin nor sorrow any more. He was a gallant young man, exceeding gracious. God give you His comfort. Before his death he was so full of comfort that to Frank Russell and myself he could not express it, it was so great above his pain. This he said to us. Indeed it was advisable. A little after, he said one thing lay upon his spirit. I asked him what it was. He told me that it was, that God had not suffered him to be no more the executioner of His enemies. At his fall, his horse being killed with the bullet, and as I am informed three horses more, I am told that he did them open to the right and left, that he might see the rogues run. Truly he was exceedingly beloved in the Army, of all that knew him. But few knew him, for he was a precious young man, fit for God. You have cause to bless the Lord. He is a glorious saint in Heaven, wherein you ought exceedingly to rejoice. Let this drink up your sorrow; seeing these are not feigned words to comfort you, but the thing is so real and undoubted a truth. You may do all things by the strength of Christ. Seek that, and you shall easily bear your trial. Let this public mercy to the Church of God make you to forget your private sorrow. The Lord be your strength; so prays,

> Your truly faithful and loving brother,
> OLIVER CROMWELL

July 5th 1644

(P.S.) My love to your daughter, and to my Cousin Percevall, Sister Desboure and all friends with you.[8]

(c) HENRY VAUGHAN (1621–1695), poet and mystic, whose whole being yearned after peace in God, here testifies to his mental suffering during the Civil War, including his grief at the death of friends:

From *An Elegy on the Death of Mr R. W. Slain in the late unfortunate differences at Routon Heath, near Chester, 1645.*

> I am confirm'd, and so much wing is given
> To my wild thoughts, that they dare strike at heav'n.
> A full year's grief I struggled with, and stood
> Still on my sandy hopes' uncertain good,
> So loth was I to yield; to all those fears
> I still oppos'd thee, and denied my tears.
> But thou art gone! and the untimely loss
> Like that one day hath made all others cross . . .
> The world scarce knew him yet, his early soul
> Had but new-broke her day, and rather stole
> A sight than gave one; as if subtly she
> Would learn our stock, but hid his treasury.
> His years—should Time lay both his wings and glass
> Unto his charge—could not be summ'd—alas!—
> To a full score; though in so short a span
> His riper thoughts had purchas'd more of man
> Than all those worthless livers, which yet quick
> Have quite outgone their own arithmetic.
> He seiz'd perfections, and without a dull
> And mossy grey possess'd a solid skull;
> No crooked knowledge neither, nor did he
> Wear the friend's name for ends and policy,
> And then lay't by; as those lost youths of th'stage

Who only flourish'd for the Play's short age
And then retir'd; like jewels, in each part
He wore his friends, but chiefly at his heart.
  Nor was it only in this he did excel,
His equal valour could as much, as well.
He knew no fear but of his God; yet durst
No injury, nor—as some have—e'er purs'd
The sweat and tears of others, yet would be
More forward in a royal gallantry
Than all those vast pretenders, which of late
Swell'd in the ruins of their king and State.
He weav'd not self-ends and the public good
Into one piece, nor with the people's blood
Fill'd his own veins; in all the doubtful way
Conscience and honour rul'd him. O that day
When like the fathers in the fire and cloud
I miss'd thy face! I might in ev'ry crowd
See arms like thine, and men advance, but none
So near to lightning mov'd, nor so fell on.
Have you observ'd how soon the nimble eye
Brings th'object to conceit, and doth so vie
Performance with the soul, that you would swear
The act and apprehension both lodg'd there;
Just so mov'd he: like shot his active hand
Drew blood, ere well the foe could understand
But here I lost him. Whether the last turn
Of thy few sands call'd on thy hasty urn,
Or some fierce rapid fate—hid from the eye—
Hath hurl'd thee pris'ner to some distant sky,
I cannot tell, but that I do believe
Thy courage such as scorn'd a base reprieve.
Whatever 'twas, whether that day thy breath
Suffer'd a civil or the common death,
Which I do most suspect, and that I have
Fail'd in the glories of so known a grave;
Though thy lov'd ashes miss me, and mine eyes
Had no acquaintance with thy exequies,
Nor at the last farewell, torn from thy sight
On the cold sheet have fix'd a sad delight,
Yet whate'er pious hand—instead of mine—
Hath done this office to that dust of thine,
And till thou rise again from thy low bed
Lent a cheap pillow to thy quiet head,

Though but a private turf, it can do more
To keep thy name and memory in store
Than all those lordly fools which lock their bones
In the dumb piles of chested brass, and stones.
Th'art rich in thy own fame, and needest not
These marble-frailties, nor the gilded blot
Of posthume honours; there is not one sand
Sleeps o'er thy grave, but can outbid that hand
And pencil too, so that of force we must
Confess their heaps show lesser than thy dust.
   And—blessed soul!—though this my sorrow can
Add nought to thy perfections, yet as man
Subject to envy, and the common fate,
It may redeem thee to a fairer date.
As some blind dial, when the day is done,
Can tell us at midnight there was a sun,
So these perhaps, though much beneath thy fame,
May keep some weak remembrance of thy name,
And to the faith of better times commend
Thy loyal upright life, and gallant end.[9]

7.5 The Distresses of the Soldiers
Literary Evidence

In his standard work on the subject, *Cromwell's Army*, C. H.
Firth points out that there was no systematic arrangement for
the collection or transportation of soldiers wounded in battle.
The badly wounded would be left to their own resources and
to the charity of sympathizers in villages near the battlefield.
The provision for the permanently disabled soldier and for
dead soldiers' widows and orphans was also inadequate. 'The
treasurers for maimed soldiers,' writes Firth, 'found themselves
besieged by claimants whom they were unable to help.'

At the Restoration what military hospitals and pensions
had been introduced under Cromwell were wound up altogether. Although Cromwell had attempted to ease the restrictions (relating to Parish Settlements and Apprenticeship
Laws) for ex-soldiers to earn their livings at civilian trades

anywhere in England a great many had no alternative but to beg their way home: 'In Red-coat rags attired I wander up and down' (Anon.).

(a) ANON. *Single Sheet, Dublin, 18 February 1647.* (Reprinted in J. Ashton, op. cit., p. 274.)

> The humble Petition of us the Parliaments poore Souldiers in the Army of Ireland, whereof many are starved already, and many dead for want of Chirurgions.

> That we the poor distressed Souldiery under the Parliaments Service in Ireland, having heretofore served the Parliament under the Lord Generall Essex, Valiant Massey, and noble Sir William Waller, and the rest, &c, did in all faithfulnesse, hardship and desperate service as ever any, hazzard our lives and fortunes, and did according to order obey and disband, then not so much as doubting of all our Arreares, and now have almost served you two years in all integrity and faithfulnesse both Winter and Summer, wet and dry, frost and Snow, having no other bedding than the bare ground for our beds, and the skies for their covering, and when dry in the day and night, no other signe to drink at but the Sun and Moone, and nothing but water, having no plenty, but cold backs, hungrie bellies, and puddle water, and when sore wounded, not a Surgeon to dresse us, or if a Surgeon, no chest, nor salve, nor oyntments; and for bread many times not a loafe of two pence under sixpence, and rotten Cheese sent, not fit for a dog, and for butter, it went from London to Dover, and mistook Dublin and went to Dunkirk, and for our new Cloathes all made of the French fashion, and being too little for any of us, were carried to France to cloath them, hardly hats to our heads but what our haire growes through, and neither hose or shooes, doublet or breeches, tearing our Snapsacks to patch a hole to hide our naked and starved flesh, and our swords naked for want to scabberds: Thus with our backs without cloaths and our bellies without food, and not a penny to buy anything, and the kernes having burnt all the corne and destroyed all fit for succour, we forced to march bare legged and bare footed, having neither fire nor food, we perish in misery, and our Commanders being in a manner in the same case, having nothing but good words to pay us with, shewing us often your Orders upon Orders for our pay, plentifully promising but not performing, and thus wee dropping downe dead

daily in our marching, and so feeble and so weak, being not able to fight or do any more service without some supply, but all like to starve and die in misery, when all meanes is anticipated, and the Tax of 60000l. wholly ingrossed by your Army from us, and your Souldiery quartered in Kings houses, and clad Gentile like, and fed in Freequarter to the full, and lie in good beds, and take their pleasure and ease in rest and peace.

We humbly desire our hungry bellies may once be filled, and our naked backs be cloathed, and our legs and feet be hosed and shooed, and our Surgeons once more fitted, and all recruited with food to supply us once more, that we may go out again to finish that work we have begun, and not to lie like Drones to eat up others meat, and we do not doubt, but with Gods blessing to give you a happy account of the Conquest of the whole Land, and shall ever pray for a happy Parliament.

(b) ANON. *The Maunding Soldier, or the Fruit of War is Beggary.*

> Good your worship, cast your eyes
> Upon a souldier's miseries;
> Let not my leane cheeks, I pray,
> Your bounty from a souldier stay,
>   But like a noble friend
>   Some silver lend,
> And Jove will pay you in the end.
>
> Twice through the bulke have I been shot,
> My braynes have boyled like a pot:
> I have at least these dozen times
> Been blowne up by those roguish mines.
>
> I pray your worship, **think** on me,
> That am what I do seeme to be,
> No rooking rascalle, nor no cheat,
> But a souldier every way compleat:
>   I have wounds to show
>   That prove it so;
> Then courteous good sir, ease my woe,
>   And I for you will pray,
>   Both night and day,
> That your substance never may decay.

(Roxburghe Ballads, iii, 111)

7.6 Contemporary Poets' Horror at the Phenomenon of War

The cruelty, waste and futility of competitions in killing—familiar poetic indictments from Euripides to Brecht—are all brought out in the seventeenth-century poems below:

ABRAHAM COWLEY, from *A Poem on the late Civil War.*

> . . . What *English* ground but still some Moisture bears,
> Of Young Mens Blood, and more of Mother Tears!
> What Airs unthickened with the Sighs of Wives,
> Tho' more of Maids for their dear Lovers Lives. . . .

> . . . What Fights did this sad Winter see each day,
> Her winds and Storms came not so thick as they! . . .

> . . . Why will you die fond men, why will you buy,
> At this fond rate, your Country's slavery?

ANON. *The Dominion of the Sword.*

A song made in the Rebellion

Lay by your pleading,
Law lies a-bleeding;
Burn all your studies down, and throw away your reading.

Small pow'r the word has,
And can afford us
Not half so much privilege as the sword does.

It softers your masters,
It plaisters disasters,
It makes the servants quickly greater than their masters.

It venters, it enters,
It seeks and it centers,
It makes a 'prentice free in spite of his indentures.

It talks of small things,
But it sets up all things;
This masters money, though money masters all things.

It is not season
To talk of reason
Nor call it loyalty, when the sword will have it treason.

It conquers the crown, too,
The grave and the gown, too;
First it sets up a Presbyter, and then it pulls him down too. . . .

No gospel can guide it,
No law can decide it,
In Church or State, till the sword has sanctified it. . . .

He that can tower,
Or he that is lower,
Would be judg'd a fool to put away his power.

Take books and rent 'um,
Who can invent 'um,
When that the sword replies, '*Negatur argumentum.*'

Your brave college-butlers,
Must stoop to the sutlers,
There's ne'er a library like to the cutler's.

The blood that was spilt, sir,
Hath gain'd all the gilt, sir,
Thus have you seen me run my sword up to the hilt, sir.

SHIRLEY, 'Death the Leveller', from *Ajax and Ulysses*, 1659.

The glories of our blood and state
　　Are shadows, not substantial things;
There is no armour against Fate;
　　Death lays his icy hand on kings:
　　　　Sceptre and Crown
　　　　Must tumble down,
And in the dust be equal made
With the poor crooked scythe and spade.

Some men with swords may reap the field,
　　And plant fresh laurels where they kill:
But their strong nerves at last must yield;
　　They tame but one another still:
　　　　Early or late
　　　　They stoop to fate,
And must give up their murmuring breath
When they, pale captives, creep to death.

The garlands wither on your brow;
   Then boast no more your mighty deeds!
Upon Death's purple altar now
   See where the victor-victim bleeds.
     Your heads must come
     To the cold tomb:
Only the actions of the just
Smell sweet and blossom in their dust.

8

OLD SCARS UNHEALED

The scars left by the terrible experiences of war were not to heal with the Restoration of Charles II. They were not intended to do so by those who executed the Clarendon Code. Shaftesbury saw the Corporation Act of 1661—with its wounding requirement on nonconformists to renounce the Covenant and to swear never to take up arms against the King—as the first step in what he called the 'State Master-Piece'[1] (8.1). Nonconformity was to be punished as the creed for rebels. Samuel Butler wrote a best-seller on that theme (8.3).

The Anglican revenge was to claim some distinguished victims. The suffering of Bunyan, Fox and Baxter is an imperishable chapter in the history of nonconformity, and we end this volume with the record of their persecution (8.7). Shaftesbury had his axe to grind, no doubt, but his picture of two nations at war with each other seems demonstrably true.

Only that is not what happened in 1688. And there are three objections to his thesis of the 'State Master-Piece'. *The first qualification is that persecution in Restoration England was a much more haphazard and inefficient process than his phrase implies.* The nonconformist Vincent Alsop could survive by varying the time of his services and by the fact that the authorities were unable to discover what was his proper Christian name and could not, therefore, legally proceed against him![2] This is not to minimize the sufferings of those who were caught. Moreover sufferings cannot always be measured by the heroics of recorded battles in the law court. Persecution could take pettier forms. For an obscure nonconformist like John Osmonton it is the dilemma of whether to give up his 4s 6d-a-week job for one with better prospects but with an employer who would link Sabbath observance with sedition (8.2). The reality was messier than Shaftesbury implies, but this does not necessarily mean that it was less painful for individuals.

The second qualification is that Shaftesbury was wrong to see the revival of persecution as the revival of Laudianism. Shaftesbury called the persecutors new Laudians; so did Zachary Crofton in 1661 when he wrote of 'the *Laudenses* of our Age'.[3] But there are several things wrong with the analysis. It implies a monolithic response from the Anglican leadership and the corollary that this response was the most important factor in the persecution: both dubious propositions.[4] It ignores the profound differences between the old leadership and the new. J. P. Kenyon got to the heart of it when he pointed out that Laud *coerced* while Sheldon *shut men out*.[5] And this, in turn, is part of a changed intellectual climate. Coercion was no longer intellectually respectable: its premises were being successfully challenged. Religious pluralism meant anarchy? There could only be *one* Church of England? Cromwell's rule gave the lie to both propositions. Religious toleration was bad for trade? The success story of the United Provinces seemed to argue the opposite, yet Goodman did try to argue that the *growth* of trade had been responsible for the recent troubles. He met with a volley of sarcasm from Alsop: 'Let men have liberty to be poor and pay their tithes . . . these creatures indeed will make fit materials for uniformity to work upon'. Samuel Parker also tried to smear trading combinations as 'so many nests of faction and sedition' but fared no better than Goodman. In reply to an attack from the Independent, John Owen, Parker beat a hasty retreat: he had not meant to attack trade but, since liberty of conscience unsettled government, it would unsettle trade too.

Coercion was still politically respectable, of course, but the change of climate is important. The Clarendon Code was persecution inspired by politics: the ideological case for intolerance was in retreat. It is against this changed background that Hobbes could now be seen as a dangerous champion of religious toleration: it is in these terms that Samuel Parker could attack him in 1670 (8.4).

We see Hobbes in a different light: as the champion of uniformity. Which view is correct? Hobbes wrote *Leviathan* on behalf of peace. He had indeed conceded, in a passage which has rarely been given proper attention, that toleration was best 'if it be without contention' (1.4). This has seemed a rather worthless concession, when set against the assumptions about the nature of Man that underlay *Leviathan* and the specific contemporary context of the ideological conflicts of the Civil War and the Thirty Years War. But Hobbes is not in the habit of making worthless concessions. The rest of the passage does not read like a *reductio ad absurdum*. Hobbes's double plea—that there ought to be no power over men's consciences but the Word, and that it was unreasonable to subordinate Man's individual reason to the 'most voices of many other men'—has an intellectual force not to be found in the famous and overrated argument for religious toleration from Locke (8.6). Hobbes's yardstick was utility, and utility—as Alsop and Owen had shown in their debates with Goodman and Parker—after the Restoration argued more for liberty of conscience than for its suppression. Hobbes had, it is true, denied 'conscience' as an excuse for resistance but in his logical way had equally denied it as an excuse for obedience. Parker, on the other hand, wanted to 'super-induce' the 'ties of conscience' upon those of secular interest (since this was now becoming a sticky wicket to defend). For Hobbes it was not a meaningless reservation to insist upon the Christian subject's rights against his sovereign in one respect: the silence of the law with regard to his thoughts and beliefs inasmuch as they were inward. Parker, not Hobbes, was the totalitarian. He wanted to extend the Prince's Power 'to the Hearts of their Subjects' and secure them 'as much from the very thoughts as Attempts of Treason'. Winston Smith must not merely give external assent: he must love Big Brother. Parker was in fact driven to the last cynical ground for intolerance: 'though Religion were a Cheat, they are apparently the greatest Enemies to Government, that tell the World it is so'. It is ironic that it is Hobbes, not his adversary, who has come down to us as the supreme cynic. Parker and Laud may both have preached and practised intolerance on behalf of the Anglican Church, but there the similarity ends. Shaftesbury blurs that distinction.

The third qualification is that Shaftesbury underrated the forces which held Anglican and nonconformist together: he could only see those which pulled them apart. He could be forgiven for doing so. We have shown in this volume a rich documentation for the view of 'two nations' in England. He was writing in 1675 as a committed Whig, just before the Popish Plot and Exclusion Crisis divided the nation. Civil

War was averted by a whisker. If he could not have anticipated a Whig *and* Tory Settlement—for that is what 1688 was
all about—he was in good company. James II had not anticipated it either. From 1685 to 1686 he had ruled with Tory
and Anglican concurrence without winning for his fellow
Catholics the repeal of the Test Acts and penal laws on which
he had set his heart. This led to James II's dramatic reversal
of alliances. This was his attempted 'bourgeois revolution' of
1687 to 1688 when he sought to win over the nonconformist
middle classes in the towns by a policy of religious toleration
and opposition to the landowning aristocracy and gentry. It
has been shown that the strategy might have succeeded, and
Alsop has been praised for the realism with which he welcomed the 1687 Declaration of Intelligence, which had 'at a
touch, irretrievably broken the web of Anglican authority
over the religious life of the nation'.[6] But Alsop was not
typical. His nonconformist colleagues responded to this
Declaration of Indulgence as they had to previous ones from
Charles II. They preferred persecution by Protestants to
toleration alongside Papists. The Anglicans were forced to
outbid James's initiative with promises of their own to their
new allies. These promises had to be honoured in 1689. The
limited freedom secured for nonconformists by the Toleration
Act of that date was the result, although it fell short, not only
of what John Locke had hoped for, but of what James II had
been prepared to give.

Why did the nonconformists reject James II? They could
have had no illusions about the men who had persecuted
Bunyan, Fox and Baxter. But Baxter himself had given the
nonconformist answer a year before James II had asked the
question. Baxter's reply, in the face of the bullying of Judge
Jeffreys (8.7), was not a retreat into Republicanism or resistance theorizing but a quiet reaffirmation in his prison cell
of the imperial faith in the civil magistrate which had sustained
him throughout his life (1.3). The year 1688 showed the sound-
ness of Barlow's argument; the Protestant consensus was no
myth (8.5). Anglicans and Presbyterians came together to
oppose a Christian Emperor who had destroyed the moral
basis of his rule by alliance with Rome. James II's imaginative
initiative in 1687 foundered on the rocks of Protestant imperialism. There *were* old scars that would not heal; 1688
demonstrated, however, they were not of the Civil War but of
the Reformation.

8.1 From The Corporation Act, 1661

The Corporation Act was the first major assault on nonconformity after the break-down of the Savoy Conference. It was passed in 1661 and excluded from the government or management of borough corporations those who would not take the Anglican sacrament and the oaths of allegiance and supremacy, and make the two solemn declarations reproduced in this extract. Crown commissioners administered the Act and had the power to remove officials from corporations without even tendering the oaths to them: we get a rare insight into their methods through the preliminary warning to the Rye Town Clerk from a friend as early as 21 July 1661 (8.2). William Prynne, however, in opposing it was as much concerned with its affront to the Lords ('it gives the numerous Commissioners named in the Bill, or any five of them (who are all Comoners) an absolute arbitrary power over the greatest Peers of the Realm') as with its punitive Anglicanism. When his opposition was defeated in the Commons he turned (as always) to the printed word; then wrote an anonymous pamphlet, *Summary Reasons, Humbly Tendered to the Most Honourable House of Peeres*, which the Commons adjudged to be seditious; and finally made a spectacularly, and quite atypically, abject recantation to the Commons of the wrong that he had done. No wonder that Lord Herbert described the curious episode to his wife as 'a conquest worthy to be bragged of, and therefore I cannot forbeare letting you know it'.[7]

. . . III And be it further enacted . . . that all persons who upon 24 December 1661, shall be mayors, aldermen, recorders, bailiffs, town clerks, common councilmen and other persons then bearing any office or offices of magistracy, or places or trusts or other employment relating to or concerning the government of the said respective cities, corporations and boroughs and cinque ports and their members, and other port towns, shall at any time before 25 March 1663, when they shall be thereunto required by the said respective commissioners or any three of them, take the Oaths of Allegiance and Supremacy and this oath following:

I, A.B., do declare and believe that it is not lawful upon any pretence whatsoever to take arms against the King, and that I do abhor the traitorous position of taking arms by his authority against his person or against those that are commissioned by him. So help me God.

And also at the same time shall publicly subscribe before the said commissioners or any three of them the following declaration:

I, A.B., do declare that I hold that there lies no obligation upon me or any other person from the oath commonly called the Solemn League and Covenant, and that the same was in itself an unlawful oath and imposed upon the subjects of this realm against the known laws and liberties of the kingdom. . . .

8.2 From *J. O. [John Osmonton]* to *Samuel Jeake*, 26 August 1670

In Samuel Jeake the Elder (1623–1690), Osmonton was assured of a sympathetic listener. Jeake was Town Clerk of Rye from 1651, but on being attacked by the Vicar of Rye for his nonconformity he was eventually obliged to retire from the town to London in the 1680s. The kind of needling persecution that nonconformists were subjected to is illustrated here in Osmonton's letter. But some years earlier Jeake himself had received a warning from a Henry Bromfield about an ominous conversation with some men who had been deputed to implement the Corporation Act: 'I did informe them of yor unspotted life and conversason and yor meekenesse of spirits even to yor enemies and that in my judgement a person so quallified as I tooke you to be could not bee an incendiary and promoter of rebellion but it was answered you might be the more earnest to carry on any designes.' [8]

. . . A factor in Cheapside his Brother being lately dead is unwiling to take a Prentice, but wiling to take a man, now I wold faine know in contradiction to my hesitateing struggling spirit whether this thing be of God, that I shold leave my small Imployment which brings in 4s 6d a week an may ebb away in winter, for this that seems so reasonablely to prosper it self, the man being but a modderate morall, and I suppose Episcopall man, which being no more in him, may in this time of persecution by fear of men or flattery by the wicked subtill generation, may be reduced in time to ther popish faction, to my great disadvantage, and befooling my self of a breathing life for a shaddow of further advantage for the future . . . though in other things, hee may prove civill, his words were these in Answer to my demand of fredome one Lords day without scruple, hee said many had liberty and by it, wrought sedishion and conspiracies against the powers, I tould him I humblely apprehended, that the faithfull ones, that had no such intentions in assembleings, were the greater tride by every ones sencur beside other hard sircomstances, that might awaite them. . . .

8.3 Samuel Butler, from *Hudibras* (London, 1663)

Samuel Butler (1613–1680) brought out the First Part of *Hudibras* in December 1662: in that same month Pepys wrote how 'all the world cries it up to be the example of wit'. This excerpt is from the Second Part, which appeared a year later (Canto II, lines 133–196): it is a good example of the anti-Puritan wit that won Pepys's admiration. The target is an easy one. Butler is hitting at the slipperiness of the Puritan saint: that antinomian refusal to be bound by past oaths, which has been sympathetically explained as the doctrine of 'progressive comprehension'.[9] Less sympathetically, contemporary critics, like Ireton at Putney, saw it as eroding the foundations of society.

> For breaking of an oath and lying
> Is but a kind of self-denying,
> A saint-like virtue, and from hence,
> Some have broke oaths by providence,
> Some to the glory of the Lord
> Perjured themselves and broke their word,
> And this the constant rule and practice
> Of all our late apostles' acts is.
> Was not the cause at first begun
> With perjury, and carried on?
> Was there an oath the godly took
> But, in due time and place, they broke?

Did we not bring our oaths in first
Before our plate, to have them burst
And cast in fitter models for
The present use of church and war?
Did not our worthies of the House,
Before they broke the peace, break vows?
And having freed us first from both
Th' Allegiance and Supremacy Oath,
Did they not next compel the nation
To take, and break, the Protestation?
To swear, and after to recant
The Solemn League and Covenant?
To take th' Engagement, and disclaim it,
Enforced by those who first did frame it?
Did they not swear at first to fight
For the King's safety and his right?
And after marched to find him out,
And charged him home with horse and foot?
And yet still had the confidence
To swear it was in his defence?
Did they not swear to live and die
With Essex, and straight laid him by?
If that were all, for some have swore
And false as they, if th'did no more.
Did they not swear to maintain law,
In which that swearing made a flaw?
For protestant religion vow
That did that voting disallow?
For privilege of parliament,
In which that swearing made a rent?
And since, of all the three, not one
Is left in being, 'tis well known.
Did they not swear, in express words,
To prop and back the House of Lords,
And after turned out the whole houseful
Of peers as dangerous and unuseful?
So Cromwell, with deep oaths and vows,
Swore all the Commons out o'th' House,
Vowed that the redcoats would disband
Ay, many would they, at their command!—
And trolled 'em on, and swore and swore,
Till th'army turned 'em out of door.
This tells us plainly what they thought:

That oaths and swearing go for nought,
And that by them th'were only meant
To serve for an expedient.
What was the public faith found out for,
But to slur men of what they fought for?
The public faith, which everyone
Is bound to'observe, yet kept by none.
And if that go for nothing, why
Should private faith have such a tie?

8.4 Samuel Parker, from *A Discourse of Ecclesiastical Politie* (London, 1670)

Samuel Parker (1640–1688), later to be made Bishop of Oxford by James II as a reward for his Erastianism, wrote this pamphlet in 1670 to uphold the power of the civil magistrate. Parker himself disliked the label, 'Erastian'. He once called Stillingfleet 'an old knave' for the Erastian views that he expressed, and later partly retracted, in his *Irenicum*. He deserved a colleague's rebuke: 'Mr. Chetwin replied to the Dr. if he be a Knave that writ so much for erastianism and hath retracted it, what a knave is he that hath writ more for it, as you have done Dr., and never retracted it.'[10] In the correct sense of the word—as a description of the philosophy of Erastus—Parker certainly was not an Erastian. In the popular, pejorative sense of the word, however, that is precisely what he was. The difference between a true Erastian and a time-server is clear in this fifth chapter of Parker's work, which is devoted to a refutation of Hobbes. Hobbes had been useful up to a point—and there is much cribbing from *Leviathan* in Parker's work—but his defence of the civil magistracy and intolerance had rested, not on Divine Right or prescription, but on *utility*. The argument for intolerance had a utilitarian force in the 1640s which had, however, been decisively sapped in the 1650s.

CHAP. V: A Confutation of the Consequences that some men draw from Mr. Hobs's Principles in behalf of Liberty of Conscience.

THE CONTENTS

How a belief of the Imposture of all Religions is become the most powerful and fashionable Argument for the Toleration of all. Though Religion were a Cheat, yet because the World cannot be govern'd without it, they are the most mischievous Enemies to Government that tell the World it is so. Religion is useful or dangerous in a State, as the temper of mind it breeds is peaceable or turbulent. The dread of Invisible Powers is not of itself sufficient to awe People into Subjection, but tends more probably to Tumults and Seditions. This largely proved by the ungovernableness of the Principles and Tempers of some Sects. Fanaticism is as natural to the Common People, as Folly and Ignorance; and yet is more mischievous to Government, than Vice and Debauchery. How the Fanaticks of all Nations and Religions agree in the same Principles of Sedition. To permit different Sects of Religion in a Commonwealth is only, to keep up so many incurable Pretenses and Occasions of Publick Disturbance. The corrupt Passions and Humours of Men make toleration infinitely unsafe. Toleration only cried up by opprest Parties, because it gives them Opportunity to overturn the Setled frame of Things. Every man that desires Indulgence is engaged by his Principles to endeavour Changes and Alterations. A bare Indulgence of men in any Religion, different from the establish'd way of Worship, does but exasperate them against the State.

1. And now the Reason why I have thus far pursued this Principle, is, because 'tis become the most powerful Patron of the Fanatick Interest; and a Belief of the Indifferency, or rather Imposture of all Religion, is now made the most Effectual (not to say most Fashionable) Argument for Liberty of Conscience. For when Men have once swallowed this Principle, That Mankind is free from all Obligations antecedent to the Laws of the Commonwealth, and that the Will of the Sovereign Power is the only measure of Good and Evil; they proceed sutably to their Principles, to believe, That no Religion can obtain the force of a Law, till 'tis establish'd for such by Supreme Authority; that the Holy Scriptures were not Laws to any man, till they were enjoyn'd by the Christian Magistrate; that no man is under any Obligation to assent to their Truth, unles the Governours of the Common-wealth require it; and that setting aside their Commands, 'tis no sin to believe our blessed Saviour a villanous and lewd Impostor; and that, if the Sovereign Power would

declare the *Alcoran* to be Canonical Scripture, it would be as much the Word of God as the four Gospels. *Leviath* p. 3, c. 33 for if Sovereigns in their own Dominions are the sole Legislators, then those Books only are Canonical, that is Law, in every Nation, which are establish'd for such by the Sovereign Authority. So that all Religions are in reality nothing but Cheats and Impostures, and at best but so many Tales of Imaginary and Invisible Powers Publickly allowed and encouraged to awe the Common People to Obedience. *Leviath* p. 1, c. 12. Who are betrayed into it by these four Follies, A false Opinion of Ghosts and immaterial Substances that neither are, nor ever can be; Ignorance of Second Causes; Devotion towards what men groundlesly fear; and mistaking things Casual for Divine Prognosticks. In brief, all Religion is nothing but a Cheat of Policy, and was at first invented by the Founders and Legislators of Common-wealths, and by them obtruded upon the credulous Rabble for the Ends of Government. And therefore, though Princes may wisely make use of Fables of Religion to serve their own turns upon the silly Multitude, yet 'tis below their Wisdom to be seriously concern'd themselves for such Fooleries; so that, provided their Subjects will befool themselves with any one Imposture, 'tis not material which they single out; in that all Religions equally oblige to the belief of Invisible Powers, which is all that is requisite to the Designs of Policy. And as long as a Prince can keep up any apprehension of Religion in the minds of his Subjects, 'tis no Policy to disoblige and exasperate any of them, by interesting his Power for one Party more than another, and by forcing all other Sects against their own Inclinations to conform their Belief to the Perswasions of one Faction; but rather to endear them all to himself, by Indulging them their Liberty in their different Follies: and so he may with more ease secure his Government by abusing all, and yet disobliging none.

2. In answer to this Objection, 'tis not material to my present Purpose largely to examine and refute these Wild and extravagant Pretenses, by asserting the Truth and Divine Authority of Religion, and giving a Rational Account of the Grounds and Principles on which it stands: only let me observe that this Discourse lies under no less Prejudice than this, that If any of the Principles of Religion be true, then is all these mens Policy false: but waving this too great advantage, I shall content myself only to discover of what noisome and per-

nicious consequences such Principles are to the Common-
wealth, though it were granted that all Religion were nothing
but Imposture. And this I shall do without reminding the
Reader how I have already prevented this Objection in the
first Part of the Discourse when I shew'd what good or bad
Influence upon the State mens Perswasions about Religion
have, by these four ensuing considerations.

First, Then me thinks his Majesty is bound to con these
men thanks for endeavouring to render the Truth of Religion
suspected, and to posses mens minds with apprehensions of
its being false whereby they effectually rob him of the best
security of his Crown, and strongest inducement of Obedience
to his Laws. There being for certain nothing so absolutely
necessary to the Reverence of Government, the Peace of
Societies, and common Interests of Mankind, as a sense of
Conscience and Religion: This is the strongest Bond of Laws,
and only support of Government; without it the most absolute
and unlimited Powers in the World must be for ever miserably
weak and precarious, and lie alwaies at the mercy of every
Subjects Passion and Private Interest. For when the Obligations of Conscience, and Religion are cashier'd, men can have
no higher Inducements to Loyalty and Obedience, than the
Considerations of their own Private interest and Security; and
then whenever these happen to fail, and Interest and Advantage invite to Disobedience, men may do as they please:
and when they have Power to shake off Authority, they have
Right too; and a prosperous Usurper shall have as fair a
Title to his Crown as the most lawful Prince; all Government
will be founded upon Force and Violence, and Kings nothing
but terrible men with long Swords. But when the Ties of
Conscience are super-induced upon those of Secular Interest,
this extends the Power of Princes to the Hearts of their
Subjects, and secures them as much from the very Thoughts
as Attempts of Treason. For nothing so strongly influences
the Minds of men, or so Authoritatively commands, their
Passions and Inclinations as Religion, forasmuch as no fears
are (not only to the considerate part of Mankind, but ruder
sort) so vehement as those of Hell nor hopes so active as those
of Heaven and therefore the Commands of Religion on being
back'd with such mighty Sanctions, they must needs have
infinitely more force to Awe or Allure the minds of men to a
compliance, than any Secular Interests. Whereas those men
that think themselves above the Follies of conscience, and

either believe or regard not the Evils threatned hereafter (an Attainment to which these our Modern Politicians do not blush to pretend though it be but an odd piece of Policy openly to own and proclaim it) must make their present Interest the Rule and measure of all their Actions; and can have no other Obligation to obey their Lawful Superiours, in what they command, than they have to disobey them, viz. their own Security and Self-preservation. Whereas if these men lived under the Restraint of Conscience, and the serious Apprehensions of Religion, and believed the Laws of their Prince to be bound upon them by the Laws of God, and that under the threatnings of Everlasting misery; their Loyalty would be tied up on them by all that men can either hope or fear, and they would have all the Engagements to Obedience that the serious reflections upon a Happy or Miserable Eternity could lay upon them. But if the Principles of Government have so Essential a dependence upon those of Religion, if nothing be powerful enough to secure Obedience but the hopes and fears of another Life, if all Humane Laws have their main force and efficacy from the Apprehensions of Religion, if Oaths, Promises, and Covenants, and whatever else whereby Civil Societies are upheld, are made firm by nothing but the Bonds of Religion: then let Authority judge, how much it is beholden to those men, who labour to bring it into Publick disreputation, and to possess their Subjects with an Opinion of its falshood: whereby they not only set them loose from their Authority, but enrage them against it, by persuading them they are governed by Cheats and Impostures, and that the Magistrate builds his Dominion upon their Folly and Simplicity, there being nothing more hateful to Mankind than to be imposed upon: So that though Religion were a Cheat, they are apparently the greatest Enemies to Government, that tell the World it is so.

8.5 Thomas Barlow, from *Popery* . . . (London, 1679)

Thomas Barlow (1607–1691) might be said to have acted out in his career the principles (or lack of them) which Samuel Parker

(8.4) had urged upon his readers. He was an Arminian in Laud's Oxford; a staunch Protestant when it fell to Fairfax; escaped ejection at the Restoration and indeed became Bishop of Lincoln in 1675; anti-popish at the time of the Popish Plot; one of the first to declare loyalty to James II and turned Whig at William III's accession. There have been more heroic lives. But *Popery* should not, for that reason, be dismissed as the ephemeral product of his anti-Popish period. It is true that it was a polemical work, written in 1679, to show that the Popish treachery revealed by Titus Oates was intelligible against the background of Popish anti-imperialism. But in making this debating point, and however slippery the man, Barlow gives us in 1679 one of the most powerful coherent statements of seventeenth-century Protestant imperialism. He shows the historic roots of the Royal Supremacy in England. He also shows the consistency of the Jesuit attempts to subvert it: the Gunpowder Plot, the Irish Massacre that began the Civil War, the Habernfeld Plot *against* Charles I and Laud[11] and the Jesuit part in the regicide. The 'Reverend and Learned Person', to whom Barlow was indebted for insights into the two latter plots, was William Prynne. Professor Abbott has indeed shown that Titus Oates's revelations of the 'Popish Plot' derived less from generalized anti-Papist sources than from two specific accounts: the contemporary narratives of the Gunpowder Plot and Prynne's account of the Habernfeld Plot. What the three have in common, apart from stock allegations of conspiracy against the life of the King and a projected change of government, are these details: (i) Catholic authorities were aware of, or directed, the Plot, (ii) a Catholic in the King's immediate entourage stood ready to kill him, (iii) a Catholic rising was to be followed by a Scots' rising and the aid of disaffected Englishmen, (iv) the Plot was betrayed by a penitent conspirator to a friend, who communicated it to the government, (v) Lord Arundel of Wardour had a part, through three generations of that name—and three variations of the Plot, (vi) there was a list of persons assigned to the leading parts. Prynne, moreover, first used the idea of drawing up information in separate articles, which was to be imitated in the accounts of Oates and Tonge.[12] Through Barlow we not only get to Titus Oates's sources but understand why he was believed.

FOR MY HONORED FRIEND. L. N. P.

SIR,

    I Received and read your Letter, and this comes to (bring my humble Service, and) tell you so. In your Letter you tell me, *First,* Of an Inhumane and Bloody Design and Popish Plot, a Traiterous and Roman-Catholick Conspiracy (as you call it)

against the Sacred Person and Life of our Gracious KING,
(whom GOD preserve) and many more (by them) design'd for
Ruine, and for the Subversion of the true Religion Establish'd by Law, and introducing Papal Tyranny, Superstition
and Idolatry. A Design not only Unchristian, but Inhumane
and Barbarous; beyond all example of Turkish or Pagan
Cruelty, nor has it (in any story) any parallel Impiety; unless perhaps that Bloody *French Massacre* or the *Gun-powder-
Treason*; all contriv'd and carry'd on, by Men of the same
desperate Principles and (though with the blood and ruine of
many thousand innocent persons) to advance the Papal
Interest. *Secondly*, You say, That the Popish Party decry
this Impious Conspiracy, as a State-Trial (without truth or
reality) to make Catholicks (as they commonly mis-call themselves) odious to the people, and this whole Nation. This I
believe (and know) they do. As their Plots and Conspiracies, so
their Impudence to deny or lessen them, (when discover'd) is
monstrous, and (were not their Persons and Principles known)
incredible. So they did, (where, and when they durst) and still
do call the *Gun-powder-Treason*, a State-Design, to make
them (though they were innocent) seem guilty, and Criminals.
Thirdly, Lastly, you say, that several Papists tell you, (in
excuse of Popery, and their Party) That if indeed there be
such a Plot and Conspiracy, (as is pretended) yet it is the
only fault of those persons concern'd in it, not of Popery, or
their Religion; the Principles and Doctrine of their Church,
giving no ground or incouragement to such impious and Anti-
Monarchical practices. This I believe too; because I find them
making the same Apology for themselves, to take off the guilt
of the *Gun-powder-Treason*. For (without all truth or modesty),
they tell us in Print; *That the Gun-powder-Treason was* MORE
THAN SUSPECTED, *to be the* CONTRIVANCE *of* Cecil, *the
great Politician*; TO RENDER CATHOLICKS ODIOUS: *and
that there were but* VERY FEW *of that Religion* (AND THOSE
DESPERADOES TOO) *detected of it, etc. All sober Catholicks
detesting that, and all such Conspiracies.*

Now these things premis'd you desire to know of me,
whether I think these their Allegations and Apologies true; or
if I think them untrue and insignificant (as you may be sure I
do) that I would give you some reasons why I do so. In
obedience therefore to your command, and to satisfie that
Obligation that lies up on me (so far, as I am able) to Vindicate Truth, and my Mother the Church of *England*; (though I

have little time, and few Books here (being absent from my own) save what I borrow of friends) I shall endeavour to say something, which may (I hope) be pertinent, towards the Conviction of our Adversaries, and your satisfaction. And here, I shall plainly set down,

I. The *Position* I undertake to make good.
II. The *Proofs* and *Reasons* of it.

I. The Position is this—The Doctrine and Principles of Popery, own'd by the Church of Rome (when believed and practised) are not only dangerous, but pernicious to Kings, (especially to those who are Protestants) prejudicial to the best rights of Monarchy, and inconsistent with that Loyalty, which by the Laws of Nature and Scripture is due to them; and particularly to our Kings, by the establish'd and known Laws of England, made antiently, even by Popish Kings and Parliament, against Papal Usurpations, and Anti-Monarchical Practices. And here (because it is impossible distinctly to shew, how Popish Principles are dangerous to our Kings, and prejudicial to their Just Rights, and Royal Prerogative; unless we first know, what that Prerogative, and those Rights are) I shall inquire,

1. What the Jura Coronae, the Rights and Prerogatives of the Imperial Crown of England are, as to our present concern.
2. How Popish Doctrines and Principles, may be dangerous or pernicious to them.

1. For the First; That England is a Monarchy, the Crown Imperial, and our Kings SUPREME Governors, and SOLE SUPREME Governors of this Realm, and all other their Dominions, will (I believe, I am sure it should) be granted; seeing our Authentick Laws and Statutes do so expresly, and so often say it. In our Oath of Supremacy we Swear, that the King is, the ONLY SUPREME Governor. SUPREME, so none (not the Pope) above Him: and ONLY SUPREME: so none co-ordinate, or equal to him. So that by our known Laws, our King is, Solo Deo minor, invested with such a Supremacy, as excludes both Pope and People (and all the World, God Almighty only excepted, by whom Kings Reign) from having any Power, Jurisdiction, or Authority over him. For this Soveraignty and Supremacy belonging to our Kings, and the Imperial Crown of England, is asserted,

not only by the Statutes of Q. Elizabeth, King James, and Charles the Second, (Protestant Princes) but even those Statutes made by Popish Princes and Parliaments, declare the same; I instance only in Richard the Second, Henry the Eighth, and Q. Mary, (though all the Statutes of Provisors, were pertinent to this purpose.) That Richard the Second and his Parliament were Roman-Catholicks, is manifest; and it is as certain, That Henry the Eighth and His Parliaments (when the Statutes cited were made) were so too. For 'tis evident, that those Statutes were made An. 24 and An. 25 Hen. 8 that is, An. Dom. 1532. and 1533. when neither He, nor His Adherents, were Excommunicated, but actual Members of the Roman Church then, and for some years after. For though Pope Paul the Third was angry about it, Anno 1535. yet he did not actually Excommunicate him or his Adherents, before the year 1538. which was six years after Henry the Eighth, and His Popish Parliament had Vindicated the Rights of the Imperial Crown of England, against the irrational and unjust Pretences and Usurpations of the Pope; and declared, that the Supremacy (both in Ecclesiastical and Civil things) ever did (de Jure) belong to the Imperial Crown of England, not to the Popes Mitre: He having no more to do in England (*Jure proprio*, or by any Law of God or Man) than Henry the Eighth in Italy. And that Parliament of Queen Mary, (cited in the Margent) although a Popish Parliament, yet declares fully for the Queen's Supremacy, (which, to some may seem strange:) for that Act expresly says, 1. That the IMPERIAL CROWN of this Realm, with all its Prerogatives, Jurisdictions, etc. was descended to the Queen. 2. That she was the SOVEREIGN and SUPREME Governor of all her Dominions, in AS FULL, LARGE and AMPLE MANNER, As ANY OF HER PROGENITORS, (therefore in as ample a manner as her Father Henry the Eighth.) 3. That by the MOST ANCIENT LAWS of this Realm the punishment of all OFFENDERS, against the Regality and Laws of this Realm, belong'd to the King, etc. So that even Popish Parliament acknowledges and declares, the Kings of England possess'd of such a Supremacy over all persons, and that by our MOST ANCIENT Laws, that He may punish ALL OFFENDERS (Clergy or Laity) against the Laws, and His Regality. (How contradictory to this, the Trent-Council and the Doctrine of the Roman Church is, you shall see anon.) But for the Supremacy of the Kings of England, (according to our Antient and Later

Laws, I refer you to the Learned in those Laws; who will give you a clear Declaration of this Supremacy, and just Vindication of it, from those impertinent (and seditious) Objections brought against it by some, who, inslaved to Rome, have cast off Loyalty to their King, and Love to their Country.

And Lastly, As for the Supremacy of Kings, (so far as it concerns the Laws of God, (Natural or Positive) and Divines to determine it) I refer you to the Answer of the University of Oxon, to a Letter of Henry the Eighth, requiring their Judgment in that Point: To the Articles of Edward the Sixth; Of Queen Elizabeth; The Articles of Ireland; The Injunctions of Elizabeth; The Canons of Jacobi; And the Canons (sub Carolo Martyre) 1640. (besides the Writings of many particular Learned Men:) In which you may see the Judgement of the Church of England, concerning Supremacy, and the Loyalty due to our King, clearly and fully express'd; and (in the late unhappy Rebellion) more truly profess'd and practic'd by Her Sons, than Papist, Presbyter, or Fanatique, (though some of them vainly brag of their Loyalty) can, with any just reason pretend to. If you desire further satisfaction and evidence, for the Supremacy of Kings, (particularly of our Kings, and the Roman Emperors) even in Ecclesiastical Matters; you know, and (at your leisure) may consult, the Collections of our Saxon, and the Imperial Laws; where you may have sufficient and abundant evidence, that (as to matter of Fact, never questioned in those days) those Emperors and Kings, made many Laws and Constitutions, in Ecclesiastical Matters, (which concern'd the Church) as well as Civil, (which concern'd the State.) And (if you desire it) I can shew you, an Original MS. (agreed upon, and approved by the Convocations of both Provinces, (Canterbury and York) and subscribed by both Archbishops, and several of each Province) wherein it is clearly shewn, (so far as Scripture, and other Records of those times mentions them) that Kings (from the beginning of the World, till our Blessed Saviours time) did, and *de Jure*, might exercise an Ecclesiastical, as well as Civil Jurisdiction and Supremacy; especially the Kings of the Jews, his own people; which Monarchy was of Gods own (and particularly Divine) Institution. These things premis'd, I come now to shew you, (in the second place) how dangerous, and (when, and where they have power to put them in execution) how pernicious Popish Principles are, to the Persons of Kings, and their just Rights and Prerogatives. . . .

... The Queen being dead, Popish Conspiracies did not die with her; the Pope and his Party continue as industrious and (as to their Designs and Plots) as impious as before. They saw and knew, that King James (a Protestant) was Legal Successor and Heir to the Crown of England, yet used all Roman Arts, to hinder his having possession of it; and to this end, Father Parsons (the Jesuite) writes a Book, to prove (what was evidently untrue and he could not chuse but know it) That King James had no just Title to the Crown of England; (though the whole Right of the Saxons and Normans, and of the Houses of York and Lancaster, were intirely and evidently united in him.) But when these Popish and Jesuitical Arts prevailed not, (having neither true Reason or Religion to further their Designs, which were impious and irrational) they contrive and resolve to execute such a Conspiracy, as (for barbarous and prodigious Villany) neither Heathens nor Hell had (till that time) ever put in execution. I mean the Gunpowder Treason, which was not any ordinary or before-known Wickedness; (as the Killing a King, or Poysoning a Prince, etc.) but a black and unparallell'd Villany, worthy Rome and a Jesuite; the Blowing up of a whole Parliament, King, Lords, and Commons, the Murdering of a Kingdom in its Representatives; and this in a moment, before they could see, or dream of any danger. But though this (for its impiety) was a prodigious Conspiracy, carried on with sworn secresie, and lay hid in the dark, and under ground; yet there is no Power or Policy against Providence, nor concealing any thing from the All-seeing Eye of our God; He saw, and graciously discover'd that horrid, Popish-Powder-Treason, to the Preservation of his People, the Confusion of their Adversaries, and (*nisi periisset pudor*) if they had any to the Eternal Shame of Papists, and (Popery) their Religion, which approves and encourages such abominable Impieties.

When King James slept with his Fathers, and was translated to a better Kingdom, out of the reach of such Popish Conspirators, and whither (without a serious and timely repentance of such inhumane Villanies) they can never come, their Designs slept not; they prosecute their Plots and Conspiracies, (to ruine our Church and establish'd Religion) as much in Charles the First's as in his Fathers time. And at last it came to this issue, that (other means failing) the King and the Archbishop of Canterbury must be made away. This was conceived the likeliest means to compass their Ends, and bring in that Religion they mis-call Catholick and Christian. For certainly such barbarous Murders and Assassinations may possibly promote Turcism, and the Errors of Mahomet, (and if you will, Popery) but never were (nor can be) any just means to propagate true Christianity. This Traiterous Conspiracy to Murder Charles the First, and the Archbishop, was discovered (by an Honourable Person) to the English Ambassador in Holland, and (by him) to the Archbishop, and by him, to the King. And the Original Copy of the Discovery, being found in the Archbishop's Library, after his death, was then publish'd, and is in Print, in many hands, and (amongst others) in mine. In the meantime, our unhappy Civil War began; and our Popish Conspirators, (animated by belief of such Rebellious Doctrines and Principles, as I have before mentioned, and incouraged and assisted by the Pope,) are first in Arms, and the bloody Rebellion; and (in Ireland) murdered above 100,000 Protestants in cold blood, without any provocation given but to kill Heretiques, (which according to their impious and erroneous Principles, was lawful and meritorious) and thereby promote the Catholick Cause. This is notoriously known to both Kingdoms (England and Ireland). And further, when in the process of that fatal Rebellion, (carried on openly by English, covertly by Popish Rebels) that good King was taken, imprison'd, with design to bring His Sacred Head to the Block, (for the distance is seldom great between a Princes Prison and His Grave) our Popish Conspirators had a Council of Priests and Jesuites, which sate in London, and signifi'd the condition of their Affairs here, to a Council of their Confederates at Paris; and they transmitted the Case to Rome, from whence Directions and Commands were returned (by the same way) back again to London. In short, it was determined, that it was for the interest of the Catholick Cause, that the King should die; and accordingly their Council of Priests and Jesuites in London Voted His Death. This is now Notoriously known to be true, and (in Print) publish'd to the World, by a Reverend and Learned Person, who (if any shall call him to an account for it) is so convinc'd of the truth of what he writ, that he (inscriptis) publickly offers, and promises to make it good. I do not hear that he has (as yet) been call'd to any account, to prove what he publickly, and in Print, has profess'd and professed to do: Nor do I think he will be call'd to any such account, because

I have reason to believe, that he can, and will produce such Proofs, as will evidently demonstrate both their bloody conspiracies, and the undeniable truth of what he affirm'd.

8.6 John Locke, from *A Letter Concerning Toleration* (London, 1689)

John Locke (1632–1704) published this famous letter to a Dutch friend, Limborch, in 1689, but religious toleration had occupied his mind for many years before that date. In 1660 he had written a treatise on the civil magistrate's powers which looked sceptically at extreme claims for 'general freedom' and did not want 'a liberty to be Christians so as not to be subjects'. Seven years later he had composed the draft of his unpublished *Essay Concerning Toleration*, with its explicit rejection of absolute monarchy. But 1667 and 1689 represent, in many ways, an illusory advance upon 1660, as this extract from the 1689 work shows. Locke still has a great caution about 'general freedom', and this limits his concept of religious toleration more drastically than is often realized. He has memorable thrusts at the mentality of the persecutor: 'Thou art not to punish him in this life because thou suppost that he will be miserable in that which is to come', but he would not extend toleration to atheists, because their promises and oaths do not bind; to Roman Catholics, because they are equivocators and obey a foreign prince (although Clarendon had been prepared to accept the Earl of Bristol's 'church/court' distinction among English Catholics); nor to antinomians—'but of these examples in a church are rare' (although the identification of dissent with its lunatic fringe was at the heart of the Clarendon Code). In 1644 Roger Williams had argued for toleration for Catholics against Cotton, and eight years later he had quoted Cromwell as saying 'that he had rather that Mahumetanism were permitted amongst us, than that one of God's children should be persecuted'. So, too, had said Jeremy Taylor in 1646, 'There's less malice and iniquity in sparing the guilty than in condemning the good', and he had a loop-hole, lacking in Locke's scheme, for distinguishing the *lives* of Catholics from their *doctrines*. It has been shown that the critical assault on the doctrine of eternal hell did not come from prudent thinkers like

Locke but from crazy chiliasts like Lead and the Petersens.[13]
Ragnhild Hatton has pointed out that the differences between
Hobbes and Locke were over-emphasized in their day as part of
the propagandist identification of absolute monarchy with arbitrary government, although Hobbes was not so 'absolutist' as his
critics asserted, and Locke's tyrannicide looked back, to a
vindication of the regicide, rather than forward to the Glorious
Revolution.[14]

. . . But to come to particulars. I say, first, no opinions contrary to human society, or to those moral rules which are
necessary to the preservation of civil society, are to be
tolerated by the magistrate. But of those, indeed, examples in
any church are rare. For no sect can easily arrive to such a
degree of madness as that it should think fit to teach, for
doctrines of religion, such things as manifestly undermine the
foundations of society, and are, therefore, condemned by the
judgment of all mankind; because their own interest, peace,
reputation, everything would be thereby endangered.

Another more secret evil, but more dangerous to the commonwealth, is when men arrogate to themselves, and to those
of their own sect, some peculiar prerogative covered over with
a specious show of deceitful words, but in effect opposite to the
civil right of the community. For example: we cannot find any
sect that teaches, expressly and openly, that men are not
obliged to keep their promise; that princes may be dethroned
by those that differ from them in religion; or that the dominion of all things belongs only to themselves. For these
things, proposed thus nakedly and plainly, would soon draw
on them the eye and hand of the magistrate, and awaken all
the care of the commonwealth to a watchfulness against
the spreading of so dangerous an evil. But, nevertheless, we
find those that say the same things in other words. What else
do they mean, who teach that faith is not to be kept with
heretics? Their meaning, forsooth, is that the privilege of
breaking faith belongs unto themselves; for they declare all
that are not of their communion to be heretics, or at least may
declare all that are whensoever they think fit. What can be
the meaning of their asserting that kings excommunicated
forfeit their crowns and kingdoms? It is evident that they
thereby arrogate unto themselves the power of deposing
kings, because they challenge the power of excommunication,
as the peculiar right of their hierarchy. That dominion is
founded in grace is also an assertion by which those that main-

tain it do plainly lay claim to the possession of all things. For they are not so wanting to themselves as not to believe, or at least as not to profess themselves to be the truly pious and faithful. These therefore, and the like, who attribute unto the faithful, religious, and orthodox, that is, in plain terms, unto themselves, any peculiar privilege or power above other mortals, in civil concernments, or who upon pretence of religion do challenge any manner of authority over such as are not associated with them in their ecclesiastical communion, I say these have no right to be tolerated by the magistrate; as neither those that will not own and teach the duty of tolerating all men in matters of mere religion. For what do all these and the like doctrines signify, but that they may, and are ready upon any occasion to seize the government, and possess themselves of the estates and fortunes of their fellow-subjects; and that they only ask leave to be tolerated by the magistrate so long until they find themselves strong enough to effect it?

Again: That church can have no right to be tolerated by the magistrate which is constituted upon such a bottom that all those who enter into it do thereby *ipso facto* deliver themselves up to the protection and service of another prince. For by this means the magistrate would give way to the settling of a foreign jurisdiction in his own country, and suffer his own people to be listed, as it were, for soldiers against his own government. Nor does the frivolous and fallacious distinction between the court and the church afford any remedy to this inconvenience; especially when both the one and the other are equally subject to the absolute authority of the same person, who has not only power to persuade the members of his church to whatsoever he lists, either as purely religious, or in order thereunto, but can also enjoin it them on pain of eternal fire. It is ridiculous for any one to profess himself to be a Mahometan only in his religion, but in everything else a faithful subject to a Christian magistrate, whilst at the same time he acknowledges himself bound to yield blind obedience to the Mufti of Constantinople, who himself is entirely obedient to the Ottoman Emperor, and frames the feigned oracles of that religion according to his pleasure. But this Mahometan living amongst Christians would yet more apparently renounce their government if he acknowledge the same person to be head of his church who is the supreme magistrate in the state.

Lastly, those are not at all to be tolerated who deny the being of a God. Promises, covenants, and oaths, which are the bonds of human society, can have no hold upon an atheist. The taking away of God, even though but in thought, dissolves all; besides also, those that by their atheism undermine and destroy all religion, can have no pretence of religion whereupon to challenge the privilege of a toleration. As for other practical opinions, though not absolutely free from all error, if they do not tend to establish domination over others, or civil impunity to the church in which they are taught, there can be no reason why they should not be tolerated. . . .

8.7 Contemporary Responses to Persecution

Promptly following on the heels of the Restoration, the Anglican Establishment—and a militantly anti-Puritan younger generation of Cavaliers—was back in power, literally with a vengeance. As the ballad below makes clear, the new see-saw of power led to a menacing intimidation of 'the godly' as suspect disloyal elements in the state:

ANON: from *The Courtiers' Health, or The Merry Boyes of the Times.*

> Come, boyes, fill us a bumper,
>   we'l make the nation roare;
> She's grown sick of a Rumper
>   that sticks on the old score.
> Pox on Phanatticks, rout 'um,
>   they thirst for our blood;
> We'll taxes raise without 'um,
>   and drink for the nation's good . . .
>
> I hate those strange Dissenters,
>   that strive to bawk a glass;
> He that, at all adventures,
>   will see what comes to pass:

And let the Popish faction
   disturb us if they can;
They ne'r shall breed distraction
   in a true-hearted man . . .

Let the Phanaticks grumble
   to see things cross their grain,
We'll make them now more humble
   or ease them of their pain:
They shall drink Sack amain, too,
   or else they shall be choak't;
We'l tell 'um 'tis in vain too,
   for us to be provok't; . . .

Quakers and Annabaptists,
   we'l sink them in a glass;
He deals most plain and flattest
   that sayes he loves a lass.
Then tumble down Canary,
   and let your brains go round;
For he that won't be merry,
   he can't at heart be sound.

Chorus: *Fill the pottles and gallons,*
                and bring the hogs head in;
                We'l begin with a tallen,
                A brimmer to the King.

For their part, all who could not in conscience conform themselves to the new compulsory uniformity of Anglican religious observance were hardened in their position by a sense of complete alienation from the moral laxity of Charles II's Court as is illustrated in Milton's *Of True Religion, Heresy, Schism and Toleration*:

It is a general complaint, that this nation of late years is grown more numerously and excessively vicious than heretofore; pride, luxury, drunkenness, whoredom, cursing, swearing, bold and open atheism everywhere abounding.

It was the old bitter divide of the 1630s once more, only this time the disaffected could not march to battle, they could only retreat into an 'inner emigration' of the spirit. Take, for instance, John Bunyan, in the Preface to the reader, before *The Life and Death of Mr. Badman* (1680):

That which has made me publish this book is, For that wickedness, like a flood, is like to drown our English world. It begins already to be above the tops of the mountains; it has almost swallowed up all, our youth, middle age, old age, and all, are almost carried away of this flood. O debauchery, what hast thou done in England! Thou hast corrupted our young men, and hast made our old men beasts; thou hast deflowered our virgins, and hast made matrons bawds. . . . O! that I could mourne for England, for the sins that are committed therein, even while I see that, without repentance, the men of God's wrath are about to deal with us, each having his 'slaughtering weapon in his hand' (Ezek. ix. 1, 2). Well, I have written, and by God's assistance shall pray that this flood may abate in England; and could I but see the tops of the mountains above it, I should think that these waters were abating. . . .

But O that I might not only deliver myself! O that many should hear, and turn at this my cry from sin! that they may be secured from the death and judgment that attend it.

The following section takes in mainly chronological order examples of ideological persecution, ranging from harassment to imprisonment and execution between 1660 and 1685. Following the exemplary punishment of the regicides, the period of Charles II's reign witnessed the last great wave of religious persecution in England. It should be noted, however, that whereas the *political* trials of the regicides were clearly willed by the monarch, the religious persecution was the work of the Anglican Establishment and not greatly favoured by that rather less than committed Anglican, Charles II.

(a) Revenge on the Regicides, From SAMUEL PEPYS, *Diary*

Samuel Pepys (1633–1703), whose graphic diary entries on the political executions of 1660–1662 follow, exhibits a confused response. He *wants* to 'sup full of horrors' and get a good view of the bloody proceedings, but he is also shocked; the fidelity of the regicides to their principles disturbs him, he is moved to admiration and pity, and he quickly needs to forget the whole terrible business by concentrating on his Navy affairs, eating a fine dish of oysters or refurnishing his house.

October 13th 1660
To my Lord's in the morning, where I met with Captain

Cuttance, but my Lord not being up I went out to Charing Cross, to see Major-general Harrison hanged, drawn, and quartered; which was done there, he looking as cheerful as any man could do in that condition. He was presently cut down, and his head and heart shown to the people, at which there was great shouts of joy. It is said, that he said that he was sure to come shortly at the right hand of Christ to judge them that now had judged him; and that his wife do expect his coming again. Thus it was my chance to see the King beheaded at White Hall, and to see the first blood shed in revenge for the blood of the King at Charing Cross. From thence to my Lord's, and took Captain Cuttance and Mr. Sheply to the Sun Tavern, and did give them some oysters. After that I went by water home, where I was angry with my wife for her things lying about, and in my passion kicked the little fine basket, which I bought her in Holland, and broke it, which troubled me after I had done it. Within all the afternoon setting up shelves in my study. At night to bed.

October 15th 1660

This morning Mr. Carew was hanged and quartered at Charing Cross, but his quarters, by a great favour, are not to be hanged up.

October 18th 1660

This morning, it being expected that Colonel Hacker and Axtell should die, I went to Newgate, but found they were reprieved till to-morrow.

October 19th 1660

Office in the morning. This morning my dining-room was finished with green serge hanging and gilt leather, which is very handsome. This morning Hacker and Axtell were hanged and quartered, as the rest are.

October 20th 1660

This afternoon, going through London, and calling at Crowe's the upholster's, in Saint Bartholomew's, I saw the limbs of some of our new traitors set upon Aldersgate, which was a sad sight to see; and a bloody week this and the last have been, there being ten hanged, drawn, and quartered.

March 12th 1662

This morning we have news from Mr. Coventry that Sir G.

Downing (like a perfidious rogue, though the action is good and of service to the King, yet he cannot with any good conscience do it) hath taken Okey, Corbet, and Barkestead at Delfe in Holland and sent them home in the *Blackmore*. Sir Wm. Pen, talking to me this afternoon of what a strange thing it is for Downing to do this—he told me of a speech he made to the Lords States of Holland, telling them to their faces that he observed that he was not received with the respect and observance now, that he was when he came from that Traitor and Rebell, Cromwell—by whom I am sure he hath got all he hath in the world—and they know it too.

April 19th 1662

This morning before we sat, I went to Allgate; and at the Corner Shop, a drapers, I stood and did see Barkestead, Okey, and Corbet drawne toward the gallows at Tiburne; and there they were hanged and Quarterd. They all looked very cheerfully. But I hear they all die defending what they did to the King to be just—which is very strange. So to the office. And then home to dinner.

June 14th 1662

Up by 4 a-clock in the morning and upon business at my office. Then we sat down to business; and about 11 a-clock, having a room got ready for us, we all went out to the Tower hill; and there, over against the Scaffold made on purpose this day, saw Sir Henry Vane bought. A very great press of people. He made a long speech, many times interrupted by the Sheriffe and others there; and they would have taken his paper out of his hand, but he would not let it go. But they caused all the books of those that writ after him to be given the Sheriffe; and the Trumpets were brought under the scaffold, that he might not be heard.

Then he prayed, and so fitted himself and received the blow. But the Scaffold was so crowded that we could not see it done. But Boreman, who had been upon the Scaffold, came to us and told us that first he begun to speak of the irregular proceeding against him; that he was, against Magna Charta, denied to have his exceptions against the Endictment allowed. And that there he was stopped by the Sheriffe. Then he drew out his paper of Notes and begun to tell them; first, his life, that he was born a Gentleman, that he was bred up and had the Qualitys of a Gentleman, and to make him in the opinion of the world more a Gentleman, he had been, till he was seventeen year old, a Goodfellow. But then it pleased God to pay a foundacion of grace in his heart, by which he was persuaded against his worldly interest to leave all preferment and go abroad, where he might serve God with more freedom. Then he was called home and made a member of the Long parliament; where he never did, to this day, anything against his conscience, but all for the glory of God. Here he would have given them an account of the proceedings of the Long parliament, but they so often interrupted him, that at last he was forced to give over; and so fell into prayer for England in Generall, then for the churches in England, and then for the City of London. And so fitted himself for the block and received the blow. He had a blister or Issue upon his neck which he desired them not to hurt. He changed not his colour or speech to the last, but died justifying himself and the cause he had stood for; and spoke very confidently of his being presently at the right hand of Christ. And in all things appeared the most resolved man that ever died in that manner, and showed more of heate then cowardize, but yet with all humility and gravity. One asked him why he did not pray for the King: he answered, 'Nay', says he, 'you shall see I can pray for the King: I pray, God bless him.'

The King had given his body to his friends; and therefore he told them that he hoped they would be civil to his body when dead; and desired they would let him die like a gentleman and a christian, and not crowded and pressed as he was.

June 22nd 1662

Coming home tonight, I met with Will Swan, who doth talk as high for the fanatiques as ever he did in his life; and doth pity my Lord Sandwich and me that we should be given up to the wickedness of the world, and that a fall is coming upon us all. For he finds that he and his company are the true spirit of the nation, and the greater part of the nation, too—who will have liberty of conscience in spite of this act of uniformity, or they will die; and if they may not preach abroad, they will preach in their own houses. He told me that certainly Sir H. Vane must be gone to Heaven, for he died as much a martyr and saint as ever any man died. And that the King hath lost more by that man's death then he will get again a good while. At all which, I know not what to think; but I confess I do think that the Bishops will never be able to carry it so high as they do.

(b) THEN HEY HO HUGH PETERS.

This ballad is a nauseous counterpart to the ballad jeering delightedly at the fall of Archbishop Laud, twenty years earlier (see above, 2.6).

Englands Object:

Or, Good and true Newes to all True-hearted Subjects, for the taking and apprehending of that horrid deluding Sower of Sedition Hugh Peters, by the name of Thomson, in South-warke, Saturday September the first. With his Examination and Entertainment by the rest of the Rebellious crew now in the Tower of London.

> Come let us tryumph and be jolly
>   brave Cavaleers every one,
> For I have more News to tell yee,
>   then any Diurnall can:
> Hugh Peters he is taken,
>   of a truth I tell to you,
> The Rump is not forsaken,
>   to them hee'l preach anew.
> Then hey ho, Hugh Peters,
>   cannot you find a Text,
> To please your fellow Brethren,
>   they are so highly vext.
>
> This is the man was wanting
>   above this three months space,
> And all the Rump lamenting
>   they could not see his face,
> For he was deeply learned,
>   all which they very well knew,
> But since he is returned
>   now Gallows claim thy due.
> Then hey ho Hugh Peters
>   cannot you quote a Text
> To please your holy Sisters
>   they are so highly vext.

Now having so much leisure,
 to tell what came to passe,
Concerning of his ceasure
 and how he taken was.
In Southwarke side he lodg'd,
 some-times in Kentish Town:
From place to place he doged,
 till publikely he was known.
They hey ho Hugh Peters
 how like you now the Text
Methinks the Tower Quarters
 have made you soundly vext.

He strangely turned his name,
 and Thomson he was cal'd,
Or like a Country-man
 in debts had bin inthral'd
He kept himselfe so close,
 by crafty cunning charms,
Till apprehended was
 by a Serjeant high at Armes.
Then hey ho Hugh Peters
 your wits did you deceive
To change your Surry quarters
 and come with us to liue.

Come Peters I must tell you
 your crafts beguild you now,
Sad fortune have befell you,
 and all your joviall crew.
The Rump hath got a sliding,
 Hugh Peters got a fall,
And Haslerig is chiding,
 like the Divel amongst them all.
Then hey ho Hugh Peters,
 can't you quote out a Text
To learn Sir Arthur patience
 that is so highly vext.

When to the Tower he came
 as brethren us'd to do:
There met him Henry Vain,
 both Scot and Mildmay too:

Then he to preach a Sermon,
  the Spirit did him call,
Drew forth an old Diurnal
  and preach'd before them all:
Then hey ho Hugh Peters
  they lik'd your Doctrine well.
Which gave them such direction
  how they should go to hell.

The next that came was a Rumper,
  and cal'd great Haselrig,
Ile warrant ye he was a thumper
  to dance a Parliament jigg:
He joyed to see his Chaplain,
  and did congratulate
But never was such tatling,
  concerning Church and State
As was between these creatures
  I must tell to you
Sir Arthur and Hugh Peters
  the Gallows claim his due.

Luke Robinson came after
  the Parson for to view,
And asked if Sir Arthur
  had heard his Sermon new,
Who said that he had quoted
  a noble Rumping Text,
For which he should be Voted
  at Tyburn to preach next.
Then hey ho Hugh Peters
  my heart shall never rue
In such a worthy pention
  Esquire Dun shall pay thy due.

The Tower is strongly made
  and Peters he is within
I'm sure he had a hand
  in mattering of our King.
Now all will be disclosed
  and brought to publick view.
If that he be opposed
  then Gallows claim thy due.

Then hey ho Hugh Peters
   you are fast within our locks,
Therefore declare the persons
   disguised in white Frocks.

These that had on long Vizards
   did on the Scaffold stand
Like base presumptuous Wizards
   plac'd by the Divels hand.
So expert and so even
   was one 'tis thought 'twas you
The blow was fatal given
   come Peters tell me true.
Examine all your fellows
   prove it perfectlie
Or else on Tyburn Gallows
   your neck shall hanged be.

(c) LUCY HUTCHINSON, from *Memoirs of the Life of Colonel Hutchinson.*

The following passage reveals how Hutchinson suffered inwardly at his own reprieve and reports how the Attorney-General subpoenaed him to appear at the trial of his fellow regicides. It vividly evokes his sickened loathing of the whole proceedings and determination to testify *against* the court and *for* the cause if called upon to speak.

When the colonel saw how the other poor gentlemen were trepanned that were brought in by proclamation, and how the whole cause itself, from the beginning to the ending, was betrayed and condemned, notwithstanding that he himself, by a wonderfully overruling providence of God, in that day was preserved; yet he looked upon himself as judged in their judgment, and executed in their execution; and although he was most thankful to God, yet he was not very well satisfied in himself for accepting the deliverance. His wife, who thought she had never deserved so well of him, as in the endeavours and labours she exercised to bring him off, never displeased him more in her life, and had much ado to persuade him to be contented with his deliverance; which as it was eminently wrought by God, he acknowledged it with thankfulness. But while he saw others suffer, he suffered with them in his mind, and, had not his wife persuaded him, he had offered himself a voluntary sacrifice; but being by her convinced that God's eminent appearance seemed to have singled him out for preservation, he with thanks acquiesced in that thing; and further remembering that he was but young at the time when he entered into this engagement, and that many who had preached and led the people into it, and many of that parliament who had declared it to be treason not to advance and promote that cause, were all now apostatised, and as much preached against it, and called it rebellion and murder, and sat on the tribunal to judge it; he again reflected seriously upon all that was past, and begged humbly of God to enlighten him and show him his sin if ignorance or misunderstanding had led him into error. But the more he examined the cause from the first, the more he became confirmed in it, and from that time set himself to a more diligent study of the scriptures, whereby he attained confirmation in many principles he had before, and daily greater enlightenings concerning the free grace and love of God in Jesus Christ, and the spiritual worship under the gospel, and the gospel liberty, which ought not to be subjected to the wills and ordinances of men in the service of God. This made him rejoice in all he had done in the Lord's cause, and he would often say, the Lord had not thus eminently preserved him for nothing, but that he was yet kept for some eminent service or suffering in this cause; although having been freely pardoned by the present powers, he resolved not to do anything against the King, but thought himself obliged to sit still and wish his prosperity in all things that were not destructive to the interest of Christ and his members on earth; yet as he could not wish well to any ill way, so he believed that God had set him aside, and that therefore he ought to mourn in silence and retiredness, while he lay under this obligation.

He had not been long at home before a pursuivant from the council was sent to fetch him from his house at Owthorpe, who carried him to the attorney-general. He, with all preparatory insinuations, how much he would express his gratitude to the king and his repentance for his error, if he would now deal ingenuously, in bearing testimony to what he should be examined, sifted him very thoroughly; but the colonel, who was piqued at heart that they should thus use him, to reserve him with an imagination that he would serve their turns in witnessing to the destruction of the rest, composed himself as well as he could, and resolved upon another testimony than

they expected, if they had really called him to any. But the
attorney-general was so ill-satisfied with his private examination that he would not venture a public one. He dealt with
him with all the art and flatteries that could be, to make him
but appear, in the least thing, to have deserted his own and
embraced the king's party; and he brought the warrant of
execution to the colonel, and would fain have persuaded him
to own some of the hands, and to have imparted some circumstances of the sealing, because himself was present. But
the colonel answered him, that in a business transacted so
many years ago, wherein life was concerned, he durst not
bear a testimony, having at that time been so little an observer, that he could not remember the least tittle of that
most eminent circumstance, of Cromwell's forcing Colonel
Ingoldsby to set his unwilling hand, which, if his life had
depended on that circumstance, he could not have affirmed.
'And then, Sir,' said he, 'if I have lost so great a thing as that,
it cannot be expected less eminent passages remain with me.'
Then being shown the gentlemen's hands, he told him he was
not well acquainted with them, as having had commerce with
but few of them by letters; and those he could own, he could
only say they resembled the writings which he was acquainted
with; among these he only picked out Cromwell's, Ireton's,
and my Lord Grey's. The attorney-general, very ill-satisfied
with his private examination, dismissed him; yet was he
served with a writ to appear in the court the next day. The
colonel had been told that, when they were in distress for
witnesses to make up their formality, Colonel Ingoldsby had
put them upon sending for him, which made him give that
instance to the attorney. The next day the court sat, and the
colonel was fetched in and made to pass before the prisoners'
faces, but examined in nothing; which he much waited for,
for the sight of the prisoners, with whom he believed himself
to stand at the bar; and the sight of their judges, among
whom was that *vile traitor* who had sold the men that trusted
him; and he that openly said he abhorred the word *accommodation*, when moderate men would have prevented the war;
and the colonel's own *dear friend*, who had wished damnation
to his soul if he ever suffered penny of any man's estate, or
hair of any man's head, to be touched;—the sight of these
had so provoked his spirit that, if he had been called to speak,
he was resolved to have borne testimony to the cause and
against the court; but they asking him nothing, he went to

his lodging, and so out of town; and would not come any more into their court, but sent the attorney-general word he could witness nothing, and was sick with being kept in the crowd and in the press, and therefore desired to be excused from coming any more thither. . . .

(d) The Experience of Religious Persecution: from JOHN BUNYAN, *Grace Abounding to the Chief of Sinners.*

John Bunyan suffered intermittent imprisonment over a period of twelve years for persisting in unlicensed preaching to his Baptist congregation:

Here is the Sum of my Examination before Justice Keelin, Justice Chester, Justice Blundale, Justice Beecher, and Justice Snagg, etc.

After I had lain in prison above seven weeks, the quarter-sessions was to be kept in Bedford, for the county thereof, unto which I was to be brought; and when my jailer had set me before those justices, there was a bill of indictment preferred against me. The extent thereof was as followeth: 'That John Bunyan, of the town of Bedford, labourer, being a person of such and such conditions, he hath, since such a time, devilishly and perniciously abstained from coming to church to hear Divine service, and is a common upholder of several unlawful meetings and conventicles, to the great disturbance and distraction of the good subjects of this kingdom, contrary to the laws of our sovereign lord the King,' etc.

The Clerk. When this was read, the clerk of the sessions said unto me, What say you to this?

Bun. I said, that as to the first part of it, I was a common frequenter of the church of God. And was also, by grace, a member with the people over whom Christ is the Head.

Keelin. But, saith Justice Keelin, who was the judge in that court? Do you come to church, you know what I mean; to the parish church, to hear Divine service?

Bun. I answered, No, I did not.

Keel. He asked me why?

Bun. I said, Because I did not find it commanded in the Word of God.

Keel. He said, We were commanded to pray.

Bun. I said, But not by the Common Prayer Book.

Keel. He said, How then?

Bun. I said, With the Spirit. As the apostle saith, 'I will pray with the Spirit with understanding' (I Cor. xiv. 15). . . .

Keel. But, says Justice Keelin, what have you against the Common Prayer Book?

Bun. I said, Sir, if you will hear me, I shall lay down my reasons against it.

Keel. He said, I should have liberty; but first, said he, let me give you one caution; take heed of speaking irreverently of the Common Prayer Book; for if you do so, you will bring great damage upon yourself.

Bun. So I proceeded, and said, My first reason was, because it was not commanded in the Word of God, and therefore I could not use it.

Another. One of them said, Where do you find it commanded in the Scripture, that you should go to Elstow, or Bedford, and yet it is lawful to go to either of them, is it not?

Bun. I said, To go to Elstow, or Bedford, was a civil thing, and not material, though not commanded, and yet God's Word allowed me to go about my calling, and therefore if it lay there, then to go thither, etc. But to pray was a great part of the Divine worship of God, and therefore it ought to be done according to the rule of God's Word.

Another. One of them said, He will do harm; let him speak no further.

Keel. Justice Keelin said, No, no, never fear him, we are better established than so; he can do no harm; we know the Common Prayer Book hath been ever since the apostles' time, and is lawful for it to be used in the church.

Bun. I said, Show me the place in the epistles where the Common Prayer Book is written, or one text of Scripture that commands me to read it, and I will use it. But yet, notwithstanding, said I, they that have a mind to use it, they have their liberty; that is, I would not keep them from it; but for our parts, we can pray to God without it. Blessed be his name.

With that, one of them said, Who is your God? Beelzebub? Moreover, they often said that I was possessed with the spirit of delusion, and of the devil. All which sayings I passed over; the Lord forgive them! And further, I said, Blessed be the Lord for it, we are encouraged to meet together, and to pray, and exhort one another; for we have had the comfortable presence of God among us. For ever blessed be his holy name!

Keel. Justice Keelin called this pedlar's French, saying, that I must leave off my canting. The Lord open his eyes!

Bun. I said, that we ought to 'exhort one another daily, while it is called to-day,' etc. (Heb. iii. 13).

Keel. Justice Keelin said, that I ought not to preach; and asked me where I had my authority? With other suchlike words.

Bun. I said, that I would prove that it was lawful for me, and such as I am, to preach the Word of God.

Keel. He said unto me, By what scripture?

I said, By that in the first epistle of Peter, chap. iv., the 10th verse, and Acts xviii, with other scriptures, which he would not suffer me to mention. But said, Hold; not so many, which is the first?

Bun. I said, This: 'As every man hath received the gift, *even so* minister the same one to another, as good stewards of the manifold grace of God. If any man speak, *let him speak* as the oracles of God,' etc.

Keel. He said, Let me a little open that scripture to you: 'As every man hath received the gift'; that is, said he, as everyone hath received a trade, so let him follow it. If any man have received a gift of tinkering, as thou hast done, let him follow his tinkering. And so other men their trades; and the divine his calling, etc.

Bun. Nay, sir, said I, but it is most clear, that the apostle speaks here of preaching the Word; if you do but compare both the verses together, the next verse explains this gift what it is, saying, 'If any man speak, *let him speak* as the oracles of God.' So that it is plain, that the Holy Ghost doth not so much in this place exhort to civil callings, as to the exercising of those gifts that we have received from God. I would have gone on, but he would not give me leave.

Keel. He said, We might do it in our families, but not otherwise.

Bun. I said, If it was lawful to do good to some, it was lawful to do good to more. If it was a good duty to exhort our families, it is good to exhort others; but if they held it a sin to meet together to seek the face of God, and exhort one another to follow Christ, I should sin still; for so we should do.

Keel. He said he was not so well versed in Scripture as to dispute, or words to that purpose. And said, moreover, that they could not wait upon me any longer; but said to me, Then you confess the indictment, do you not? Now, and not till now, I saw I was indicted.

Bun. I said, This I confess, we have had many meetings together, both to pray to God, and to exhort one another, and that we had the sweet comforting presence of the Lord among us for our encouragement; blessed be his name therefor. I confessed myself guilty no otherwise.

Keel. Then, said he, hear your judgment. You must be had back again to prison, and therelie for three months following; and at three months' end, if you do not submit to go to church to hear Divine service, and leave your preaching, you must be banished the realm: and if, after such a day as shall be appointed you to be gone, you shall be found in this realm, etc., or be found to come over again without special licence from the king, etc., you must stretch by the neck for it, I tell you plainly; and so he bid my jailer have me away. . . .

(e) From GEORGE FOX'S *Journal.*

George Fox and his Quaker followers were among the most stubbornly persecuted, precisely because they were the most stubbornly non-cooperative (albeit non-violently so). Pepys in his diary on 7 August 1664 says: 'While we were talking, came by several poor creatures carried by Constables for being at a conventicle. They go like lambs, without any resistance. I would to God they would either conform, or be more wise and not be ketched.' Not only would they not attend Anglican services in place of their own Friends' Meetings, but they would also not take any oath in a Court, raise their hats or acknowledge the validity of any social hierachy by addressing their 'Superiors' by their accepted titles.

I was kept till the Assize; and Judge Turner and Judge Twisden coming that circuit, I was brought before Judge Twisden on the 14th day of the First Month, called March, in the latter end of the year 1663. When I was set up to the Bar, I said, 'Peace be amongst you all.' The judge looked upon me, and said, 'What! do you come into the Court with your hat on?' Upon which, the jailer taking it off, I said, 'The hat is not the honour that comes from God.' Then said the judge to me, 'Will you take the oath of Allegiance, George Fox?' I said, 'I never took any oath in my life, nor any covenant or engagement.' 'Well,' said he, 'will you swear or no?' I answered, 'I am a Christian, and Christ commands me not to swear, and so does the apostle James, and whether I should obey God or man, do thou judge.' 'I ask you again,' said he, 'whether you will swear or not.' I told him they had had experience enough, how many men had first sworn for the King and then against him. But as for me, I had never taken an oath in all my life; and my allegiance did not lie in swearing, but in truth and faithfulness; for I honour all men, much more the King. Then I asked the judge if he did own the King. 'Yes,' said he, 'I do own the King.' 'Why then,' said I, 'dost thou not observe his declaration from Breda, and his promises made since he came into England, that no man should be called in question for matters of religion, so long as they lived peaceable? Now if thou ownest the King, why dost thou call me into question, and put me upon taking an oath which is a matter of religion, seeing neither thou nor any else can charge me with unpeaceable living?'

Upon this he was moved, and looking angrily at me, said, 'Sirrah! will you swear?' I told him I was none of his sirrahs, I was a Christian; and for him, an old man and a judge, to sit there and give names to prisoners, it did not become either his gray hairs or his office. 'Well,' said he, 'I am a Christian too.' 'Then do Christian works,' said I. 'Sirrah!' said he, 'thou thinkest to frighten me with thy words.' Then catching himself and looking aside, he said, 'Hark! I am using the word again'; and so checked himself. I said, 'I spake to thee in love; for that language did not become thee, a judge. Thou oughtest to instruct a prisoner in the law, if he were ignorant and out of the way.' 'And I speak in love to thee too,' said he. 'But', said I, 'love gives no names.' Then he roused himself up, and said, 'I will not be afraid of thee, George Fox; thou speakest so loud, thy voice drowns mine and the Court's; I must call for three or four criers to drown thy voice: thou hast good lungs.' 'I am a prisoner here,' said I, 'for the Lord Jesus Christ's sake; for His sake do I suffer, for Him do I stand this day; and if my voice were five times louder, I should lift it up, and sound it for Christ's sake, for whose cause I stand this day before your judgment-seat in obedience to Christ who commands not to swear; before whose judgment seat you must all be brought and must give an account.' 'Well,' said the judge, 'George Fox, say whether thou wilt take the oath, yea or nay.' I replied, 'I say, as I said before, whether ought I to obey God or man, judge thou. If I could take any oath at all, I should take this; for I do not deny some oaths only, or on some occasions, but all oaths, according to Christ's doctrine, who hath commanded His followers not to swear at all.'

'Then you will not swear,' said the judge; 'take him away,

jailer.' I said, 'It is for Christ's sake that I cannot swear, and for obedience to His command I suffer, and so the Lord forgive you all.' So the jailer took me away; but I felt the mighty power of the Lord was over them all.

The sixteenth day of the same month I was brought before Judge Twisden again: he was somewhat offended at my hat; but it being the last morning of the Assize before he was to go out of town, and not many people there, he made the less of it. He asked me whether I would traverse, stand mute, or submit. But he spake so fast that it was hard to know what he said. However, I told him I desired I might have liberty to traverse the indictment, and try it. Then said he, 'Take him away, I will have nothing to do with him; take him away.' I said, 'Well, live in the fear of God and do justice.' 'Why,' said he, 'have not I done you justice?' I replied, 'That which thou hast done has been against the command of Christ.' So I was taken to the jail again, and kept prisoner till the next Assizes. . . .

. . . Then I was put into a tower, where the smoke of the other rooms came up so thick, that it stood as dew upon the walls, and sometimes it was so thick that I could hardly see the candle when it burned; and I being locked under three locks, the under-jailer, when the smoke was great, would hardly be persuaded to come up to unlock one of the upper doors, for fear of the smoke, so that I was almost smothered. Besides it rained in upon my bed; and many times, when I went to stop out the rain in the cold winter season, my shift would be as wet as much with the rain that came in upon me. And the place being high and open to the wind, sometimes as fast as I stopt it, the wind being high and fierce, would blow it out again. In this manner did I lie all that long cold winter, till the next Assize; in which time I was so starved with cold and rain, that my body was greatly swelled, and my limbs much numbed.

. . . Persecution was stirred up and wicked Informers set to work, so that a Friend could hardly speak a few words in a private family before they sate down to eat meat, but some were ready to inform against them. It was a cruel, bloody, persecuting time, but as persecution began to cease I began to arise out of my sufferings. Many precious Friends came far and near to see me and attended upon me; and towards the Spring I began to recover and to walk up and down, to the astonishment of Friends and others.

When I had recovered I went from Enfield to Gerrard Roberts's again, and thence to London, where, though I was yet but weak, the Lord's power upheld and enabled me to declare His eternal Word of life.

About this time I was moved to pray to the Lord as follows:

O Lord God Almighty! Prosper truth, and preserve justice and equity in the land! Bring down all injustice and iniquity, oppression and falsehood, and cruelty and unmercifulness in the land; that mercy and righteousness may flourish!

O Lord God! Set up and establish verity, and preserve it in the land! Bring down in the land all debauchery and vice, and whoredoms and fornication, and this raping spirit which causeth people to have no esteem of Thee, O God, nor of their own souls or bodies; nor of Christianity, modesty, or humanity. And, O Lord! Put it in the magistrates' hearts to bring down all this ungodliness, and violence, and cruelty, profaneness, cursing, and swearing; and to put down all these whore-houses and play-houses, which do corrupt youth and people, and lead them from the kingdom of God, where no unclean thing can enter, neither shall come! Such works lead people to hell! And the Lord in mercy bring down all these things in the nation, to stop Thy wrath, O God! from coming on the land.

G. F.

This Prayer was writ at night, the
17th of the 2nd Month, 1671. . . .

(f) *The Last Trial of Richard Baxter before Judge Jeffreys*, from BAXTER'S *Autobiography*.

In 1685 at the age of seventy, bent double and in pain from an incurable disease, Baxter was arrested for publishing 'A scandalous and seditious book' entitled *A Paraphrase of the New Testament* on the grounds that his commentary on the Greek text covertly attacked the bishops and rulers of his own day. (Cf. 1.3.)

He had to be held up by two friends in order to stand in the dock. An anonymous eye-witness has reported the inimitable Judge Jeffreys' Squire Western-like mode of attack:

Lord Chief Justice: This is an old rogue, and hath poisoned the world with his Kidderminster doctrine. Do not we know how he preached formerly, 'Curse ye, Meroz, curse them bitterly that come not to help the Lord against the mighty,' and encouraged all the women and maids to bring in the bodkins and thimbles to carry on the war against that king of ever-blessed memory; an old schismatical knave, a hypocritical villain!

Pollexfen: I beseech your lordship, suffer me a word for my client. It is well known to all intelligible men of age in this nation, that these things agree not at all to the character of Mr. Baxter, who wished as well to the King and royal family, as Mr. Love that lost his head for endeavouring to bring in the son long before he was restored; and, my lord, Mr. Baxter's loyal and peaceable spirit King Charles II would have rewarded with a bishopric, when he came in, if he could have conformed.

Lord C.J.: Oy! Oy! we know that: but what ailed the old stockcole, unthankful villain that he could not conform—was he better or wiser than other men? He hath been ever since the spring of the faction; I am sure he hath poisoned the world with his linsey-wolsey doctrine.

And here I thought he would have run stark staring mad . . . and yet his larum was not run down yet neither; for 'he was a conceited, stubborn, fanatical dog, that did not conform when he might have been preferred; hang him! This one old fellow hath cast more reproach upon the constitution and excellent discipline of our Church than will be wiped out this hundred years; but I will handle him for it, for, by God! he deserves to be whipped through the city.'

Pol.: My lord, I am sure these things are not *ad rem* . . . I come not to justify men's Nonconformity, nor to give here the reasons of their scruples why they cannot accept of beneficial places, but had rather suffer anything. My lord, I know not what reasons sway other men's consciences; my business is to plead for my client, and to answer the charge of dangerous sedition that is alleged to be in this Paraphrase of his upon the New Testament.

Then my lord took breath a little, and turning his eyes all around, I suppose to see how the multitude liked this harangue, spies Dr. Bates laughing, and pierces him through like a vulture; but Dr. Bates not caring, I suppose, to be stared upon by him, steps down, and Jeffreys took notice of it, and said, 'There is Bates, I saw him just now—I will say that for him, he is a gentleman and a scholar, and the best of the whole pack of them; he hath always taken care to keep his pitcher whole and his water clear: but this old rogue hath been always a troublesome factious fellow.' So I saw Dr. Bates afterwards in the court, and told him of it; and he smiled and shook his head, and answered as one said, 'What evil have I done, etc., that this wicked man praiseth me?'

Pol.: My lord, my client, Mr. Baxter, is a man of another spirit; he hath written a book for episcopal government, etc., and that is his judgment, my lord; I have it in court and will show it your lordship, if you please.

Lord C.J.: I will see none of his books; it is for primitive Episcopacy, I will warrant you—a bishop in every parish. Pox take 'em, we know their bishops well enough.

Pol.: Nay, my lord, it is the same with Archbishop Usher's. (But a silly jerk he had at him too, though he mumbled it so softly I could not well hear it.) My lord, Mr. Baxter was a commissioner, appointed by the king at the Savoy, to settle ecclesiastical affairs, and he never offered anything for agreement and accommodation but Archbishop Usher's Reduction of Episcopacy and nothing at all against liturgies, as such.

Lord C.J.: It is no matter what he or Bishop Usher offers; our Church is established, and we will bate nothing; neither do we care what such a company of whining hypocritical fellows talk of, and this is one of the ring-leaders of them; but I will handle him well enough, I'll warrant you.

Now Dr. Oates being whipped a little before, and my lord and the government being in a whipping mood, for Dangerfield was condemned this very morning, at Westminster Hall, by my Lord (whose trial I heard, too), the people, especially the ladies, of whom there were some of good quality, burst out a-weeping, and amongst the rest a Conformist in his gown and scarf, one Dr. Ford, a comely, grave man, who stood near my lord upon his left hand, who seemed not at all to like these things. But Jeffreys, turning his wall-eyes hither and thither, and seeing all the persons upon the bench almost (except himself) in tears, he calls out to Mr. Baxter, saying to this effect:

Lord C.J.: Come you, what do you say for yourself, you old knave! Come, speak up: what doth he say? I am not afraid of you for all the snivelling calves that are got about you.

Mr. Baxter: Your lordship need not, for I will not hurt you. But these things will surely be understood one day, what tools one sort of Protestants are made to persecute and vex the other. (And lifting up his eyes to heaven, said:) I am not concerned to answer such stuff, but am ready to produce my writings for the confutation of all this, and my life and conversation is known to many in this nation, etc. . . .

. . . Baxter was again about to speak, but Jeffreys checked him, 'Richard, Richard, dost thou think we'll hear thee poison the court? Richard, thou art an old fellow, an old knave; thou hast written books enough to load a cart, every one as full of sedition, I might say treason, as an egg is full of meat. Hadst thou been whipped out of thy writing-trade forty years ago, it had been happy. Thou pretendest to be a preacher of the Gospel of Peace, and thou hast one foot in the grave: it is time for thee to begin to think what account thou intendest to give. But leave thee to thyself, and I see thou'lt go on as thou hast begun; but, by the grace of God, I'll look after thee.'

When Mr. Rotherham had sat down Mr. Atwood tried to get a hearing, and beginning to read from the text of Mr. Baxter's book, Jeffreys broke forth again, 'You shan't draw me into a conventicle with your annotations nor your snivelling parson, neither.' 'My Lord,' pleaded Atwood, 'that I may use the best authority, permit me to repeat your lordship's own words.' 'No, you shan't, you need not speak, for you are an author already; though you speak and write impertinently.' Atwood replied, 'I can't help that, my lord, if my talent be no better, but it is my duty to do my best for my client.'

Jeffreys ordered him several times to sit down, but Atwood persisted. 'Well,' said Jeffreys at last, 'you have had your say.' Williams and Phipps saw it was useless to attempt to speak, and were silent. Jeffreys summed up in a long harangue. It was notoriously known, he said, there had been a design to ruin the king and the nation. The old game had been renewed: and this person had been the main incendiary. 'He is as modest now as can be, but time was when no man was so ready at 'Bind your king in chains, and your nobles in fetters of iron'; and 'To your tents, O Israel.' Gentlemen, for God's sake, don't let us be gulled twice in an age.' When he had finished Baxter said to him, 'Does your lordship think any jury will pretend to pass a verdict upon me upon such a trial?' 'I'll warrant you, Mr. Baxter,' said he; 'don't you trouble yourself about that.' . . .

The packed jury did not even retire, but, after a brief consultation at the Bar, brought in a verdict of Guilty.

L'ENVOI

Oh, England!
    Sick in head and sick in heart,
    Sick in whole and every part:
    And yet sicker thou art still
    For thinking that thou art not ill.

        Anon. written before 1675.
        Collected in Ault, *Seventeenth Century Lyrics*

Notes

LITERARY INTRODUCTION

1 Kierkegaard, *Concluding Unscientific Postscripts*, pp. 169 ff.
2 William Blake, *The Marriage of Heaven and Hell.*
3 Lucy Hutchinson, *Memoirs of Colonel Hutchinson* (Everyman ed.).
4 Ibid.
5 Golo Mann, 'Wer War Wallenstein?', *Zeit Magazin* (15 September 1971).
6 John Ashton, *Humour, Wit and Satire in the Seventeenth Century* (1883).
7 Abraham Cowley, *Essays, Plays and Verses*, ed. A. Waller (1906).
8 *Roxburghe Ballads*, Coll. iii.
9 T. S. Eliot, *Burnt Norton.*

HISTORICAL INTRODUCTION

1 Keith Lindley, 'The Part Played by the Catholics' in Brian Manning ed., *Politics, Religion and the English Civil War* (1973), pp. 127–79.
2 Blair Worden, *The Rump Parliament* (Cambridge, 1974); Gerald Aylmer, *The State's Servants* (1974).
3 W. F. Church, *Constitutional Thought in Sixteenth-Century France* (Harvard, 1941).
4 Thomas Edwards, *Gangraena* (1946), pp. 47–9.
5 E. P. Thompson, *The Making of the English Working Class* (1963), pp. 34–5; Bernard Semmel, *The Methodist Revolution* (New York, 1973).
6 John Bossy, 'The English Catholic Community 1603–1625' in A. G. R. Smith ed., *The Reign of James VI and I* (1973), pp. 104–5.
7 N. H. Keeble ed., *The Autobiography of Richard Baxter* (Everyman's University Library ed., 1974), p. 7.
8 J. P. Cooper ed., *Wentworth Papers* (Camden Society, Fourth Series, 12, 1973), p. 8.
9 N. Tyacke, 'Puritanism, Arminianism and Counter-Revolution' in *The Origins of the English Civil War*, C. Russell ed. (1973), pp. 119–44; C. Bangs, 'All the Best Bishoprics and Deaneries: The Enigma of Arminian Politics', *Church History*, 42, 1 (1973), pp. 5–16.
10 Anon., *A Friendly Debate* (1689), p. 6.

I KING-WORSHIP

1   A. G. R. Smith ed., *The Reign of James VI and I* (1973).
2   M. H. Curtis, 'The Hampton Court Conference and its Aftermath', *History*, XLVI (1961), pp. 1–16, is a good corrective to Barlow's account.
3   On this dating see: J. N. Figgis, *The Divine Right of Kings* (1965), p. 138.
4   Keith Thomas, *Religion and the Decline of Magic* (1971); Frances Yates, *The Rosicrucian Enlightenment* (1973); Marc Bloch, *The Royal Touch* (1973).
5   J. G. A. Pocock, 'Time, History and Eschatology in the Thought of Thomas Hobbes' in *The Diversity of History*, J. H. Elliott and H. G. Koenigsberger eds. (1970), pp. 149–98.
6   J. G. A. Pocock, *The Ancient Constitution and the Feudal Law* (Cambridge, 1957); Margaret Judson, *The Crisis of the Constitution* (New Brunswick, 1957).
7   Christopher Hill, 'The Norman Yoke' in his *Puritanism and Revolution* (1965), pp. 62–3.
8   Quentin Skinner, 'History and Ideology in the English Revolution', *Historical Journal*, 8, 2 (1965), pp. 151–78.
9   Nathaniel Hardy, *The Arraignment of Licentious Libertie* (1647), dedicatory epistle.
10 Quentin Skinner, 'Conquest and Consent: Thomas Hobbes and the Engagement Controversy' in *The Interregnum*, G. E. Aylmer ed. (1972), pp. 79–99.
11 William Laud, *Works*, iv, p. 156.

2 THE DIVIDE OF THE 1630S

1   Norman Ault, *Seventeenth Century Lyrics* (New York, 1928).
2   Ibid.
3   Valerie Pearl, *London and the Outbreak of the Puritan Revolution* (1961).
4   Thomas Brande in a letter later printed in Collier's *History of English Dramatic Poetry and the Stage* (1879), quoted by G. E. Bentley, *The Jacobean and Caroline Stage* (1968), vol. 6, p. 23.
5   John Pory to Viscount Scadmore, quoted in Bentley op. cit., p. 31.
6   Office Book of the Master of the Revels, quoted in Bentley op. cit., p. 31.
7   See A. S. Knowland, *Six Caroline Plays* (Oxford, 1962), for both Shirley's and Killigrew's Comedies.
8   Izaak Walton, *The Life of Mr George Herbert* (Oxford, 1956), p. 304.
9   The Vice-Chancellor of Cambridge wanted to censor these two lines before publication but was persuaded to risk them as poetry not prophecy. Ibid., p. 315.
10 Preface of the Second Book of *The Reason of Church Government Urged Against Prelaty*.
11 For a fascinating article on these and other dreams see Peter Burke, 'L'Histoire social des rêves', *Annales*, 2 (1973), pp. 329–42.
12 W. Wilkins, *Political Ballads* (1860), vol. 1.
13 Hyder Rollins, *Cavalier and Puritan* (New York, 1923).
14 Ibid.

3 THE DEHUMANIZED IMAGE OF THE ENEMY

1 Cf. 'After the I.R.A. have murdered a retarded boy we are not going to stand any longer for what these animals have done to us in the past four years. There will be more deaths in reprisal.'—A man calling himself Captain Black claiming responsibility for two stabbings in Ulster, *The Guardian*, 27 June 1973.

2 Book of Revelation, Chapter 13.

3 *Apology for Smectymnuus.*

4 Sonnet: 'I did but prompt the age to quit their cloggs.'

5 Marchamont Needham Mercurius Pragmaticus, *The History of the English Rebellion* (1661).

6 John Cleveland, 'The Rebell Scot' (1644), reprinted in *The Poems of John Cleveland*, Morris and Withington eds. (Oxford, 1967).

7 Cleveland, 'On the Archbishop of Canterbury', op. cit.

8 Samuel Butler, *A Republican in Characters*, C. W. Daves ed. (Cleveland, 1970).

9 'Picture of an English Antick' (18 November 1646), reprinted in John Ashton, op. cit., p. 346.

10 Richard Baxter, *Autobiography* (Everyman's University Library, Chapter III).

11 John Bunyan, *The Pilgrim's Progress* (Everyman ed.).

12 Lucy Hutchinson, op. cit.

13 Peter Verney, *The Standard Bearer* (1963), Chapter IX.

14 *The Reason of Church Government Urged Against Prelaty*, Book I (1641).

15 *Idem.*

16 Richard Baxter, *Autobiography*, Chapter III.

17 Cromwell, letter 107 in *Letters*, Carlyle ed., 3 vols.

18 Cromwell, letter 116, op. cit.

19 Lucy Hutchinson, op. cit.

20 The second of *The Two Speeches of the Lord Wharton Spoken in Guild-Hall, 21st October 1642*, quoted in Commentary, p. 125 to *The Poems of John Cleveland*, op. cit.

21 Lady Sussex to Ralph Verney, November 1643 (Verney, *Letters*).

22 Thomas Stanford, *Sussex in the Great Civil War and the Interregnum* (1910), Chapter 14.

23 W. Wilkins, *Political Ballads* (1860), Vol. I.

24 *Hudibras*, Part I, Canto I.

25 Reprinted in V. Sola Pinto, *The Common Muse* (1965).

26 See Introduction to Cleveland, *Poems*, op. cit.

27 W. Wilkins, op. cit.

28 *Idem.*

29 Bishop Henry King, *A Deepe Groane, fetched at the Funeral of that Incomparable and glorious Monarch, Charles the First.*

4 THE CAVALIER AND PURITAN SELF-IMAGE

Part 1: The Cavalier Self-Image

1 Clarendon, *Selections*, Huehns ed. (Oxford, 1955), pp. 255–8.

2 *Idem.*

3 'When the King enjoys his own again' in Wilkins, *Political Ballads*, op. cit.

4   Aubrey, 'Sir John Suckling' in *Brief Lives* (1949).
5   *Idem.*
6   Reflections on the French Revolution (1790).
7   King, *Poems*, Crum ed. (Oxford, 1965), p. 102.
8   Clarendon, op. cit., pp. 50–67.
9   Clarendon, op. cit., pp. 249–50.
10 Alexander Brome, *Songs and Poems* (1668).
11 'Lucasta' in *The Poems of Richard Lovelace Esq.*, W. Carew
    Hazlitt ed. (1897), p. 45.
12 Reprinted in Ault, op. cit.
13 *The Knyvett Letters 1620–1664*, Bertram Schofield ed. (1949).

Part 2: The Puritan Self-Image

1   Clarendon, op. cit., p. 268.
2   W. K. Jordan, *Men of Substance* (Chicago, 1942), p. 93, has queried
    Parker's authorship but for the opposite view see William Lamont,
    Marginal Prynne (1963), p. 171, and Margaret Judson, *The Crisis
    of the Constitution* (New Brunswick, 1949), pp. 426–7.
3   Lucy Hutchinson, op. cit.
4   *Scottish Ballads and Songs*, J. Maidment ed. (Edinburgh, 1868),
    vol. 1.
5   *Idem.*
6   Sonnet: 'On the new Forcers of Conscience.'
7   Translation of Psalm 136.
8   Hymn: 'On the Morning of Christ's Nativity.'
9   Sonnet VII.
10 *Apology for Smectymnuus.*
11 *Doctrine and Discipline of Divorce*, Chapters 4 and 6.
12 *Areopagitica.*
13 Sonnet XII.
14 Psalm I: Done into English verse, 1653.

5 CHARLES I: ROYAL MARTYR OR 'POPISH FAVOURITE'?

1   David Underdown, *Pride's Purge* (Oxford, 1971), especially pp.
    117–85.
2   Radical and millenarian pamphlets are available to students in a
    number of useful texts. Especially to be commended are: A. S. P.
    Woodhouse, *Puritanism and Liberty* (1950); S. E. Prall, *The Puritan
    Revolution* (1969); William Haller and Godfrey Davies, *The
    Leveller Tracts* (New York, 1944); C. Hill ed., *Winstanley: The
    Law of Freedom and Other Writings* (1973). Because of the acces-
    sibility of this material, we chose to omit from our volume this
    aspect of seventeenth-century thought when we were pressed for
    space: not because we felt this to be unimportant, as is pointed
    out in the Preface.
3   Roger Williams, *The Bloudy Tenent . . .* (1644), p. 224.
4   Cf. for instance—as the anonymous author of that pamphlet did—
    the views of Prynne's *The Popish Royall Favourite* (1643) with
    those expressed in his *The Substance of a Speech* (1649).
5   Among them: Peter du Moulin, White Kennett, Bishop Ussher,
    Bishop Bramhall, Richard Baxter and Sir William Morice!
6   Anon., *A Friendly Debate* (1689), pp. 52–3; William Lamont, 'The

Rise and Fall of Bishop Bilson', *The Journal of British Studies*,
V, 2, pp. 22–32.
7 David Underdown, op. cit., especially pp. 148–50.
8 *Eikon Basilike*, ed. Philip Knachel (New York, 1966), pp. xi–
xxxii.
9 R. C. Latham, 'Roger Lowe, Shopkeeper and Nonconformist',
History, xxvi (June 1941), pp. 19–36.
10 Alan Macfarlane, *The Family Life of Ralph Josselin* (Cambridge,
1970). I owe the latter point to a private communication from Dr
Macfarlane, who is now producing a modern edition of Josselin's
diary.
11 W. Wilkins, *Political Ballads* (1860), vol. I.
12 C. V. Wedgwood, *Poetry and Politics under the Stuarts* (Cambridge,
1960), Chapter 3.
13 For a most helpful discussion of the attempted Parliamentary
censorship of Royalist ballads see the introduction to Hyder E.
Rollins, *Cavalier and Puritan* (New York, 1923).

6 CROMWELL: FOR AND AGAINST

1 Flora Thompson, *Lark Rise to Candleford* (1973), p. 215.
2 G. E. Aylmer, 'Englands Spirit Unfoulded, or an Incouragement to
take the Engagement', *Past and Present*, 40 (July 1968), pp. 1–5.
3 A. E. Barker, *Milton and the Puritan Dilemma* (Toronto, 1942), pp.
382–3.
4 William Prynne, *Loyalty Banished* (1659); *The Weekly Post*, No. 7
(14–21 June 1659); *The Faithful Scout*, No. 9 (17–24 June 1659).
5 Christopher Hill, *God's Englishman* (1970), pp. 234–5.
6 Ibid., p. 193.
7 *Baxter Treatises* (Dr Williams's Library), ix, ff. 30–1.
8 Claire Cross, 'The Church in England 1646–1660' in *The Interregnum*, G. E. Aylmer ed. (1972), pp. 99–121.
9 Thomas Carlyle ed., *Oliver Cromwell's Letters and Speeches*, iii, p.
295.
10 B. H. G. Wormald, *Clarendon: Politics, History, Religion* (Cambridge, 1951).
11 G. R. Abernathy Jnr., 'Clarendon and the Declaration of Indulgence', *Journal of Ecclesiastical History*, XI, 1 (1960).
12 J. P. Cooper, 'Social and Economic Policies Under the Common-
wealth' in *The Interregnum*, G. E. Aylmer ed. (1972), pp. 121–42.
13 *Baxter MSS.* (Dr Williams's Library), 59.1, f. 261.
14 Abraham Cowley, *A Discourse . . . Concerning the Government of
Oliver Cromwell* (1659): 'I began to reflect on the whole life of this
Prodigious Man, and sometimes I was filled with horror and de-
testation of his actions, and sometimes I inclined a little to reverence and admiration of his courage, conduct and success.' But
Cowley only allowed the Devil to speak well of Cromwell in the
main body of this unfinished work.
15 J. Ashton, op. cit., p. 44.
16 Ibid., pp. 214–15.
17 Marchamont Needham, *History of the English Rebellion*.

18   Hyder Rollins, *Cavalier and Puritan*, pp. 222–3.
19   Waller, *Poems*, Thora Drury ed. (1905).

7 THE WRETCHEDNESS OF WAR

1   Schofield ed., op. cit., p. 133.
2   Ibid., p. 149.
3   Marvell, 'The Nymph Complaining for the Death of her Fawn'.
4   Sonnet: 'On the Lord General Fairfax at the Seige of Colchester'
      (1648).
5   Milton, 'The Second Defence of the People of England' in *Milton's
      Prose Works*, Bohn ed. (1848), vol. i, p. 295 et seq.
6   Quoted in Peter Verney, op. cit., pp. 179 and 187.
7   Ibid., p. 203.
8   W. C. Abbott ed., *Writings and Speeches of Oliver Cromwell* (Har-
      vard, 1937), pp. 287–8.
9   *Olor Iscanus* (1651).

8 OLD SCARS UNHEALED

1   Lord Shaftesbury, *A Letter from A Person of Quality* (1675), pp. 1–2.
2   R. A. Beddard, 'Vincent Alsop and the Emancipation of Restora-
      tion Dissent', *Journal of Ecclesiastical History*, XXIV, 2 (1973),
      p. 170.
3   Zachary Crofton, *A Serious Review of Presbyters Reordination by
      Bishops* (1661), p. 15.
4   R. S. Bosher, *The Making of the Restoration Settlement* (1951) is the
      best refutation of both propositions, despite using the term
      'Laudian' himself.
5   J. P. Kenyon, *The Stuart Constitution* (Cambridge, 1966), p. 364.
6   J. R. Jones, *The Revolution of 1688 in England* (1973); Beddard,
      loc. cit., p. 177.
7   Historical Manuscripts Commission, *12th Report*, ix, pp. 50–1.
8   Frewen MSS. D677/712 (East Sussex Record Office).
9   A. S. P. Woodhouse, *Puritanism and Liberty* (1950), p. 43.
10   Beddard, loc. cit., pp. 161–84.
11   For details of this little-known, absurd and yet important 'plot',
      see William Lamont, *Marginal Prynne* (1963), pp. 113–14.
12   W. C. Abbott, 'The Origins of Titus Oates' Story', *English Historical
      Review*, XXV (1910), pp. 126–9.
13   D. P. Walker, *The Decline of Hell* (Chicago, 1964).
14   Ragnhild Hatton, *Europe in the Age of Louis XIV* (1969), p. 80.